PORT OUT, STARBOARD HOME

'A wonderful book on the origins of well-known words and phrases . . . Every page of this book is a sheer delight. For anyone who writes, or who gives lectures or sermons, or for anyone who just loves the highways and byways of the English language, it will be an invaluable addition to a personal reference library. My advice is to go the whole nine yards and buy it' *Catholic Herald*

'Quinion's scholarship is impeccable, but borne lightly. He strikes a fine balance between erudition and entertainment . . . Anyone with a genuine interest in the English language will want to own a copy of this book' Dr Patrick Hanks, former editor, the *New Oxford Dictionary of English*

'Explodes myths about the words we use' *Sunday Post* (Dundee)

'Quinion's chatty and erudite book should sit nicely next to Fowler, Brewer and Partridge' Dianne Dempsey, *The Age* (Melbourne)

'Whether he's dealing with truth or tall tales, Quinion aims to provide the whole ball of wax, and as an etymologizer he more than cuts the mustard' Jan Freeman, *Boston Globe*

'Everybody knows that posh comes from Indian civil servants having their steamer tickets booked as "Port Out, Starboard Home". But everybody is wrong, as Michael Quinion entertainingly demonstrates in his rambles through the thickets of English etymology' *Tablet*

Michael Quinion has spent the past forty years struggling with the English language and considers he has now fought it to a draw. He has written almost every sort of text except obituaries and sports reports, having been variously a BBC radio reporter and features producer, writer and director of audio-visual programmes for museums and visitor centres, a museum curator, an exhibition scriptwriter, and a heritage interpreter. For the past decade he has been a field researcher and advisor to the *Oxford English Dictionary*, writer of much of the second edition of the *Oxford Dictionary of New Words* and author of *Ologies and Isms: A Dictionary of Affixes* (OUP). He is perhaps best known as writer and editor of the e-mail newsletter and website, both called World Wide Words (http://www.worldwidewords.org/), which feature the idiosyncrasies and oddities of our language.

Port Out, Starboard Home

and other language myths

Michael Quinion

PENGUIN BOOKS

PENGUIN BOOKS

Published by the Penguin Group
Penguin Books Ltd, 80 Strand, London WC2R ORL, England
Penguin Group (USA) Inc., 375 Hudson Street, New York, New York 10014, USA
Penguin Group (Canada), 10 Alcorn Avenue, Toronto, Ontario, Canada M4V 3B2
(a division of Pearson Penguin Canada Inc.)
Penguin Ireland, 25 St Stephen's Green, Dublin 2, Ireland
(a division of Penguin Books Ltd)
Penguin Group (Australia), 250 Camberwell Road, Camberwell, Victoria 3124, Australia
(a division of Pearson Australia Group Pty Ltd)
Penguin Books India Pvt Ltd, 11 Community Centre, Panchsheel Park, New Delhi – 110 017, India
Penguin Group (NZ), cnr Airborne and Rosedale Roads, Albany, Auckland 1310, New Zealand
(a division of Pearson New Zealand Ltd)
Penguin Books (South Africa) (Pty) Ltd, 24 Sturdee Avenue, Rosebank 2196, South Africa

Penguin Books Ltd, Registered Offices: 80 Strand, London WC2R ORL, England

www.penguin.com

First published 2000
Published in Penguin Books 2005
1

Copyright © Michael Quinion, 2000
All rights reserved

The moral right of the author has been asserted

Designed by Richard Marston
Typeset by Rowland Phototypesetting Ltd, Bury St Edmunds, Suffolk
Printed in England by Clays Ltd, St Ives plc

Contents

Introduction

Stories about words

You're with a friend, and you get talking about language, probably because one of you has just uttered some expression that you've never thought about before, like ONE FELL SWOOP or DRESSED TO THE NINES (words and phrases in SMALL CAPITAL LETTERS have entries in this book). Your friend tells you an interesting story about where the saying comes from, such that the word HONEYMOON derives from an old Persian custom of giving the happy couple mead for the first month after the wedding, or that a HOOKER is so called after the camp followers who flocked around the headquarters of the American Civil War general Joseph Hooker.

Well, you believe it, don't you? Who wouldn't? The story is convincing, often backed up with extraneous but significant detail drawn from the teller's personal experience or background knowledge. And, most of all, you have nothing to measure it against. It all sounds very reasonable. You are impressed with your friend's superior knowledge about language and history. At the next opportunity, you mention the story to somebody else. Each time you do so, or hear somebody else repeat it, the tale becomes more familiar, above all, more *true*. After a while, it's as though you have always known it. You may even become a little possessive about it, so that somebody who attempts to argue differently seems to be telling you that you're a fool and that you don't know what you're talking about.

We're suckers for a really good story – it's one way we make sense of the world around us and so turn the unfamiliar (which is much the same thing as the dangerous and the frightening) into the known and the comfortable. So it's important that we have stories that explain things, but it's much less important that the stories we tell are verifiably true. Much of this book is a testament to that insouciance about origins.

Such stories about language must satisfy on a number of levels: they must reassure and convince, but above all they must interest and entertain. Stories that are boring, mundane or inconclusive will not survive. Unfortunately, real word histories are often all of these things.

Back in Elizabethan times, an early economist called Sir Thomas Gresham promulgated the rule that 'bad money drives out good' – that good-quality coins mixed with debased ones will be hoarded or exported, leaving only the rubbish in circulation. It's much the same with etymology, alas. Only an etymologist could or would be expected to take the time to exhaustively research the history and evidence behind such stories, and in these days of electronic communications an entertaining but false word history will race twice round the world before the etymologist has had time to put fingers to keyboard.

Etymythology

Some experts call the creation of such stories about the origins of words *popular etymology* or *folk etymology*. A large part of this book retells such mythic tales and also tries to find and explain the true stories behind them. You might like to think of it as a group of illustrations of the imaginative ways in which people can work very hard to make sense of the unknown. Better names might be *pseudo-etymology*, *mythic etymology* or *etymological myth* – one worker in the field, Professor Laurence Horn, has collapsed those terms into the neatly abbreviated *etymythology*.

There are two specific kinds of etymythology that continually recur. One argues that a given word has been created as an acronym, from the initial letters of a phrase. This is a common suggestion, for words as widely differentiated as COP, 'Constable On Patrol', FUCK, supposedly 'Fornication Under Consent of the King', POSH, 'Port Out, Starboard Home' (from sailing-ship days), or TIP, money given to a waiter 'To Insure Promptness'.

People think this is a sensible sort of suggestion because we are surrounded by an alphabet soup of acronyms these days, such as *GIFT* (Gamete Intrafallopian Transfer), *NATO* (North Atlantic Treaty Organization), *SARS* (Severe Acute Respiratory Syndrome) or *POTUS* (President Of The United States). Some acronyms are now so accepted as words in their own right that few know their origins: *radar* is from Radio Detection And Ranging, *laser* from Light Amplification by Stimulated Emission of Radiation, and *scuba* from Self Contained Underwater Breathing Apparatus.

The fashion for acronymic creation is actually a military one dating from around the time of the First World War (an early example is *AWOL*, 'Absent Without Leave', though even this wasn't consistently pronounced as a word until the Second World War), and acronyms didn't get into wide general circulation until the Second World War and after. There are almost no examples of words of acronymic origin before 1900 (though some writers will argue that our modern sense of CABAL was at least influenced by initials). Indeed, the very word *acronym* to describe them wasn't coined until 1943.

Another, more erudite, mistake is to assume that because a word exists in English, and a similar sounding word with much the same meaning exists in another language, that the two must necessarily be connected. One of the more famous examples here is that OK derives from the Choctaw *okah*, all right; it was also thought at one time that YANKEE came from Cherokee *eankke*, a slave.

To discover similarities like these can be a heady experience: it takes no more than a moment to construct a plausible-sounding theory of the way that such a word might have been introduced into English. The truth (and I ask you to bear this in mind should you ever find such a coincidence) is that chance sound resemblances across languages, even among words with similar senses, are surprisingly easy to find and mean nothing in themselves.

Folk etymology

The term *etymythology* is especially useful because it allows *folk etymology* to be reserved for a related but significantly different process for which many language experts prefer to retain it.

What often happens here is that a term really is borrowed from another language or another dialect. Or it may be that a word, or one element of the word, that was once common, has become archaic or rare. Either way, it is strange, and has to be modified into something that sounds like a current English form if it is to be accepted and continue to be used. Our minds search for familiar patterns and make mistakes.

For example, when the second half of *bridegome* for the male half of a marrying couple became obsolete, people borrowed *groom* instead (making BRIDEGROOM). The Spanish *cucaracha* made no sense to English speakers, so they transmogrified it into COCKROACH; the Native American term for a water-loving rodent became MUSKRAT. People translate the defunct word *umbles* for the innards of a deer into *humble*, as in HUMBLE PIE. British Tommies in France in the first years of the First World War heard *il n'y en a plus*, 'there is no more', and condensed it into *napoo*, 'finished, done for, dead'; they did much the same with *ça ne fait rien*, 'it does not matter', into *san fairy ann*. So few Americans now know the old comic strip that some write Mutton Jeff instead of Mutt 'n' Jeff; people talk about *having another thing coming* instead of *think*; New Yorkers have so often heard *an arm and a leg* (as in 'this is costing me an arm and a leg', for a thing that is outrageously expensive) that they have created from it *a nominal egg* with the same sense; you may occasionally come across *bag of shells* when the writer has meant *bagatelle*.

There are hundreds of such examples, and some of them feature here. When they first appear, they are often viewed as mistakes, as indeed they are, but they can become accepted in time. Entries of this sort may be dismissed by experts of a conservative persuasion as dignifying errors rather than chronicling language evolution in action. I have avoided examples that are no more than obvious homophonic mistakes (*his interest was peaked, home one's skills, bare with me*), limiting discussion to those which have attained some measure of acceptance or are at least widely encountered.

A few terms that are commonly thought to be folk etymologies may not in fact be so and a couple of the articles in this book take time out to argue the opposite point of view. CARD SHARP is one such, which is quite often written and said as *card shark*. This looks like a folk etymology, but research shows that it is more probable the two forms arose independently. Another of a similar kind is STRAIGHT AND NARROW.

Sensitive senses

Some misunderstandings about etymology can have serious consequences.

We have seen a number of serious disputes arise in the USA in recent years because someone thinks a person has used racist language. Almost any word beginning in *black* or which implies a dark colour is open to suspicion. A member of the Mayor's staff in Washington was disciplined because he used the word NIGGARDLY, because it was supposedly linked to *nigger* (it isn't). A row broke out more recently because a West Coast American council member used the phrase CALL A SPADE A SPADE and a black colleague accused him of using racist language (he didn't). There have been false stories concerning the origin of PICNIC, NITTY-GRITTY and SQUAW, either as malicious attempts to increase racial tension, or as the result of misunderstandings that have been seized on for propaganda purposes.

Where there is intent to make a racial taunt, it is entirely reasonable to complain and try to stop it. On the other hand, the process of making people more aware of the implications of the words they use can only be hampered by vociferous objection to benign words and phrases that are innocent of racial associations.

Confusion over meaning

There is one further source of confusion that features in some entries, which stands to one side of the other types of mistake. Sometimes a phrase turns into an idiom, a saying whose meaning cannot be worked out from the individual words alone. In such cases the meaning can become so detached from literalness that it shifts, because people have misunderstood what it means and end up inventing a completely new sense. Examples include BEG THE QUESTION, CHEAP AT HALF THE PRICE, THE EXCEPTION PROVES THE RULE and MOOT POINT.

What isn't here

You won't find *spoonerisms* ('Young man, you have tasted your worm, and you must leave Oxford by the town drain', a sentence that the Reverend Archibald Spooner never actually uttered); *mala-propisms* ('She's as headstrong as an allegory on the banks of the

Nile', from Mrs Malaprop, a character in Sheridan's play *The Rivals*); or *mondegreens* (mishearings of song lyrics, as in ' 'Scuse me while I kiss this guy'). Also omitted are words that have been transformed through linguistic processes, including *metanalysis* (in which letters move about within a word or between words, as *a napron* became *an apron* and *an ewt* turned into *a newt*) or *metathesis* (in which letters within a word are transposed, as *bird* was long ago formed from *brid* and *wasp* from *wops*).

Canute was right

Trying to hold back shifts in language is useless. If people ignorant of cricket start to say *off one's own back* for something done solely by a person's own exertions, instead of OFF ONE'S OWN BAT, that's something no writer on words, however persuasive, may reverse. I will explain how errors have arisen, but I am too aware of the impossibility of holding back the tide of language change to do other than sadly regret the loss of an interesting sporting image. However (to invent a folk etymology, a step I hope will not rebound on me), if somebody were to suggest that the phrase came about because stevedores at London Docks were paid at piece rates for each sack they unloaded from a ship by lifting it up from the hold on their shoulders, then I would be forthright in saying that, from the evidence, the story is wrong.

In recent years, the growth of the Internet and e-mail has hugely increased the speed and distance by which such tales can circulate. This has led to a curious phenomenon in which writers have spirited up tales based on stories about word origins and sent them out on the Net by e-mail. Such pieces are often clever and entertaining, and many of them, like one that supposedly explains about life in 1500, circulate endlessly online, to the frustration and annoyance of people like me who get sent half a dozen copies a week by people asking if they are true or not (for example, whether a *wake* really was so called because the family sat around the coffin to see whether the corpse would wake up). Almost universally, they're not true, though they mix a drop of real information with a bucketful of false in a way that's convincing to a reader who doesn't have the necessary background knowledge. My view of such pieces, when I've stopped laughing, is that we word sleuths have enough trouble with mistakes that are caused by ignorance or misunderstanding without having deliberate obfuscation added to the mix. BI (Before the Internet), hoaxes were limited in circulation because most publicly available text was first subjected to the well-stocked mind of a copy editor, though a few are notorious, such as zzxjoanw.

I don't imagine for a moment that writing this book will by itself reduce the mountain of disinformation that exists on the subject of word origins, but it will at least supply you with the evidence you need to rebut the most egregious tales, and in the process I hope provide a few entertaining moments.

Acknowledgements

This book arose in part out of the online newsletter and website, both called *World Wide Words* (see www.worldwidewords.org), that I have been writing since 1995. In that time, thousands of questions have come in from subscribers and visitors. Many of them refer to stories about the origin of some word or phrase that the writers have heard about and often end with some variation on 'This seems a bit suspicious. What do you think?' My thanks to you all for your queries (with apologies to the many whose enquiries I never got around to answering). There could have been no better way of alerting me to the need for this work.

The World Wide Web, among many other things, is a research tool for busy writers that has had no equal in human history. To list all the sites that have contributed background information to this book would make it half as large again, though I should mention in particular the *Making of America* and *American Memory* databases. A great number of sites are non-commercial, run by individuals who make the results of their private passions and deep personal knowledge available to all. Though I can't mention them all by name, a few of those that specialize in language and word histories are listed at the end of the book.

Collective and individual acknowledgements are also owed to the members of the American Dialect Society, whose mailing list is a perpetually refreshed cornucopia of research materials on the origins of many kinds of term, folk etymologies and etymythologies among them. My thanks go in particular to Fred Shapiro, Jesse Sheidlower, Laurence Horn and Frank Abate for helping to tease out word histories or providing raw research material. Barry

Popik and Gerald Cohen deserve special acknowledgement because of their work on a number of iconic American terms that has refuted long-standing folk tales about their origins, among them BIG APPLE, HOT DOG, JAZZ, JINX, SHYSTER, SMART ALEC and WINDY CITY.

Thanks also to Joost Lemmens, Julane Marx, Nigel Rees, Jonathon Green, Nicholas Shearing and David Wilton for their help in sorting out the facts behind a number of expressions.

My wife deserves special mention for listening patiently, sometimes it has to be admitted with glazed eyes, to my discussions of current researches; I thank her from the bottom of my heart for her never-failing support and encouragement.

The fact is that some among us have put almost as much
ingenuity into misexplaining the origins of words and phrases
as the race has put into making language.

John Ciardi, *A Browser's Dictionary* (1980)

Man is an etymologizing animal. He abhors the vacuum of
an unmeaning word. If it seems lifeless, he reads a new soul into it,
and often, like an unskilful necromancer, spirits the wrong soul
into the wrong body.

Reverend A. Smythe Palmer, *Folk-Etymology* (1882)

Akimbo

This must be one of the odder-looking words in the language and puzzles us in part because it doesn't seem to have any relatives. What's more, it is now virtually a fossil word, until recently almost invariably found in *arms akimbo*, a posture in which a person stands with hands on hips and elbows sharply bent outward, one that signals impatience, hostility or contempt.

The first spelling recorded was *in kenebowe*, which turns up in a work called *The Tale of Beryn* that dates from 1400. This looks as though it ought to come from an Old Norse source that meant something bent into a curve, but it has never been found. (The last element in the word is essentially the same as our *bow* for a curve.)

It's a good example of the way that the shape of a word can buckle and twist over time when there are no related forms to help keep it straight. The phrase went through several shifts, variously being written as *on kenbow*, *on kimbow*, *a-kenbold*, *a-kimbo*, *a-kembo* and in other ways, arriving at our modern spelling as a single word without a hyphen only in the late eighteenth century.

In theory, it might be used for anything bent into the shape of a bow, but from its earliest appearance it was attached to that aggressive bent-elbow, hand-on-hip position that signals trouble in store for somebody. Charles Reade used it so in *The Cloister and the Hearth* (1861): 'Suddenly setting her arms akimbo she told him with a raised voice and flashing eyes she wondered at his cheek sitting down by that hearth of all hearths in the world.'

Up to a decade or so ago, there the matter might have rested. But if you search newspaper databases you will find lots of recent examples of *legs akimbo*. It might be that writers have creatively applied it to somebody sitting cross-legged, a position with bent knees that's similar to the elbows of *arms akimbo*, though presumably without the body language that goes with it.

But then you find this, from the *Daily Mirror* newspaper of July 2002, in a piece that refers to gym equipment: 'A quick look around reveals the absence of an inner-thigh-outer-thigh machine – the kind you sit on, legs akimbo, and squeeze your knees in and out.' Or this, from the *Ottawa Sun* in November 2001, about a police line whose members stand 'faces stoic, legs akimbo, at the steel barrier'. Or this, from the *Guardian* a year earlier: 'I spent the next 20 minutes high above him, straining over my camera with tripod legs akimbo, getting pictures of the top of his head.'

It's hard to imagine the utility of tripod legs that bend or hinge. What has happened is that writers have tried to understand the idea behind *akimbo*, but have got it wrong because it only ever turns up in the set phrase *arms akimbo* and there are no easy clues to its meaning (other than consulting a dictionary, of course). So they have reanalysed it as 'apart' or – more strongly – 'flung out widely or haphazardly'.

It's a sense that is only gradually coming to be recorded in dictionaries, but the large number of examples show it is bound to come. It's yet another example of how language so often evolves through mistakes.

All mouth and trousers

This strange expression comes from the north of England and is used, mainly by women in my experience, as a sharp-tongued and effective put-down of a certain kind of pushy, over-confident male. Proverbial expressions like this are notoriously hard to pin down: we have no idea exactly where it comes from nor when it first appeared, though it is recorded from the latter part of the nineteenth century onwards. However, we're fairly sure that it is a pairing of *mouth*, meaning insolence or cheekiness, with *trousers*, a pushy sexual bravado. It's a wonderful example of metonymy ('a container for the thing contained').

The phrase seems to have become known, and surprisingly popular, among southern English writers in the last decades of the twentieth century, perhaps as a result of the airing of a series of television comedies based in the north, such as the BBC's *Last of the Summer Wine*. What is interesting about the saying from a folk etymological point of view is that its opaqueness has led its modern users to reinterpret it as *all mouth and no trousers*.

For example, an article in the *Daily Record* in 2002 quoted a Scottish politician as saying, 'The First Minister is all mouth and no trousers'; a piece in the *People* newspaper described a pop group in the same terms; the *Guardian* in June 2002 said: 'Bloody men. All mouth and no trousers.' It has reached the stage at which the older non-negative form is in great danger of vanishing, though Australia and New Zealand seem to be staying with it (when they use it at all, which isn't often).

Metropolitan writers are trying here to make sense of something obscure that they have not often heard in its native surroundings, and are getting it muddled. They confuse it with other put-downs that are conventionally phrased with a negative, such as *all talk and no action*, or *all fur coat and no knickers*. To have no trousers on is not only embarrassing, the argument seems to go, but is a state in which one is not ready for action (outside the bedroom, that is).

It's a pity it should be changing through ignorance. It's a lovely phrase, as effective a snub as anyone could want – all the better for being slightly obscure – and it's one that ought to be preserved pristine. Eliminate the negative!

Alligator *See* AVOCADO

Aluminium

A story is sometimes told about how the American spelling *aluminum* for this metal came about. It is said that the infant Aluminium Company of America had a problem when the typesetter accident-ally left out the second i in the name in the firm's stationery. There wasn't enough money in the kitty to reset and reprint it, the tale goes, so the spelling perforce remained.

Few people will be taken in by this modern Just So story, but it provides a good excuse to look into the history of this troubling couplet, as good an example of etymological and orthographical confusion as you may ever encounter.

The metal was named by the English chemist Sir Humphry Davy in the first years of the nineteenth century, even though he was unable to isolate it – that took another two decades' work by others. He derived the name from the mineral called *alumina*, which itself had been so named in English by the chemist Joseph Black in 1790. Black borrowed his term from French, which had based it on *alum*, a white mineral containing aluminium that had been used since ancient times for dyeing and tanning, among other things.

Sir Humphry made a mess of naming this new element, at first spelling it *alumium* (this was in 1807) then changing it to *aluminum*, and finally settling on *aluminium* in 1812. His classically educated colleagues preferred *aluminium*, because it had a Latinate ring and chimed harmoniously with other elements whose names ended in -ium, such as *potassium*, *sodium* and *magnesium*, all of which Davy had named (the -ium ending has since become standard for the names of metallic elements).

The -um spelling continued in occasional use in Britain for a while, though -ium soon predominated. In the USA the standard scientific spelling was *aluminium* right from the start. This is the only form given in Noah Webster's Dictionary of 1828, and seems to have been usual among US chemists throughout the nineteenth century; it was the preferred version in *The Century Dictionary* of 1889 and is the only spelling given in *Webster's Unabridged Dictionary* of 1913. However, there's plenty of evidence that the spelling without the final i was used in various trades and professions in the USA from the 1830s onwards and that as early as the 1860s it had become the more common one outside science. Why this should have happened is a mystery.

For a long time this didn't matter much, since it was only at the end of the century that the name of the metal gained much currency among ordinary people. For most of the nineteenth century it was rare and costly. When the cap of the Washington Monument was cast from aluminium in 1884, it was still an expensive choice (it cost about the same as silver), as it was when the metal was used for the statue of Eros in Piccadilly Circus in London in 1893. The price dropped dramatically when a way of extracting the metal using inexpensive hydroelectricity was developed in the 1890s.

In 1907, a pioneering business in this technique that had been formed in 1888 as The Pittsburgh Reduction Company was renamed the Aluminum Company of America (it is known today as Alcoa Inc.). Oddly enough, and as a further illustration of American indecision about the spelling, the first name proposed for the business, in the minutes of 31 July 1888, was 'Pittsburgh Aluminium Company', so spelled.

It would seem that the 1907 spelling was a reflection of its popularity among non-technical users in the USA; because of the high profile of the company it was also influential in further encouraging the form without the second i (if the founders had stuck to their first suggestion, Americans might by now be using the British spelling). In 1925 the American Chemical Society adopted *aluminum* as standard.

The International Union of Pure and Applied Chemistry (IUPAC) officially standardized on *aluminium* in 1990, though this has done nothing, of course, to change the way people in the USA spell it for day-to-day purposes.

Apple-pie order

Something that is in *apple-pie order* is in perfect order or arrangement. Motherhood and apple pie being so much the traditional essence of the USA, you will not be surprised to hear that a story about where the phrase comes from links it with a New England house-wife and her apple pies. Being a person of foresight and application, we are told, each weekend she would bake seven pies for the week ahead, ranging them neatly in order on the larder shelves, carefully checking each evening that she had the remaining pies lined up neatly.

There's a big snag with any belief you might have in this tale of a wife, even if she wasn't an old wife: *apple-pie order* seems to be British, not American. It is first recorded in 1780 in the sea journals of an Englishman named Pasley, and it appears next in a letter by Sir Walter Scott in 1813.

There are two slightly more respectable theories about the true origin of the phrase. One links it with the much older phrase *cap-à-pie*, a French phrase meaning 'head to foot', which was used in reference to a soldier's being fully equipped with armour or other equipment, the implication being that someone so arrayed was in good order. The other theory also suggests a French origin, from *nappe pliée*, folded linen, on the presumption that household linen so folded was the epitome of neatness.

Unfortunately for the proponents of these theories, there's no evidence that links *apple-pie order* with either, raising the suspicion that they are as much folk etymology as the one about the New England cook. The only gem of comfort is that *apple-pie bed*, for one made up with sheets so folded that you can't sleep full-length, is known from about the same period and could have the same source. If so, the French folded linen origin seems the best bet.

Artichoke

This much travelled plant, also called the *globe artichoke*, has had its name transformed by mishearings and folk etymology during its travels around the shores of the Mediterranean. The name was originally Arabic, *al-karsufa*, which travelled via Moorish Spanish *alcarchofa* into Northern Italy as *articiocco* (perhaps influenced by *ciocco*, a stump).

People had all sorts of goes at converting this into something that sounded sensible when the plant was first brought into Britain ('in the time of Henry VIII' according to Richard Hakluyt, writing in 1599), variously trying out *archecock*, *hortichock*, *artichoux*, *hortichoke* and even *heartychoke*. The last element may have become *choke* because the plant grows rather too well in Britain and will overrun the garden if not vigorously controlled. *Choke* is also the name given to the inedible upper part of the artichoke head; people sometimes say that *choke* forms part of the name because that part of the artichoke will choke you if you try to eat it, but that's folk etymology derived from the modern name.

The name didn't finally settle down to the modern spelling until the eighteenth century.

See also JERUSALEM ARTICHOKE.

Asparagus

This delightful vegetable has had its name battered so much by Latin scholars and folk etymologists during its history in English that if it were sentient it would be terminally confused.

It first appears in English around the year 1000. The name was taken from the medieval Latin *sparagus* or *sparagi* and after going through various forms it had settled down by the sixteenth century to *sparage* or *sperage*. It might well have stayed like that had it not been for Latin scholars during and after the Renaissance. They made knowledge of Latin (and Greek) a fashionable and lofty ideal among educated laypeople. They knew that the classical Latin word was *asparagus*, which itself had been borrowed from Greek and which was well known among botanists. By force of example, they changed the word back to its classical Latin form, which became moderately well known during the sixteenth and seventeenth centuries.

Ordinary people had trouble with *asparagus* and tended to do what the medieval Latin scholars had done with it – leave off the unstressed initial vowel, so making it *sparagus* again. But they went one step further still, converting it by folk etymology into forms that made more sense, either as *sparagrass* or *sparrowgrass*. The latter in particular became common in the seventeenth and eighteenth centuries. Samuel Pepys wrote in his diary for 20 April 1667: 'So home, and having brought home with me from Fenchurch Street a hundred of sparrowgrass, cost 18d.' In the eighteenth century *sparrowgrass* was so much the standard term that John Walker commented in his *Critical Pronouncing Dictionary and Exposition of the English Language* of 1791 that 'Sparrow-grass is so general that *asparagus* has an air of stiffness and pedantry.'

During the nineteenth century, the wheel turned yet again, in part because of pedagogical opposition to a form considered to be no more than an ignorant mistake, bringing *asparagus* to the fore and relegating *sparrowgrass* to what the first edition of the *Oxford English Dictionary* rather loftily described as 'dialect or vulgar' status. It's still around, though rarely to be seen in print.

At sixes and sevens

This expression is commoner in Britain and Commonwealth countries than in the USA. It can mean something that's in a state of total confusion or disarray, or people who are collectively in a muddle or at loggerheads about how to deal with some situation. For example, a British newspaper article in 2002 reported that the Conservative opposition had accused the Government of being 'at sixes and sevens' over what to do with the rail network.

But what could possibly be the *sixes* and the *sevens* that are involved? There are two old stories that try to explain this. One tries to find it in the King James Version of the Bible; Job 5: 19 has: 'He shall deliver thee in six troubles; yea, in seven shall no evil touch thee', a couplet that makes no sense to us today and which doesn't seem to link to any known use of the expression. The other story, more common and very widely believed, traces it back to a dispute between two of the ancient livery companies in the City of London.

These companies, trade guilds, grew up from the latter part of the twelfth century as associations to protect their members' interests. (They were called livery companies because members had the right to wear a distinctive costume or *livery*.) There was a lot of squabbling with other guilds about precedence in the early days. One especially troublesome dispute concerned the Merchant Taylors Company, whose members were tailors, and the Skinners Company, whose members controlled the trade in furs. In 1484 the then Lord Mayor, Sir Robert Billesden, settled the dispute in a judgement of Solomon by ruling that the two companies should alternate between the sixth and seventh positions in successive years, a ruling still in force. This might seem to settle the matter. What could be clearer? The two companies were permanently *at sixes and sevens* with each other.

The problem lies in the brute force of the evidence. The first form of the phrase was *set on six and seven*. Geoffrey Chaucer uses it like this ('to set the world on six and seven') in his *Troilus and Criseyde*, dated about 1375. There are several other examples in the following century, which show that Chaucer was making use of an expression already well known (to the extent that he didn't feel the need to explain it). The appearance in Chaucer was rather more than a century before the dispute between the guilds was settled, so can't have been created as a result of it (though I can imagine people using the saying to make a joke about the dispute after it had been settled).

We can't be absolutely sure of where the phrase comes from, but the most probable explanation is that it arose out of an old game of dice called hazard, in which one's chances of winning were controlled by a set of rather arbitrary and complicated rules. It is thought that the expression was originally *to set on cinque and sice* (from the Old French numerals for five and six). These were apparently the most risky numbers to shoot for ('to set on') and anyone who tried for them was considered careless or confused. Later, the number words shifted to their modern values as a result of folk etymology among individuals who knew no French and misheard the words. The link with the game (and the original French words) must by then have been severed, or perhaps it was a joke, as seven is an impossible number to throw with one die. The change may also be linked to the sum of the new numbers being thirteen, long considered unlucky.

The phrase has been common since Chaucer's day, to the extent that we can trace in detail the way its form has shifted down the centuries, including *set at six and seven*, *stand on six and seven*, and *to be left at six and seven*. Shakespeare used it in this last form in *Richard III*, in which the Duke of York says:

> I should to Plashy too,
> But time will not permit. All is uneven,
> And everything is left at six and seven.

It took until the eighteenth century for people to commonly put the numbers in the plural; for example, Captain Francis Grose included it in his *Dictionary of the Vulgar Tongue* in 1785 as 'Left at sixes and sevens, in confusion, commonly said of a room where the furniture, etc. is scattered about, or of a business left unsettled'.

Incidentally, our word *hazard* first came into the language to refer to the dice game (via the Old French *hasard* and the Spanish *azar* from the Arabic *az-zahr* 'luck, chance', based on an Arabic or Turkish word for dice), and only later took on the meaning of danger or risk, or as a verb, to venture something, because the dice game was so risky to bet on. The modern game called craps is a simplified form of hazard.

Avocado

Popular etymology isn't confined to English, of course. When the Spanish came across this fruit in Central America they learned that the native Aztecs called it *ahuacatl*, but the Spanish converted this into *aguacate* and then into *avocado*, their word for a lawyer that's closely related to our *advocate*. The word moved across into English at the end of the seventeenth century (it's first mentioned in William Dampier's *A Voyage Round the World* of 1697). He and other English writers usually called it an *avocado pear*, because the fruit is indeed pear-shaped and grows on a tall tree which does look like an overgrown pear (except that it's evergreen).

The British cultivated the tree in the West Indies in the eighteenth century and it was there that they confused matters still further by adding another layer of folk etymology. Not being familiar with the Spanish word, they changed it to *alligator pear*, perhaps because the tree grows in tropical conditions in which one also finds alligators, or because the green warty skin of some types reminded people of the saurian. Even today that name is not entirely defunct, though *avocado* has almost completely superseded it.

Incidentally, *alligator* is itself another example of folk etymology, this time an English corruption of the Spanish *el lagarto*, the lizard, the term that the Spanish applied to the beasts when they first encountered them in the New World.

Back to square one *See* SQUARE ONE

Ball of wax *See* WHOLE BALL OF WAX

Ballyhoo

Ballyhoo is exaggerated publicity or advertisement, what the *Times Literary Supplement* of 19 July 1934 described as 'eloquence aimed at the pocket book', often with the most extravagant disregard for the truth.

It's an expressive word. Most dictionaries say simply 'origin unknown'. This doesn't satisfy those whose enthusiasm outweighs their concern for evidence, so we have a number of proposals in the literature:

- It's from the town of Ballyhooly in County Cork, Ireland (roughly halfway between Ballydesmond and Ballyduff), supposedly renowned for the unruliness of its inhabitants.

- Bailinghadh (pronounced ballyhoo), is an Irish verb meaning 'to collect'. Irish fairground touts in the nineteenth century shouted bailinghadh anois! ('collection now!') when they were passing around the hat at the end of a performance.

- It's a modification of hullabaloo or a blend of ballet and whoop.

- The origin lies in the Arabic cry of b'allah hoo, 'through God it is', used by the fake dervishes in the Oriental Village in the 1893 World's Fair in Chicago.

- It's a shortened form of ballyhooly truth, a lie, said to be music-hall slang of the nineteenth century, possibly derived from the whole bloody truth, with bloody modified to the euphemistic bally.

We can disregard some of these stories straightaway, since we know ballyhoo was originally American. It came from the circus and fairground, where it was the name barkers gave to a flamboyant free performance outside an attraction to encourage the punters to pay their money and see the full show. It's on record from the very beginning of the twentieth century.

We do also know that in the nineteenth century it was the name given to an unseaworthy or slovenly ship. An excellent illustration of its use is in Thomas Warren's book Dust and Foam of 1859:

> During my wanderings about the world, I had fallen in with a good many forlorn craft; but I had never met a more perfect type of what a sailor calls a ballyhoo, than was this one. In model she looked like a Dutch galiot; her rigging untarred, and hanging in a bight, swayed to and fro in the wind; her decks, rough and greasy, appeared never to have been washed down, and the cabin was in a state of dire confusion, the rats making a violent stampede as I entered.

There's also *ballyhoo of blazes*, the last word of contempt for a slovenly ship, which Herman Melville used in *Omoo* in 1847 and which is known to the end of that century, when Kipling included it in *Captains Courageous* in 1897. It's thought this word comes from the Spanish word *balahu* for a type of ungainly schooner used in the West Indies. However, nobody can propose a method by which this nautical term came to be picked up by landlubbers and had its sense so dramatically changed.

A possible clue lies in a story in *Harper's New Monthly Magazine* in June 1880, recounting a joke played on inexperienced shooters in a Long Island club of sportsmen:

> *Another green South-Sider was sent in pursuit of birds as remarkable as anything in the mythology of the ancients: they were provided with four wings and two heads, and possessed the wonderful power of whistling through one bill while they sang through the other. They inhabited a marsh about a mile east of the club-house, and were only to be taken at daybreak. The ambitious hunter rose early, and went breakfastless to the field indicated. He waited till long after sunrise, but saw no sign of the curious production of ornithology, and he went there three days in succession, only to be disappointed. Finally, on the fourth morning he discovered a bird answering to the description, and after creeping through the wet grass, and nearly getting mired in a bog, he fired, and brought down a clever composition of wood and pasteboard. Subsequent references to the 'ballyhoo bird' were never relished by the victim of the practical joke.*

This looks like a more direct ancestor of the American fairground term, but even then the connection is more than a little opaque. Whilst dismissing the more fanciful interpretations, the experts have to admit that the problem of the origin of *ballyhoo* is as yet far from solved.

Bamboozle

To bamboozle somebody is to trick, deceive or cheat them.

One story suggests it's a slang variant of *bombazine*, a fabric that is a mixture of silk with wool or cotton; dyed black, it was once commonly used for mourning clothes. The idea behind the association was that a woman so dressed was able to play a confidence trick as a grieving widow. I sit open-mouthed in admiration at the ingenuity of this explanation, not least because I can find not a shred of evidence that connects *bombazine* with *bamboozle*. The only connection between the words is that both start with the same letter and both contain a z.

A more respectable theory was put forward in 1860 by the English writer John Camden Hotten, in his *Dictionary of Modern Slang, Cant, and Vulgar Words*. He argued that it came from Romany, the language of the British gypsies, and developed in the late seventeenth century from a word meaning 'to perplex or mislead by hiding'. However, nobody has identified this word and modern etymologists dismiss the idea out of hand.

So where, then, does it come from? Put simply, we don't know. It appears in print for the first time in a play by Colley Cibber in 1703, *She Wou'd, and She Wou'd Not*: 'Sham Proofs, that they propos'd to bamboozle me with.' Seven years later, Jonathan Swift wrote a letter to the *Tatler* to complain about 'the continual Corruption of our English Tongue'. He wrote: 'The third Refinement observeable in the Letter I send you, consisteth in the Choice of certain Words invented by some *pretty Fellows*, such as *Banter*, *Bamboozle*, *Country Put*, and *Kidney*, as it is there applied; some of which are now struggling for the Vogue, and others are in Possession of it.'

There's just a chance that it may be linked to the Scots word *bumbaze* or *bombaze*, which means to be perplexed, confused or stupefied; however, the *Concise Scots Dictionary* prefers to assert the journey was in the other direction and that the word comes from *bamboozle* by conflation with another Scots word, *baise*, with similar meaning.

Otherwise, it seems likely that the word came out of some cant word of the London criminal underworld of the period.

Bankrupt

The great Dr Johnson told the story in his dictionary that when a medieval Italian moneychanger became insolvent, he was forced to break his dealing bench. Hence *bankrupt*, where the second part is from the same source as words like *rupture* that are derived from the medieval Latin *ruptus*, broken, the past participle of *rumpere*, to break. The same tale has been repeated in some recent books on word history.

Bankrupt is actually from Italian *banca rotta*, a broken bench (not a rotten one, as the false friend represented by Italian *rotta* might suggest – it's likewise from Latin *rumpere*). Italians know as much about figurative uses of language as anybody else and *rotta* was a good example, since it could also mean 'shipwrecked' or 'defeated' as well as 'failed' or 'ruined'. The bench was real, though: it was the usual word in Italian for a money dealer's table (and is the origin of our *bank* for a financial institution).

Bankrupt arrived in English around the middle of the sixteenth century via the equivalent French form of *banqueroute*. It was changed into our modern form by a learned folk etymology based on the known Italian sense. We English also borrowed the figurative idea to create our sense of *break* in phrases like *he's gone broke* and *to break the bank*. The first appearance of the latter was not in the gambling sense but meant to become bankrupt.

Barbecue

Some authorities, especially in parts of the USA, will argue that the back-garden device for cooking over charcoal or gas is no more than an outdoor grill. A *real* barbecue, they hold, is a festival at which the central element is a beef or hog dressed whole and roasted on a spit over a pit fire. The *Oxford English Dictionary*'s definition includes this evocative description: 'to split a hog to the backbone, fill the belly with wine and stuffing, and cook it on a huge gridiron, basting with wine'.

Disagreement about the word extends to where it comes from. It is often said to derive from the French *barbe à queue*, that is, 'from beard to tail', signifying the whole of the pig being roasted. Leaving aside the fact that pigs don't have beards (though the allusion would work for goats), the true origin is well authenticated, and the story is just another example of a well-meaning but false attempt to explain the apparently inexplicable.

We have to go back to the West Indian island of Hispaniola in the early days of European exploration to begin the search for this word. The local Arawakan Indians had a method of erecting a wooden frame over a fire in order to dry or cure meat and fish. In their language, Taino, they called the frame a *barbacoa*, which the Spanish explorers borrowed.

This word seems also to have been applied to sleeping platforms raised off the ground to reduce the risk of snakebite, presumably without the fire underneath. That extraordinary seaman William Dampier is the first recorded user of the noun in this sense, in his *New Voyage round the World* of 1699: 'And lay there all night, upon our Borbecu's, or frames of Sticks, raised about 3 foot from the Ground.'

It seems that Europeans who settled in the North American colonies began to apply the word to cooking meat rather than drying it, and that such outdoor cooking soon became a social event. The first example known in this sense is of the verb, in a work by Aphra Behn of 1690: 'Let's barbicu this fat rogue', showing that it was well enough known even then to be used figuratively.

In 1733, Benjamin Lynde, then Chief Justice of Massachusetts, wrote in his diary, 'Fair and hot; Browne, barbacue; hack overset.' This is cryptic, but he could hardly have known that nearly three centuries later his jotted note would be celebrated as the first ever recorded usage of our modern noun. It seems that on this pleasant summer's day he went to some neighbours called Browne to have a barbecue, but that at some point, presumably on the way back, his hack – possibly his hired horse but from context more probably his carriage – had an accident.

William Dampier, by the way, had a varied and controversial career: the *Dictionary of National Biography* describes him as 'buccaneer, pirate, circumnavigator, captain in the navy, and hydrographer'. It is appropriate that the man so closely associated with the early days of the word *barbecue* should be called a *buccaneer*, since that comes from the French *boucanier*, which probably derives from *mocaém*, a word used by a group of Brazilian Indians, the Tupi, for a wooden framework on which meat was dried.

Barefaced lie

To judge from my electronic postbag, this expression worries people. When I used it in a newsletter, subscribers wrote to suggest that it should instead be *baldfaced lie* or *boldfaced lie*, with or without a hyphen. A few were quite vehement in their belief that I was making a serious mistake. Having looked at the evidence, I can see why they were confused.

The original is certainly *barefaced lie*. The first example on record is in an American book of 1836, *George Balcombe* by Nathaniel

Tucker: 'Would you palm such a barefaced lie upon me, as well as on that poor, confiding, generous, true-hearted girl? I will undeceive her instantly.' There are enough examples from the 1840s on in US sources to suggest that the expression was coined there. It was only taken up by British authors later in the century.

At some point – exactly when my sources can't make clear but it seems to be in recent decades, since the earliest example I've been told about is from 1961 – the saying has shifted in North America towards *baldfaced lie*, so much so that it is now the more common form in newspapers, though the other is still found in dictionaries. In Britain, we have largely retained *barefaced lie*.

Both forms are based on colloquial uses that go back into the seventeenth century. Someone *barefaced* originally had the face uncovered, and hence was figuratively acting in an unconcealed or open way (Shakespeare is the first known user of both literal and figurative senses). From the latter part of the seventeenth century, it took on a sense of something or someone who was audacious, shameless or impudent, so that a *barefaced lie* was one in which the speaker made no attempt to disguise it as truth.

An animal that is *baldfaced* has a white face or a white mark on the head. (Today, *bald* refers to someone or something that lacks hair, but that's a medieval extension on the basis that a bald pate looks whitish.) Examples of the white sense include *bald coot* (from the white flash on the forehead of this waterbird, a phrase which was changed by a bit of folk etymology into the slang insult *bald as a coot*, totally bald), *bald-faced stag* (one likewise with a white flash on the head) and *baldfaced cattle* (Herefords, which have white faces). In mid-nineteenth-century America, a *baldfaced shirt* was a dress shirt with a starched white front. It seems that *baldfaced* is sufficiently common in America, compared with *barefaced*, to have influenced the expression.

An even more recent introduction is *boldfaced lie*. It is sometimes argued in defence of this version that such a lie is told with a shamelessly bold face. I can't really dispute that, since it makes sense. However, the other story one sometimes hears in support of it falls firmly into the area of folk etymology – it is said that it comes from a lie knowingly told in print because it was printed for emphasis in bold type.

Boldfaced lie is usually regarded as an error. Oddly, the databases record it earlier than either of the others; it appeared in 1607 in a work in verse by Robert Pricket, *The Jesuits Miracles, or New Popish Wonders*: 'Who so beleeues this Popish bold facest lie . . .' It should not be taken as a precedent, though, since it is an isolated instance with almost no further examples until very recent times.

Barking

This informal British term, used for somebody thought to be totally mad or demented, has led people to try to connect it with the East London suburb of Barking, which on the face of it seems reasonable.

I've heard someone described as 'one stop short of Barking', referring to the London District Line railway station, as one might say someone is 'two sandwiches short of a picnic', 'three sheep short in the top paddock', or 'two bricks short of a load'. I've even heard a person described as *Dagenham*, explained as being 'three stops on from Barking', which on that line indeed it is. Peter Ackroyd, in his book *London: The Biography*, dating from 2000, suggests that monks in medieval times had a lunatic asylum there, which gave rise to the term. The problem with Mr Ackroyd's hypothesis is that the evidence strongly suggests the term is nothing like so old as that.

The second edition of the *Oxford English Dictionary* contains not a single reference to *barking* in the sense of mad and I can't find an example in my electronic database of more than 7,000 works of literature. Eric Partridge, in his *Dictionary of Slang and Unconventional English*, dates it to about 1965, as does Jonathon Green in *The Cassell Dictionary of Slang*.

Nicholas Shearing of the OED kindly hunted through Oxford's database of citations for me and found that the earliest reference they have is from as far back as 1933, from *Mr Jiggins of Jigginstown* by Christine Packenham (Countess Longford): 'But he was mad! Barking mad!' That gives the clue to the origin: *barking* is an elliptical form of the full expression *barking mad*, for a person who is so deranged that he or she barks like a dog, or resembles a rabid dog, or one that howls at the full moon.

By the 1960s, *barking* was being used alone. Anne Hegerty found this for me in a Nancy Mitford story, *Don't Tell Alfred*, of 1960: 'If Dr Jore comes here every day like he says he's going to he will drive me mad. Really, properly barking.'

Bated breath

It's so common these days to see this phrase written *baited breath* that there is every chance that it will soon become the usual form. Examples in newspapers and magazines are legion; this one appeared in the *Daily Mirror* on 12 April 2003: 'She hasn't responded yet but Michael is waiting with baited breath.'

It's easy to mock, but there's a real problem. *Bated* and *baited* sound the same and we no longer use *bated*, let alone its verb *to bate*, outside this one phrase. Confusion is almost inevitable. *Bated* here is a contraction of *abated* through loss of the first vowel (a process called aphesis); it has the meaning 'reduced, lessened, lowered in force'. So *bated breath* refers to a state in which you almost stop breathing through terror, awe, extreme anticipation or anxiety.

Shakespeare is the first writer known to use it, in *The Merchant of Venice*:

> *Shall I bend low and, in a bondman's key,*
> *With bated breath and whisp'ring humbleness,*
> *Say this . . .*

Mark Twain employed it, too, in *The Adventures of Tom Sawyer* in 1876: 'Every eye fixed itself upon him; with parted lips and bated breath the audience hung upon his words, taking no note of time, rapt in the ghastly fascinations of the tale.'

Bee's knees

Something that is the *bee's knees* is stylish and the height of excellence. It is sometimes explained as being from an Italian-American way of saying *business*. I've also heard it argued that it is properly *Bs and Es*, an abbreviation for *be-alls and end-alls*.

Both are without doubt wrong. *Bee's knees* is actually one of a set of nonsense catchphrases from 1920s America, the period of the flappers. You might at that time have heard such curious concoctions as *cat's miaow, elephant's adenoids, tiger's spots, bullfrog's beard, elephant's instep, caterpillar's kimono, turtle's neck, duck's quack, gnat's elbows, monkey's eyebrows, oyster's earrings, snake's hips, kipper's knickers, elephant's manicure, clam's garter, eel's ankle, leopard's stripes, tadpole's teddies, sardine's whiskers, pig's wings, canary's tusks, cuckoo's chin,* and *butterfly's book*. Plus many others.

None of these made much sense – but then slang fashions often don't – and their only common feature was the comparison of something of excellent quality to a part of an animal with, if possible, a bit of alliteration thrown in. Another example was *cat's whiskers*, which is sometimes said to have been the first of the bunch to arise, from the cat's whisker that was the adjustable wire in early radio crystal sets. However, *cat's miaow* and *cat's pyjamas* (an exception to the anatomical rule, referring to the then new fashion of wearing pyjamas at night) are both recorded slightly earlier, about 1921. The first appearance of *bee's knees* so far known in print was found by Barry Popik in a flapper's dictionary in the *Appleton Post-Crescent* of Appleton, Missouri of 28 April 1922, glossed as meaning 'peachy, very nice'. Clearly, by then it must have already become well established.

It was a short-lived frivolous slang fashion and only a very few such expressions have survived, of which *bee's knees* is perhaps the best known, though *cat's pyjamas* and a few others are also still encountered. Strangely, these two examples are still quite well known, though they are considered old-fashioned and are usually said with a knowing tongue-in-cheek attitude.

A British example from the same period is the rather rude *dog's bollocks*, the second word being a low slang term for testicles. This, too, indicates something excellent, admirable or first-rate. Eric Partridge suggests it arose as a term for the printer's mark of a colon followed by a dash. This fits the pattern and period of the others, and might have been influenced by it, but its first sense suggests it came out of a different tradition. Certainly it only became a general slang term much later.

Beg the question

Casual and common usage of this phrase annoys people who know some logic and are familiar with the classical languages. From my attempts to research the point, it also seems to cause trouble for dictionary writers and compilers of style guides, so much so that I've not found two authorities that entirely agree on the nature of the problem or which senses of *beg the question* are acceptable.

What has happened is that the phrase has become an idiom,

whose sense is far from obvious, and that people have guessed its meaning, as a result coming up with incorrect usages that have fogged its meaning and diluted its value.

You can easily find examples of it being used just as though one might say 'prompts the question' or 'forces one to ask why'. Here's an example from the *Independent on Sunday* in February 1995 about gay weddings: 'It begs the question why the Church ever sanctioned . . . something it now abominates?' This meaning of the phrase seems to have grown up because people have turned for a model to other phrases in *beg*, especially the well-known I *beg your pardon* and I *beg to differ*, where *beg* is a fossil verb that actually used to mean 'humbly submit, request'. The way we use *beg to differ* makes *beg the question* look the same as 'wish to ask'. It doesn't – or at least, it didn't.

The original sense is of a logical fallacy, taking for granted or assuming something that as much needs to be proved as your assertion. You might say that 'capital punishment is necessary because without it murders would increase' or that 'fox hunting is acceptable because the fox enjoys the chase'. A closely related idea is that of circular reasoning, of assuming the conclusion as part of your argument. Examples here include 'lying is wrong because we ought always to tell the truth' and 'democracy must be the best form of government because the majority is always right'.

The fallacy was described by Aristotle in his book on logic in about 350 BC. His Greek name for it was turned into Latin as *petitio principii* and then into English around the 1580s as *beg the question*. Most of our problems arise because whoever translated it made a mess of the job. The Latin might better be translated as 'laying claim to the principle', that is, assuming something which needs first to be proved.

Very often, the fact that you are using the matter to be proved as part of your argument is a good deal more subtle than in these examples. It comes across rather as an attempt to evade the issue or avoid giving a straight answer, making the phrase mean 'avoid the question'. This meaning of the phrase is common and many authorities agree it is now part of standard English. The sense of 'prompt the question' that I gave above is another that has a long history. It is gaining ground, and some recent dictionaries include it as an alternative – the *Oxford Dictionary of English* (the single-volume work of 2003, not to be confused with the *Oxford English Dictionary*), for example, says it is 'widely accepted in modern standard English'.

Because the phrase can be used in several different ways, and because it's often used in a way that the purists among us consider to be wrong, it's probably safest to avoid the phrase altogether.

Belfry

What else, you might ask, would one put in a *belfry* but bells? It was that thought that persuaded people to spell and say it like that. However, the Middle English word was *berfrey*, and at first referred to a siege tower, a wooden construction designed to protect besiegers while they were attacking a fortification. The word shifted its meaning around the fifteenth century to mean a tower where a watchman was based. Because such towers often had an alarm bell with which to warn local people of some impending disaster, the name later came to be applied to the bell tower of a church. The shift of pronunciation from r to l is not uncommon: in this case the association with *bell* made the change all the more likely.

Between the devil and the deep blue sea

By this we mean that we're trapped between two equally unpleasant alternatives; another idiom with the same meaning is *on
the horns of a dilemma*.

A persistent story holds that the *devil* was a seam between the
planks of a sailing ship, one that was particularly hard to get at; it
required the sailors set the task of caulking it at sea to hang over
the side in bosun's chairs, so forcing them to be precariously
situated between the devil and the sea.

The association of names between a hard seam to caulk and
devil also turns up in THE DEVIL TO PAY and is likely to be just as
spurious. The evidence is not absolutely convincing, but it looks
very likely that it evolved from the perspective of a landsman, for
whom the sea was an alien and frightening element (one which
even today can hardly be considered safe for those who venture
on it). It would be difficult to decide which would be the greater
peril for such a person: being grabbed by Satan or taking a sea
voyage.

The first examples have the form *between the devil and the dead sea*
and date from the seventeenth century. Others are phrased as
between the devil and the deep sea; only in comparatively modern times
does our version appear. One example is in *The Life and Adventures of
Sir Launcelot Greaves* by Tobias Smollett, dated 1762: 'The conjurer
having no subterfuge left, but a great many particular reasons for
avoiding an explanation with the justice, like the man between
the devil and the deep sea, of two evils chose the least.' None of
the examples I can find makes reference to actual caulking, or even
to sailors' lives.

The desire of writers to romanticize sailing-ship days, or to
assume that an expression that mentions the sea must refer to
sailors, has led them to accept this origin without questioning
dates and sources.

Beyond the pale

Because *pale* is now a rare word, this expression often appears these days as *beyond the pail*, lending yet another layer of confusion to an already rather opaque expression.

Pale here is from Latin *palus*, a stake. A *pale* is a pointed stake driven into the ground to form an element of a fence and – by extension – to the whole barrier made of such stakes (*paling* survives from the same source). This meaning has been around in English since the fourteenth century. By 1400 it had taken on various figurative senses, such as a defence, a safeguard, a barrier, an enclosure within a barrier, or a limit beyond which it was not permissible to go.

In particular, it was used to describe various defended enclosures of English territory inside other countries. The *English pale* in the fourteenth century was the territory of Calais, the last English possession in France. The *Irish Pale* is the more famous one, that part of the country over which England had direct jurisdiction – it varied in size from time to time, but was an area containing several counties centred on Dublin. The first mention of the Irish Pale is in a document of 1446–7. Though there was an attempt later in the century to enclose this Pale by a bank and ditch (never completed), no literal fence was ever constructed around it.

The expression *beyond the pale*, outside the bounds of acceptable behaviour, came much later. The idea behind it was that civilization stopped at the boundary and beyond lay those whose behaviour therefore was not that of gentlemen. A classic example appears in *The Pickwick Papers* by Charles Dickens of 1837: 'I look upon you, sir, as a man who has placed himself beyond the pale of society, by his most audacious, disgraceful, and abominable public conduct.' The earliest example I've found in the modern sense is from Sir Walter Scott in 1819, though it is older in a simple figurative sense of a boundary.

It is frequently said that *beyond the pale* refers to the Irish Pale. Though it must surely be older than 1819, it certainly doesn't date back to the period of the Pale itself. It may be that it actually came to public attention in England as the result of the establishment of the Russian Pales in 1791, specified provinces and districts within which Russian Jews were required to live. The Russian name for these was usually translated into English as *pales of settlement*. It is very probable that writers such as Scott took the figurative sense from that.

Big Apple

In a bit of spirited boosterism that became the envy of other cities, in 1971 the New York Visitors and Convention Bureau began to encourage tourism by giving New York the nickname of *The Big Apple*. The campaign succeeded beyond the promoters' hopes and is now widely known, even beyond the shores of the USA. As a result, a perennial question to word sleuths asks where the name comes from. Was it perhaps invented by the Bureau?

No, they didn't invent it. But where it actually came from has been the subject of much argument and misinformation, leading at times to bad-tempered exchanges between individuals claiming to be experts. One idea puts the origin as far back as the early 1800s and a French émigrée known as Eve; she is said to have established a brothel in the city, whose clients became known as Eve's Apples, leading to *apple* gaining an unsavoury sexual connotation. Some say instead that the nickname appeared during the years after the Wall Street Crash of 1929, when out-of-work financiers sold apples on the city's streets. Others link it to a dance of the late 1930s with that name, popular in New York. However, none of these fits the known dates. As we shall see, the name has been known since 1921, which rules out all but the first, the derivation of which doesn't account for the century or so of silence before the term first reaches print.

The real story is now known, as the result of a decade-long detective hunt through old newspapers by American researchers Barry Popik and Gerald Cohen. They have found that the first printed evidence actually comes from a racing writer named John J. Fitz Gerald, who wrote a regular column in the old *New York Morning Telegraph*, which he eventually renamed *Around the Big Apple*. He first used it in 1921 to refer to the racetracks of New York: 'The L. T. Bauer string is scheduled to start for "the big apple" tomorrow.' He broadened the term to refer to the whole of New York in February 1924: 'The Big Apple, the dream of every lad that ever threw a leg over a thoroughbred and the goal of all horsemen. There's only one Big Apple. That's New York.'

After a lot of work, the researchers found that Fitz Gerald had written in 1924 that he had first heard the term from a couple of black stable hands in New Orleans in 1920, for whom the *big apple* was their name for the New York racetracks that represented the big time, the goal of every aspiring jockey and trainer.

It seems that Fitz Gerald popularized the name to the extent that it was picked up by others. Walter Witchell used it for the entertainment district of New York in 1927: 'To the lonely and aspiring hoofer, the fannie-falling comedian, Broadway is the Big Apple, the Main Stem, the goal of all ambition.' Jazz musicians also used it the same way, which led to the late 1930s' dance name, possibly through a New York club also called the *Big Apple*. The expansion of the term to the whole of New York seems to have become common around the 1940s.

This solves the immediate problem, but – as so often in etymology – merely takes it back one step. Where did those New Orleans stable hands get the phrase from, since it seemed to be well known?

Some writers point to the Spanish phrase manzana principal, 'main apple', for a city centre or the main downtown area. That's from an idiomatic usage of manzana for a city block, probably from manzanar, an apple orchard, hence a plot of land. It is suggested that it was being used by the New Orleans men Fitz Gerald talked to in the more general sense of the place to be, the place where the main action is. The problem with this story is that Spanish wasn't a language especially well known among black stable hands in New Orleans in 1920, though they might have picked it up from racetracks in Spanish-speaking areas. However, Barry Popik has found that manzana principal isn't recorded until later; in fact it's a loan translation from 'big apple' into Spanish rather than the other way around. Scotch yet another folk etymology, albeit a more learned one than most.

It seems from an early example of the phrase that people were thinking of an apple as a treat, and that for those New Orleans stable hands the New York racing scene was a supreme opportunity, like an attractive big red apple.

The Bill

In British slang The Bill is the police, in particular the Metropolitan Police, best known to many people through a long-running television series with that title.

Like so many slang terms, its history is obscure: it appears near the end of last century (the Oxford English Dictionary hasn't been able to trace it back further than a glossary in the Daily Mirror in October 1969, though Eric Partridge, in A Dictionary of Slang and Unconventional English, dates it to the 1950s from anecdotal evidence). An older and fuller form is Old Bill, which is now much less well known, but which is recorded from 1958.

Absence of evidence is fertile ground for inventors of anecdotes. The Metropolitan Police Historical Museum claims to have traced no less than thirteen different stories for where it comes from. I won't bore you with them all, but a selection will once again point up the inventiveness of amateur etymologists:

- The original 'Old Bill' was King William IV, whose constables were an early form of police.

- It is said that constables of the watch, forerunners of the police, were given this name because of the bills or billhooks they carried as weapons.

- The old bill was, in Victorian times, a banknote passed to a policeman as a bribe to turn a blind eye on some illegal activity.

- It might be a blend of Bill Bailey (from the music hall song 'Won't You Come Home, Bill Bailey?') with The Old Bailey, the Central Criminal Court.

- The original vehicles used by the Flying Squad all had the registration letters BYL, so the squad became known as the Bill.

The Oxford English Dictionary is fairly sure the origin lies in the cartoon character Old Bill. He was created during the First World War, in 1915, by Captain Bruce Bairnsfather. Old Bill was a Cockney veteran soldier with a walrus moustache, the epitome of the grumbling but loveable foot-soldier. In a famous cartoon, he was the one who told an unhappy recruit sheltering with him in a shell hole, 'If you knows a better 'ole, go to it', a saying that became a catchphrase.

Bruce Bairnsfather's cartoons and stories became hugely popular during the War and immediately afterwards. The name Old Bill remained in the language as a term for a man with a heavy, drooping moustache. It is often assumed that the name became applied to the police, perhaps sometime in the 1930s. Eric Partridge said it was because many London policemen wore walrus moustaches in the inter-war years, but the evidence we have doesn't confirm that.

Billy-o

This common (though informal) expression is sometimes spelled *billy-oh*. It usually appears in the phrase *like billy-o*, which means to do something with energy or effort, perhaps in an instruction to somebody to 'Pull like billy-o!' or this from John Buchan's *Mr Standfast* of 1919: 'I lied like billy-o and said I had never heard of you.'

It's not often a folk etymology comes with a heritage plaque attached, but at the end of April 2003 a marker was placed on the United Reformed Church in Market Hill, Maldon, Essex, to commemorate a Nonconformist minister, the Reverend Joseph Billio. He came to the town in 1696, built a chapel that would hold 400 and made his name locally through his impassioned sermons – hence preaching *like billio*. Unfortunately, the word is first recorded only from the end of the nineteenth century, which makes it much too recent to be linked with Mr Billio (and would seem to render the plaque a permanent record that the civic pride of the people of Maldon is greater than their etymological knowledge, though there's nothing unexpected in that – see LYNCH LAW for another case).

Other stories I've come across online link the word to an Italian soldier at the time of Garibaldi, Lieutenant Nino Bixio (a Genoese name that's pronounced rather like 'billio'); it is said he would enter battle encouraging his men to follow him and 'fight like Bixio' (presumably in Italian, so how it passed into English is not explained). It has also been associated with William Hedley's early steam engine, *Puffing Billy*, and with Good King Billy, William III.

In truth, nobody knows where the word comes from, though

the first part might indeed be from the name Billy, a pet form of *William*, which has been a common generic term for a man in parts of Scotland and the north of England for centuries. The first recorded use is in the phrase 'Shure it'll rain like billy-oh!', from the *Referee* of 1885, in which the spelling of *sure* hints at an Irish origin. If it is Irish it might indeed be thought to have something to do with William III, who burned his name into Irish memory at the Battle of the Boyne in 1690. But two centuries is a long time.

It is rather more probable that it's a euphemistic reformulation of the much older phrase *like the devil*, which dates back to Shake-spearean times. There are expressions, older than billy-o, in which Billy is a euphemism for the devil – *billy-be-damned* and giving somebody *all billy hell* – so it would seem that there's very likely a devilish connection there.

Black Maria

A play on BBC radio not long ago attributed the source of this term for a police or prison van to a lady who came to court in London wearing black dresses of exceeding splendour. This is a fine example of a sort of folk etymology that grows out of nowhere except the fertile imagination of its inventor. We can dispose of this person straight away, as the expression is quite certainly American in origin (though it was adopted in London from the 1860s). We can't be totally certain where the name comes from, though the standard story that is often told about it also looks likely to be wrong.

This story points to Maria Lee, a black woman who kept a boarding house in Boston in the early 1800s. She did so with such severity that she became more feared than the police, who called on her to help them catch and restrain criminals. The story almost certainly became attached to her because she was well known, black, named Maria, and associated with the police, but there's no evidence that she was the source of the name for the police vans. The first reference we have to such a vehicle in Boston is dated 1847, which might seem to be rather too long after her heyday for there to be a direct connection.

Eric Partridge mentions a book of 1844 with the title *Peter Ploddy, and Other Oddities*, by Joseph Clay Neal, a well-known American journalist and humorist of the period. It contains the story *The Prison Van; or, The Black Maria*, whose title has been for many years the first known use of the term. In it, the author wrote: 'In Philadelphia . . . the popular voice applies the name of "Black Maria" to each of these melancholy vehicles.'

We now know, as the result of research by George A. Thompson of New York University, that the term was in use in New York about a decade earlier, since it turned up in at least two newspaper reports, one of 1835 and the other of 1836. The former was in the *New York Transcript* of 24 December 1835 and said: 'A man named Henry Stage . . . contrived to make his escape on Saturday last while on his way from Bellevue prison to the city in the carriage generally known as "Black Maria".' However, he also found a couple of slightly earlier references in the *New York Daily Advertiser* which don't mention it by that name, but just call it a prison van (it would be the better part of another century before anybody started to call it a *paddy wagon*). It looks as though 1834–6 was the period at which the new term was just beginning to shift from low slang into a halfway respectable form that could be quoted in the public prints.

George A. Thompson suggests the name comes from a famous black racehorse of the period, also named Black Maria, which was foaled in Harlem, New York, in 1826. She won many races (her purse winnings alone amounted to nearly $15,000, a very large sum for the period), but her most famous exploit was on 13 October 1832, when she won the race for the Jockey Club purse of $600 at the Union Course. In 1870, an article about her in *Harper's New Monthly Magazine* noted that 'The track was heavy, and yet, to achieve a victory, twenty miles had to be run. We wonder if there is a horse on the turf to-day that could stand up under such a performance as this?'

The dates are suggestive. Here is a famous black racehorse whose greatest exploit is in New York in 1832, and only three years later her name is used for a horse-drawn prison van in the same city, no doubt because it got prisoners to their unwanted destination rather more quickly than they would have liked. As matters stand, it's not possible to prove – but like her many admirers, I'd put my money on her to be first past the post.

Blind man's buff

'What's this word *buff*?' people ask, since many know it as *blind man's bluff*, especially in the USA, where a book on submarine espionage during the cold war was published in 1999 under that title.

It was an effective and relevant one for its subject, and it's not hard to find other examples of the *bluff* form in book titles and texts. Many recent ones occur in newspapers in Britain, the USA, Canada and New Zealand, but it's by no means new. H. G. Wells used it in *War and the Future* in 1917: 'I feel almost like a looker-on at a game of blind-man's bluff as I watch the discussion of synthetic political ideas.' The oldest example I know of is in *'Way down East; or, Portraitures of Yankee life* by Seba Smith, from 1854 or thereabouts: 'Well, now, what's the order of the day here to-night? Dance, or forfeits, or blind man's bluff?'

The original was certainly *blind man's buff*. That last word has been archaic for more than three centuries, so one can't blame anybody for wanting to amend it. And bluff seems to make a lot of sense in the context of the game, which might be said to involve the bluffing of the blindfolded person. But the original buff was a blow or buffet (the latter being a diminutive form of buff, both having their origin in the Old French buffe, a blow). The game was once much rougher than it is today, with the central player having to run a gauntlet of blows from the other participants while he attempted to catch and identify one of them.

Blue laws

This American expression refers to any law considered to be puritanical, especially one that restricts what may be done on Sunday – for example one which prevents shops from opening, or limits what they can sell, or prohibits dancing, drinking or working. People have tried to make a link with the use of blue in the sense of a thing that offends against morals. However, blue laws came first by nearly a century and blue in this sense is an abbreviation of blue laws, a term which by the 1820s was well known down the eastern seaboard of America. It is often said that they were called that because the restrictive laws of Puritan New England colonies in the seventeenth century were published on blue paper or between blue covers (this suggestion goes back at least as far as a book on the laws that was published in Hartford in 1838).

The first blue laws in popular mythology were those enacted by the theocratic Puritan leaders of the Commonwealth of Connecticut. These are said to have been decidedly more restrictive and draconian than those of the other New England colonies of the time. You may still find descriptions of them that include such supposed rules as 'No one shall travel, cook victuals, make beds, sweep house, cut hair or shave on the Sabbath-day'; 'every male shall have his hair cut round according to a cap'; 'no woman shall kiss her child on the Sabbath or fasting day'; 'no one shall read Common Prayer, keep Christmas or saints' days, make minced pies, dance, play cards or play on any instrument of music except the drum, trumpet and jew's-harp'.

All these are fables. They were invented by the Reverend Samuel Peters of Hebron in Connecticut, in an unsuccessful little work published in London in 1781, *The General History of Connecticut*. When this was reprinted a century later it was described as 'a book which probably contains as great a number of remarkable falsehoods as any ever published' and as 'a tissue of lies from beginning to end'. He wrote it as a extravagant diatribe against his fellow countrymen while a refugee in England, having been driven out of his homeland by those favouring independence. Though many of his tales were as tall as any by Baron Münchhausen, like all good humorists he leavened his bitter jokes with much that was true. Some items in his list of laws were substantially true: 'The judges shall determine controversies without a jury'; 'married persons must live together or be imprisoned'; 'a wife shall be good evidence against her husband'; and 'the selectmen, on finding children ignorant, may take them away from their parents and put them into better hands, at the expense of their parents'.

Peters wrote that 'Even the religious fanatics of Boston and the mad zealots of Hertford . . . christened them the "Blue Laws".' Despite that comment, it's often said that he invented the term, but it has been found earlier, in a pamphlet of 1762 entitled *The Real Advantages Which Ministers and People May Enjoy, Especially in the Colonies, by Conforming to the Church of England*. Peters said this name had been given because they were 'bloody laws; for they were all sanctified with whipping, cutting off the ears, burning the tongue, and death'. His association was between *blue* and *bloody*, though it isn't immediately obvious why (what might seem a significant linguistic link, to the expression *blue blood* for a person of aristocratic breeding, wouldn't come into English until about 1830); he probably borrowed it as a catchpenny phrase to freeze the blood of his readers.

So we must disregard the Reverend Samuel Peters, but the true source of the phrase is still unknown and represents a great puzzle for etymologists.

Blunderbuss

Even before the days of accurate gunnery, this seventeenth-century weapon was known to be so stunningly imprecise that it could only be used at short range. It had a large bore with a flared muzzle, which fired a number of balls or slugs at a time. We commemorate its erratic aim by using its name to refer to something lacking in subtlety and precision.

The Reverend A. Smythe Palmer, in *Folk-Etymology* (1882), stated firmly that its name was originally *blanterbus or plantierbus*, derived from Latin *plantare*, to plant. This he justified by arguing that it was just a later version of the older arquebus or harquebus, an early gun that was so heavy that it had to be 'planted' or supported on a rest before it could be fired.

Hardly. Unfortunately for his suggestion, the blunderbuss has always been a hand-held device. And sadly for his reputation, we're fairly sure that an origin he dismisses is the right one, though it has suffered from folk etymology. It comes from Dutch *donderbus*. *Bus* here is the old Dutch and German word for a tube or gun (as in the second element of *arquebus*). The first part is the Dutch word for thunder (closely related to the German *Donner*). So it was a thundering tube, fair enough as a description for a weapon that intimidated in close combat more by the noise it made than by its accuracy.

The British knew nothing of the Dutch word for thunder, and modified the name to suit the weapon's blindly firing nature, borrowing *blunder* for the purpose (which then had the highly appropriate sense of 'confusion, bewilderment, trouble, disturbance, clamour', as the *Oxford English Dictionary* puts it), so turning the word into *blunderbuss*.

Bob's your uncle

This is a catchphrase which seemed to arise out of nowhere and yet has had a long period of fashion and is still going strong. It's known mainly in Britain and Commonwealth countries, and is really a kind of interjection. It's used to show how simple it is to do something: 'You put the plug in here, press that switch, and Bob's your uncle!'

The most attractive theory – albeit suspiciously neat – is that it derives from a prolonged act of political nepotism. The Prime Minister, Lord Salisbury (family name Robert Cecil), appointed his rather less than popular nephew Arthur Balfour to a succession of posts. The most controversial, in 1887, was Chief Secretary of Ireland, a post for which Balfour – despite his intellectual gifts – was considered unsuitable. The *Dictionary of National Biography* says: 'The country saw with something like stupefaction the appointment of the young dilettante to what was at the moment perhaps the most important, certainly the most anxious office in the administration.' As the story goes, the consensus among the irreverent in Britain was that to have Bob as your uncle was a guarantee of success, hence the expression. Since the very word *nepotism* derives from the Italian word for nephew (from the practice of Italian popes giving preferment to nephews, a euphemism for their bastard sons), the association here seems more than apt.

Actually, Balfour did rather well in the job, confounding his critics and earning the bitter nickname Bloody Balfour from the Irish, which must have quietened the accusations of undue favour-itism more than a little (he also rose to be Prime Minister from 1902 to 1905). There is another big problem: the phrase isn't recorded until 1937, in Eric Partridge's *Dictionary of Slang and Unconventional English*. Mr Partridge suggested it had been in use since the 1890s, but nobody has found an example in print. This is surprising. If public indignation or cynicism against Lord Salisbury's actions had been great enough to provoke creation of the saying, why didn't it appear – to take a case – in a satirical magazine of the time such as *Punch*?

A rather more probable, but less exciting, theory has it that it derives from the slang phrase *all is bob*, meaning that everything is safe, pleasant or satisfactory. This dates back to the seventeenth century or so (it's in Captain Francis Grose's *Dictionary of the Vulgar Tongue* of 1785). There have been several other slang expressions containing *bob*, some associated with thievery or gambling, and from the eighteenth century on it was also a common generic name for somebody you didn't know. Any or all of these might have contributed to its genesis.

Bog-standard

Bog-standard is a well-known informal term, which originated in Britain and is still best known there. It is often used in a dismissive or derogatory way to suggest something is ordinary or basic, of no more than average quality. The Prime Minister's former spokesman, Alistair Campbell, caused offence in February 2001 when he used it belittlingly to say that 'the day of the bog-standard comprehensive [school] is over'.

It's a puzzling phrase – nobody knows where it came from. It first appeared in writing in the 1980s, seemingly out of the air.

Several people have told me, however, that they remember it from the late 1960s and early 1970s in Rolls-Royce and Ford factories and from other engineering environments. This might be thought to be support for the most common story that *bog* here is an acronym from 'British Or German', on the grounds that manufacturing standards were set in Victorian times by British and German engineering, then considered the best in the world. It's an interesting example of the tendency among amateur word historians to explain away a puzzling word as an acronym, but there's no good evidence for it and it is very unlikely to be true.

The most obvious suggestion is that it has a link with *bog*. This has long been a British slang term for a lavatory or toilet. It's a shortened form of the older *bog-house* for a latrine, privy, or place of ease, which is seventeenth century and is a variation on an even older term, *boggard*. (This is unconnected with the other sense of *boggard* or *boggart* for a goblin or sprite.) The modern slang *bog* in this sense most certainly has a negative edge to it, as you might expect from anything that's linked to excretory functions, so it is plausible that it might be the origin.

However, a more convincing suggestion is that it's a corruption or variant form of *box-standard*, for something that is just how it comes out of the box, with no customization or improvement. The noun is known from the 1880s in a different sense – it's defined in *Lockwood's Dictionary of Mechanical Engineering* in 1888 as 'the standard, or main framework, of a machine or engine, which is hollowed internally to obtain the maximum of strength with the minimum of material'.

The adjectival form of *box-standard* in the same sense as *bog-standard* turns up first in print in a comment by the British computer inventor and all-round genius Sir Clive Sinclair. In February 1983, he said in an interview with the magazine *Computerworld*: 'We cannot foresee the day when a computer becomes just a standard box.

There will be box-standard machines along the road, but we do not simply have to make those.'

Box-standard has continued to appear in later decades. Though it's hard to prove, it does look as though it's the original form, with *bog-standard* being the result of a folk etymological change.

Boldfaced lie   *See* BAREFACED LIE

Brass monkey weather

The full expansion of the phrase is *cold enough to freeze the balls off a brass monkey* and is common throughout the English-speaking world, though much better known now in Australia and New Zealand than elsewhere. This is perhaps surprising, since we know it was first recorded in the USA, in the 1850s. It is often reduced to the elliptical form of the title (perhaps in deference to polite society – for the same reason, it has been modified in the USA into *freeze the tail off a brass monkey*).

There is a story, often repeated, that the phrase originated in the British Navy at the time of the Napoleonic Wars or thereabouts. It is said that the stack of cannon balls alongside each gun were arranged in a pyramid on a brass plate to save space, the plate being called a *monkey*. In very cold weather, the story goes, the cannon balls would shrink and they would fall off the stack.

Don't let anybody convince you of this. It's rubbish. There's no evidence that such brass plates existed. Although the boys bringing charges to the guns from the magazine were known as *powder monkeys* and there is evidence that a type of cannon was called a *monkey* in the mid seventeenth century, there's no evidence that the word was ever applied to a plate under a pile of cannon shot. The whole story is full of logical holes: would they pile shot into a pyramid? (hugely unsafe on a rolling and pitching deck); why a brass plate? (too expensive, and unnecessary: they actually used wooden frames with holes in, called *garlands*, fixed to the sides of the ship); was the plate and pile together actually called a monkey? (no evidence, as I say); would cold weather cause such shrinkage as to cause balls to fall off? (highly improbable, as all the cannon balls would reduce in size equally and the differential movement between the brass plate and the iron balls would be only a fraction of a millimetre).

What the written evidence shows is that the term *brass monkey* was quite widely distributed in the USA from about the middle of the nineteenth century and was applied in all sorts of situations, not just weather. For example: from *The Story of Waitstill Baxter*, by Kate Douglas Wiggin (1913): 'The little feller, now, is smart's a whip, an' could talk the tail off a brass monkey'; and from *The Ivory Trail*, by Talbot Mundy (1919): 'He has the gall of a brass monkey.' Even when weather was involved, it was often heat rather than cold that was meant, as in the oldest example known, from Herman Melville's *Omoo* (1847): 'It was so excessively hot in this still, brooding valley, shut out from the Trades, and only open toward the leeward side of the island, that labor in the sun was out of the question. To use a hyperbolical phrase of Shorty's, "It was 'ot enough to melt the nose h'off a brass monkey." '

It seems much more likely that the image here is of a real brass monkey, or more probably a set of them. Do you remember those sculptured groups of three wise monkeys, 'Hear no evil, See no evil, Speak no evil'? Though the term *three wise monkeys* isn't recorded before the 1920s, the images themselves were common throughout the nineteenth century. It's more than likely the term came from them, as an image of something solid and inert that could only be affected by extremes.

Brass tacks

The meaning of *to get down to brass tacks* is clear enough: to concern oneself with basic facts or realities, to focus on the business at hand. In unedited text, you sometimes see this as *brass tax*, an obvious error caused through the two words sounding alike, and because there is no very obvious image on which to hang the expression.

Its origin is unclear; it appears, seemingly out of the blue, in a letter written by the American painter, sculptor and writer Frederic Remington in 1895. We do know it is American, but otherwise facts are sparse. This has led – in the usual way of things – to a set of more or less fanciful stories:

- It refers to the cleaning of the hull of a wooden ship, scraping off the weed and barnacles until the bolts that held its hull together (the *brass tacks* of the expression) were exposed.

- Concealed brass tacks were used in upholstery because they would not rust and stain the fabric. To reupholster a chair would require the craftsman to get down to the brass tacks.

- It is Cockney rhyming slang for 'facts'.

We can dismiss all of these for various good reasons. The expression has no known connection with the sea and hull fastenings were always of copper, not brass. Though brass tacks were used in furnishings, the association with the phrase seems more than a little stretched, not least because the tacks were mostly visible, not hidden. The last suggestion was put forward by Eric Partridge, but as the idiom is quite certainly American in origin, it seems unlikely.

That leaves us with a fourth idea, that it refers to brass tacks set into the counter of a hardware store or draper's shop to measure lengths of material. The idea here is that measurements were often casually made by the almost immemorial method of holding one end to the nose and marking the end of the arm as being a yard away. Since this was imprecise, requesting an exact measurement using the brass tacks on the counter would be to focus on the realities of the situation.

We can't be sure about this, but the homely analogy is seductive. The use of brass markers in this way long predates the first appearance of the idiom (though it was much more common in the nineteenth century to describe them as brass nails rather than brass tacks, the latter term only becoming common in any application quite late in the century). But we do know that *brass tacks* in this sense is known earlier than the idiom. For example, this appears in *Scribners Monthly* in August 1880: 'I hurried over to Seabright's. There was a little square counter, heaped with calicoes and other gear, except a small space clear for measuring, with the yards tacked off with brass tacks.'

Break a leg!

Of all theatrical superstitions, this attempt to ward off the forces of darkness by wishing one's fellow performers the opposite of good luck is the one that is perhaps best known outside the profession. It belongs with such other beliefs that it is bad luck to whistle in a theatre, that you should never say the final line of a play at the dress rehearsal, and that you must never say the name of the Scottish Play in the green room. Actors have always been a superstitious bunch, as you might expect from a profession in which employment is sporadic, audiences fickle and reputations fragile.

The saying is widely used among actors and musicians in the theatre today, sometimes before every performance, but more often reserved for the first night. Where it comes from has for decades been a source of dispute and I've collected the following speculations:

- In earlier times, actors wished one another 'may you break your leg', in the hope that the performance would be so successful that the performer would be called forth to take a bow – to bend his knee.

- At one time audiences showed their appreciation by throwing money on the stage; to pick the coins up, actors had to *break their legs*, that is, kneel or bend down.

- The curtains on either side of a stage were called the *legs*, so that to pass through the legs was to make it out on to the stage and thereby overcome incipient stage fright.

- The saying really refers to getting one's *big break*, that the performance will be good enough to ensure success in one's career.

- The famous French actress Sarah Bernhardt had a leg amputated in 1915, which didn't stop her performing; it is considered good luck to mention her in the hope that some of her theatrical prowess will rub off by association.

- John Wilkes Booth, the actor who assassinated President Lincoln, broke his leg when he jumped on to the stage to escape afterwards. Somehow, reminding fellow actors of this event leads to good luck in the performance.

We may discard all of these on the grounds principally of varying degrees of implausibility. A key factor is that most of the stories assume that *break a leg* is an old expression. In truth, it's actually quite modern. The earliest known example in print refers to a show with that title in 1957. The saying must, of course, be older for it to have been borrowed for the title and there is anecdotal evidence from theatrical memoirs and personal recollection that it has been around since the 1930s. But not further back.

Similar expressions are known from other languages: the

French say *Merde!* (a term that has been borrowed by dancers in the English and American theatre) and Germans say *Hals- und Beinbruch*, 'neck and leg break', as ways of wishing someone good luck without any fear of supernatural retaliation. It is sometimes said that the German expression is actually a corruption of a Hebrew blessing *hatzlacha u-brakha*, 'success and blessing'. Whatever its source, the most plausible theory is that *Hals- und Beinbruch* was transferred, perhaps via Yiddish, into the American theatre (in which Yiddish- or German-speaking immigrant Jews were strongly represented) sometime after the First World War.

Bridegroom

There's nothing new about folk etymology, as other entries will confirm. In Old English, this word was *brȳdguma*, which is a compound of *brȳd*, a bride, and *guma*, a man (the modern German *Bräutigam* comes from the same Germanic root). *Guma* was a poetic term for a man, which turns up in the epic poem *Beowulf*, as does another version of the same word, *gome*.

By the sixteenth century this had become *brydegome* (in various spellings). This was starting to look puzzling, because *gome* had become obsolete, and people didn't connect it with the old word for a man. On the other hand, they did have *groom*. In the twelfth century, this had been a term for a boy or lad, with something of the colloquial informality about it that *kid* still possesses, though it could only refer to a male child. Two centuries later it had grown up to mean an adult man, but it had also taken on the idea of a menial male, a serving-man or man-servant (its modern sense of a servant who specifically attends to horses developed a little later).

So, people casting about during the sixteenth century in an attempt to make sense of the second half of this mysterious old word *brydegome* seized upon *groom* as an alternative, despite its unfortunate associations with the menial and the lowly. We have it still.

Brouhaha

This is an over-excited and noisy argument, a commotion, or uproar. We know the word came from the French word spelled the same way; it's found in French from the fifteenth century on, but it only arrived in English at the end of the nineteenth century. It seems to have been used in French farce as a noise made by the devil, who cried *brou, ha, ha!*

Like COPACETIC, some people believe the word comes from Hebrew. The late Walther von Wartburg, an expert on the French language, suggested the source was *barukh habba*, 'welcome' – literally 'blessed be the one who comes' – a phrase that appears several times in the Book of Psalms and which is used in Synagogue prayers and as a greeting at Jewish weddings and other public occasions. Unlike folk etymologies, which often grasp uncritically at similarities between languages (see OK for a classic case), there's some support by analogy for the idea. Robert K. Barnhart points out in *The Barnhart Dictionary of Etymology* that a similar word, *barruccaba*, exists in the Arezzo dialect of Italian and is without doubt borrowed from the Hebrew, and that Italian *bandini*, a noise of people chattering, comes from Hebrew *anna 'adonai*, 'Oh Lord', which is found in prayers.

However, it's dangerous to say that because some words come from Hebrew, others must do so too. Some lexicographers think a Hebrew derivation for *brouhaha* is just plain wrong and that it's no more than an imitative nonsense exclamation. Our English word definitely sounds like a large crowd emoting noisily.

Buckaroo

It's not a word people see much these days, not even Americans, in whose country it was invented. However, even if you don't use the word every day, you may know of Buck Owens and his Buckaroos; Americans of mature years may remember the film adventures of the Bronze Buckaroo, Herb Jeffries; some movie buffs may fondly recall that weird comic-strip-cum-science-fiction film of 1984, *The Adventures of Buckaroo Banzai Across the Eighth Dimension*.

Dictionaries will tell you that a *buckaroo* is a cowboy, though those who come into contact daily with the men who work the cattle ranches of the west and who still use the word may like to tell you that he's a superior member of his type, distinctive in his methods and dress.

Some writers seek to prove African origins for American English words, often from racial pride or activist motives. They have claimed an origin for *buckaroo* in *buckra*, the word for a white man in various West African languages like Ibibio, Igbo or Efik. The related *bukra* is indeed used in Gullah (a creole language spoken in the South Carolina Sea Islands) to refer to a poor or mean white man. However, there's no evidence to show how that turned into or even influenced the development of *buckaroo*, and the theory is usually dismissed as wishful thinking.

The experts are firm in their belief that *buckaroo* is Spanish. That's not surprising, since so much of the vocabulary of cattle ranching (including *ranch* itself) is of Spanish origin: *chaps*, *sombrero*, *lasso*, *stampede*, *rodeo*. The source in this case is Spanish *vaquero* for a cowboy or cattle driver, a word that has moved unchanged into American English from Spanish America. People often heard the initial sound as a *b* rather than a *v*. From the 1820s on they began to spell it in that way, as in forms like *bakhara* (the first known version in English, from 1824). Later, it began to be influenced by folk etymological derivation from *buck*, a word that in America could mean a fellow or man (though now considered racist, because it was a derogatory term for male black slaves and native Americans), and spellings like *bocarro*, *buckhara* and *buckayro* turn up at various points through the nineteenth century.

Incidentally, *vaquero* derives from Spanish *vaca*, a cow. That has its roots in Latin *vacca*, which is also the source of our *vaccine*, since the earliest vaccines guarded against smallpox by inoculation with an extract of the less deadly cowpox.

Bug

In the sense of an error in a computer program or system, something with which the industry continues to be beset as though it was suffering one of the seven plagues of Egypt, this word is so common a slang term as to have taken on the status of colloquial, if not standard, English: 'There's a bug in the editor: it crashes if you print more than one page at a time.'

There's a widespread story, reinvigorated from time to time by its being retold by a writer with more enthusiasm than research skills, that this term results from an incident with the US Navy's Harvard Mark II computer soon after the end of the Second World War, in which a technician cured a fault by extracting a moth from between the contacts of a relay in the system. It is also said that this was the source of *debug*, the process of finding and removing errors from a computer program.

The incident really happened: the logbook containing the reference, dated 9 September 1947, survives with the actual moth taped to it. (A picture is at <http://www.history.navy.mil/photos/pers-us/uspers-h/g-hoppr.htm>, though it is wrongly dated as having happened in 1945.)

Writers who tell this story are confusing their entomology and etymology. The log entry itself blows to pieces the story about this being the origin of *bug* by noting under the insect, 'First actual case of bug being found'. This makes it clear that *bug* for a fault was already in use. Indeed, Rear Admiral Grace Hopper (an early programmer who worked on the machine and who later invented the computer language COBOL) used to tell this story in lectures and would remark that the word was applied to problems in radar electronics in the Second World War.

It's actually older still. The first recorded use is in reference to the inventor Thomas Edison and appeared in the *Pall Mall Gazette* in 1889: 'Mr. Edison, I was informed, had been up the two previous nights discovering "a bug" in his phonograph – an expression for solving a difficulty, and implying that some imaginary insect has secreted itself inside and is causing all the trouble.' It seems it wasn't new even then: an electrical handbook from 1896 suggests it was first used in telegraphs as a joke that suggested noisy lines were caused by bugs getting into the cables.

Debug is also recorded before the moth incident: a writer in the *Journal of the Royal Aeronautical Society* in 1945 wrote: 'It ranged from the pre-design development of essential components, through the stage of type test and flight test and "debugging" right through to later development of the engine.'

Those who continue to tell the moth story are doing a grave disservice to an intriguing item of old American slang.

Burger

A couple of decades ago, I was doing some work in one of the Forestry Commission's plantations, one known particularly for its deer. The ranger in charge of wildlife management was enthusiastic about selling patties from the meat of culled animals in the site café: 'You could call them veniburgers!' he enthused.

Even then, *burger* was too well known for this bit of wordplay to attract much attention beyond a polite smile. But the word is a classic example of faulty analysis that has led to the creation of a new combining word element.

The original was *Hamburger steak*, a thin patty made of ground beef seasoned with onions and fried. It originated in (or became associated with) the north German port of Hamburg in the middle decades of the nineteenth century. The ending *-er* is a standard German way of making adjectives relating to place; it also turns up – to give a couple of cases out of many – in *frankfurter* (originally in German *Frankfurter wurst*), a sausage associated with Frankfurt am Main, and in *Rottweiler*, a breed of dog associated with Rottweil in the Black Forest of southern Germany.

The early history of the introduction of the hamburger into the USA has accreted so many claims, counter-claims, legends and sheer misinformation that one must enter a discussion of it on tiptoe. It does seem though, that the concept was introduced into North America by German immigrants from the 1870s onwards. American researcher Barry Popik has found a recipe for preparing it, under the name of *Hamburger steak*, in the *Caterer and Household Magazine* for August 1885. The idea of putting it in a sandwich is known no later than the following decade (it is often said that it was invented at the 1904 World's Fair in St Louis, but it certainly predates this event). The classic bun seems to have followed shortly afterwards.

In parallel with the development of this classic American dish, its name became abbreviated just to *hamburger*. The *Caterer and Household Magazine* article also uses that form, but it seems not to have become common until the first years of the twentieth century.

Despite the fact that it was well known that hamburgers were made from beef, Americans somehow got the idea that the word was a compound of *ham* and *burger*. That opened the way, not only to further abbreviation to *burger*, but also to a number of compounds, of which the first was *cheeseburger* (known from the 1930s), followed by *nutburger, beefburger, porkburger, vegiburger* or *veggie burger* (for a vegetarian variety) and *soyaburger,* together with exotic and essentially jocular examples like *tunaburger, gatorburger* and *turtleburger.*

The oddest thing about the false analysis that spawned all these compounds is that few people make literal hamburgers, though *baconburgers* are by no means unknown.

Burton *See* GO FOR A BURTON

Busman's holiday

A *busman's holiday* is free time a person spends in an activity that is much like what he does for a living. So a carpenter who spends the weekend repairing his own house or a teacher working at summer school during the holidays are taking busman's holidays. A good example appeared in *Newsday* in August 2002: 'The court finished this year's term last month and won't begin to hear cases again until October. The break allows for trips and for busman's holidays spent lecturing law students in Italy or the Greek coast.'

Busman here is a term dating from the 1850s, and not yet quite obsolete, for the driver or conductor of a London bus (the conductor, non-Brits may need to be told, is the second man of the crew, who rides inside to collect the fares). *Busman's holiday* is also originally British, though it is now known throughout the English-speaking world. Several American writers on etymology who refer to this expression have got themselves into a mess trying to explain it.

A typical story appeared in John Ciardi's *A Browser's Dictionary* in 1980: 'British drivers of horse-drawn omnibuses, becoming attached to their teams, were uneasy about turning them over to relief drivers who might abuse them. On their days off, therefore, the drivers regularly went to the stables to see that the horses were properly harnessed, and returned at night to see that they had not been abused.' A similar tale is told by William and Mary Morris in *The Morris Dictionary of Word and Phrase Origins*, except that they assert that the most caring drivers, should they have any reason to fear abuse would occur, would sit among the passengers to observe the relief driver's behaviour.

Other writers are justly scornful of these stories. Anyone who has looked into the history of London buses in the nineteenth century will know that their horses were no better cared for than any other working nags and that they were often sweated to death (Anna Sewell's descriptions in *Black Beauty* in 1877 were not exaggerations).

The truth of the matter is mundane. A popular recreational activity among working-class Londoners in the late nineteenth century was to make an excursion by bus. A bus driver or conductor who went on such a trip was said to be taking a *busman's holiday*. The term is first recorded in print in 1893 in the *English Illustrated Magazine*: 'I shall indeed take a holiday soon . . . but it will be a "Busman's Holiday".'

Butterfly

Some charming theories exist about the origin of this name. One suggests the link with butter comes from the insect's yellow faeces. Others point to the old belief that butterflies like to land on milk or butter that are left uncovered, or that fairies and witches took on the form of butterflies at night to steal butter from the dairy. Nice stories, but lacking rather a lot on the firm-evidence front. The most common idea is that the insect's name was originally *flutter by* — which is, after all, what the creature often does — but became inverted.

It's a nicely seductive idea. There's a big problem with it, though. The famous scientist J. B. S. Haldane once spoke sadly of 'a beautiful theory, slain by an ugly fact', and I'm about to tread all over the idea with my size nine clodhoppers of evidence. The word can be traced right back to the Old English *buterflege*, found in a glossary of about the year 700. Nowhere along its trip from those times to today does it ever appear inverted. The word does indeed seem to be *butter* plus *fly*.

But why butter? We wish we knew for sure. Stephen Potter pointed out in his book *Pedigree: Words From Nature* (1973) that the most common British butterflies around habitations, such as the small white and cabbage white, are cream or pale yellow in colour, a frequent colour for butter in the days before manufacturers started to add vegetable dyes to it. This would be my first choice for an explanation, too, so making a *butterfly* literally 'a butter-coloured flying thing'.

Buy the farm

If you *buy the farm* in American slang you die in combat, in particular in a plane crash. This oblique reference has given rise to two stories about its origin that are almost certainly false but are widely believed.

One appeared in an issue of *American Speech* in 1955: 'Jet pilots say that when a jet crashes on a farm the farmer usually sues the government for damages done to his farm by the crash, and the amount demanded is always more than enough to pay off the mortgage and then buy the farm outright. Since this type of crash is nearly always fatal to the pilot, the pilot pays for the farm with his life.'

An example of the other story was told me by a *World Wide Words* subscriber: 'I understand that this term dates back at least to World War II. Each member of the U.S. armed services was issued a life insurance policy in the amount of $10,000, a great deal of money then. Many of the troops were unmarried young men who named their parents as beneficiaries. The parents were often living on a farm that was mortgaged; if their son were killed, the $10,000 would be used to pay it off.'

Let's hack through the undergrowth to uncover the hard core of evidence. The specific phrase *to buy the farm* turns out to be surprisingly recent, first recorded only in the 1950s. From the evidence that Jonathan Lighter has compiled in the *Random House Historical Dictionary of American Slang*, the first clear written evidence comes from the US Air Force, where it was slang for a fatal crash. There were other forms around at that time in the US Air Force, like *buy the plot* and *buy the lot* (presumably references to grave plots), but *buy the farm* prevailed.

Dr Lighter records people saying that they remember *buy the farm* from the US Air Force and the US Army at the time of the Korean War a few years earlier, when the idea of compensation could not apply. It is very likely that it actually dates back to the Second World War (slang terms often circulate for years before they appear in print, often only after their heyday has passed).

All of these versions seem to be related to several older British slang sayings, like *buy it* or *buy one* (usually in the form 'He's bought one!'). These are known to be British fighter pilot slang from the First World War for being wounded or killed, particularly for being shot down in combat. Both seem to be ironic references to something that one could not possibly want to buy. There was also the fuller phrase *to buy a packet* with the same sense (which is probably a combination of the Royal Flying Corps/RAF sayings with a British Army expression, *to stop a packet*, where the *packet* is a bullet, so meaning to be shot – either wounded or killed). The idea of being forced to buy something one doesn't want may be ancient military slang – the Oxford English Dictionary has an isolated example from 1825 in just the same sense, 'If we didn't buy it with his raking broadsides', which is said to be Royal Navy slang from the time of the Napoleonic Wars.

To judge from anecdotal evidence, all these terms are based on the kind of black humour so common among people in dangerous professions. It's a cliché of American war films to have a pilot or enlisted man from the heartland musing about what he will do when the conflict is over: he will go home, buy a farm and settle down. Later, the man is killed and his buddies comment that 'Well, I guess Joe has bought his farm now.'

We can't prove that's the origin, but my money's on it.

Cabal

This term for a secret political clique is sometimes said to be an acronym, from the initials of five leading members of Charles II's government of 1667–73 that covered the period of the third Anglo-Dutch War. They were Sir Thomas Clifford, Henry Bennet (Earl of Arlington), George Villiers (Duke of Buckingham), Anthony Ashley Cooper (Earl of Shaftesbury) and John Maitland (Earl of Lauderdale); so Clifford, Arlington, Buckingham, Ashley and Lauderdale – CABAL.

Even without detailed knowledge of word history this should cause your mental eyebrows to rise in scepticism. The earliest known acronyms date from around the time of the First World War (the military slang AWOL for 'Absent Without Leave' is among the earliest, recorded from 1921) and yet the source of *cabal* is dated on this theory to an acronymic origin some 250 years earlier.

What scuppers the idea completely is that *cabal* is known from earlier in the seventeenth century. It came into English via French *cabale* from medieval Latin *cabbala* (these days usually written *Kabbalah*). This is an esoteric secret Jewish system of mystical and magical practices based on a study of the Torah, the first five books of the Old Testament. Kabbalistic teaching was based on oral transmission from a personal guide, so *cabal*, at first referring directly to the Kabbalah, came to mean some private or semi-secret interpretation. By the middle of the seventeenth century it had developed further to mean some intrigue entered into by a small group – perhaps not sinister enough to be called a conspiracy, but certainly underhand – and also referred to the group of people so involved.

The word was indeed applied to the five ministers (in a pamphlet issued in 1673), but it was no more than a scurrilous joke based on the accident of their initials. Unfortunately, it's a joke that has long since gone sour on etymologists, who have to keep explaining the facts, a problem compounded by historians, who continue to refer to the *Cabal ministry* as a convenient shorthand.

Call a spade a spade

Most people know that *to call a spade a spade* means that we should avoid euphemism, be straightforward, use blunt or plain language, to tell it how it is. Most also know that *spade* is a rather outmoded derogatory slang term for an African-American. Putting the two ideas together, however, can only be done by someone whose sensitivity to possibly offensive language is greater than their knowledge of word history. Nothing new about that, though, as you can tell from the entries on NIGGARDLY, NITTY-GRITTY, PICNIC and SQUAW.

Many people in the USA regard *call a spade a spade* as a racist comparison – or at least worry that it might be thought so – and there have been complaints about people who have used it. It is rare to find it in American newspapers these days, and writers are often advised to avoid it. For example, Rosalie Maggio, in *The Bias-Free Word-Finder* (1992), writes: 'The expression is associated with a racial slur and is to be avoided', and recommends using 'to speak plainly' or other alternatives instead.

There's a considerable misunderstanding behind all this. The spade in the idiom isn't the same spade as in the slang term. The first is undoubtedly the digging implement; the second is the suit of cards. In the latter case, the allusion was to the colour of the suit, and originally appeared in the fuller form *as black as the ace of spades*. The abbreviated form *spade* seems to have grown up sometime in the early part of the last century (it appears in print first in the 1920s). Though they're the same word historically – both derive from Greek *spathē*, for a blade or paddle – the one you dig with came into Old English from an intermediate Germanic source, while the card sense arrived via Italian *spade*, the plural of *spada*, a sword.

An oddity is that *to call a spade a spade* was actually a mistranslation. The original was an ancient Greek proverb which might be translated as 'to call a fig a fig, a trough a trough'. This appears in Aristophanes' play *The Clouds*, dated 423 BC, and the Greek writer Plutarch also used it. His word was *skaphe*, a hollow object, variously a trough, basin, bowl or boat. When he translated Plutarch into Latin, the medieval scholar Erasmus misread it as *skapheion*, the Greek word for a digging tool. Nicholas Udall copied him when making his 1542 English version. The phrase has been in the language ever since.

If Erasmus had got it right, we might now be telling people to *call a trough a trough*, and America would have been spared all the fuss.

Camp

This adjective describes a man who is ostentatiously and extrava-
gantly effeminate; dictionaries say it appeared in print for the first
time in 1909, in J. Redding Ware's *Passing English of the Victorian Era*,
in which he says it refers to 'actions and gestures of exaggerated
emphasis', which are used by 'persons of exceptional want of
character', by which I take it he means homosexuals. However,
the adjective *campish* was used by the gay cross-dresser Frederick
Park (see DRAG) in a letter in 1868, so the term has been around
rather longer than is usually supposed.

It is sometimes said by bar-room pundits that the word is an
acronym of *Known Associate of a Male Prostitute*, with *kamp* changed to
camp under the influence of the existing word. This is obviously
nonsense, because the word appeared before acronyms were at all
common in English. But the story has gained some currency
because its real origin is unclear. Redding Ware suggested it came
from the French, perhaps because all things risqué were considered
to be imports from across the Channel. Eric Partridge, on the other
hand, was sure that it was natively English, from a dialect word
camp or *kemp*, meaning rough or uncouth. Anthony Burgess has
argued that it might be derived from a literal camp, as in a military
or mining camp, in which the all-male society could lead gay men
to advertise their availability through an exaggerated pseudo-
femininity. Others have pointed to the slang use of *camp* to mean
a male brothel, though that term is probably of later date and
derived from it. Those theories take you as near to the true origin
as you're likely to get, I'm afraid.

As a side note, though *camp* still has close associations with the
gay world, another sense has grown up in the past half-century or
so. It can now mean a sophisticated and knowing type of amusement, based on something deliberately artistically unsophisti-
cated or self-consciously exaggerated and artificial in style. It's

an obvious enough extension of the older sense. Christopher Isherwood called it *high camp* in his novel *The World in the Evening* of 1954, in which he emphasized that 'you're not making fun of it; you're making fun out of it'. Susan Sontag famously wrote about it in the *Partisan Review* in 1964; she said that the ultimate camp statement was 'It's good because it's awful'.

Card sharp

Many Americans will wonder if there's a misprint in this heading, since the usual phrase in North America for a person who cheats at cards to win money is *card shark*. This form is now regarded as standard in that country and has penetrated to varying degrees in all English-speaking countries, though *card sharp* remains more common in Britain.

It is often assumed that *card shark* is a form of *card sharp* which has become mangled through the folk etymological reasoning that *card shark* seems to be a better label for a dishonest player. Though the evidence – as always – is clouded by omissions in the record, it looks very much as though, just for once, it isn't folk etymology but a parallel development.

Both forms are specific applications of a pair of slang terms, *shark* and *sharp*, for petty swindlers, confidence tricksters and dishonest gamblers. *Shark* is the older of the two, and appears for the first time in a play of Ben Jonson's, *Every Man Out of His Humor*, in 1599. (We have that sense today in *loan shark*, for a lender of money at inflated rates of interest backed by menaces, though that's a relatively recent creation.) A person who is *sharp* has keen wits, but may use them to take unfair advantage of other people. That sense was recorded back in the 1690s, was applied from the late eighteenth century to a confidence trickster, and survives in the phrase *sharp practice* for dealings that are dishonest or barely honest.

(As it happens, the agent nouns *sharker* and *sharper* are recorded a few years before the simple nouns, in 1594 and 1681 respectively.)

So it may reasonably be assumed that a *card sharp* or a *card shark* was a crooked person who happened to use gambling as his method of operation. Both phrases seem to be American, the first examples of the former being from the works of Bret Harte in the 1870s and 1880s, the earliest in his *Gabriel Conroy* of 1876: 'If I give ye that twenty thousand, you'll throw it away in the first skin-game in 'Frisco, and hand it over to the first short-card sharp you'll meet!' ('Short-card sharp' doesn't have a misplaced hyphen – the same form also appears in a short story of his in *Scribners Monthly* the same year. Short-card games were those such as poker, casino and seven-up in which only part of the deck was dealt in any game; it doesn't seem to be a reference to the common gambler's trick of shortening certain cards by shaving them in order to force the punter to draw the one the gambler wants.)

The assumption that *card shark* derives from *card sharp* is that the latter has been found much earlier – until recently, the earliest example of *card shark* on record was from 1942. However, now we have searchable electronic databases researchers have been able to show that *card shark* is actually not that far short of *card sharp* in age. The earliest so far known was found by Fred Shapiro of Yale Law Library in the *Brooklyn Daily Eagle* of 29 January 1899: 'An authority on this game [society calls], who modestly denies that she is "something of a 'card shark' herself."'

Both are here to stay. And it doesn't matter which you choose: everybody will know what you mean.

Carpet *See* ON THE CARPET

Cater-cornered

Americans use this term to describe things that are placed diagonally, say on opposite corners of a junction, as in the *Christian Science Monitor* in August 2000: 'Our hotel sat cater-cornered to a yellow limestone Gothic cathedral.' The oddity of this term has led people to try to turn it into a phrase whose parts are better known. There have been lots of attempts, resulting in spellings like *cata-cornered*, *catty-cornered*, *cat-a-cornered*, and *kitty-corner*, a sure sign that it puzzles users. Despite all these forms, you may not be surprised to learn that it has nothing whatever to do with cats.

The first part comes from the French word *quatre*, four. It's actually quite an old expression that first appeared in English as the name for the four in dice, soon Anglicized to *cater*. The standard placement of the four dots at the corners of a square almost certainly led to the idea of diagonals. From this came a verb *cater*, to place something diagonally opposite another or to move diagonally, which can be found from the sixteenth century. Some English dialects had it as an adverb in compounds such as *caterways* or *caterwise*. By the early years of the nineteenth century it was beginning to be recorded in the USA in the compound form *cater-cornered*.

It had by then lost any link with the French word and people invented new spellings in attempts to make sense of it. In connecting it with cats, they probably didn't think of *caterpillar*, even though that comes from Old French *chatepelose*, literally a hairy cat, because it is doubtful whether many people knew that. It's more possible they had in mind *caterwaul*, in which the first part really does refer to a feline (possibly from the Dutch *kater* for a tomcat).

Chaise longue

The audience at the Chichester Festival Theatre is often criticized for being deeply conservative, preferring older, well-made plays to modern stuff. One of the many jokes on this theme tells of a lady of mature years who exclaimed one night from the stalls as the curtain went up, 'Oh, goody! A chaise longue!' The implication she drew, I presume, was that its presence signalled a period costume drama and so an uncontroversial evening's entertainment.

But at least she knew what it was, how to say it, and no doubt how to spell it, too. Many British visitors to the USA are surprised to find that the article of furniture is not only still known, but is often called a *chaise lounge*. This spelling and pronunciation is so common that it is in standard dictionaries of American English.

The original form, *chaise longue*, is French, meaning 'long chair'. Though the *chaise lounge* form is a classic example of folk etymology changing an odd foreign word into something more meaningful, it's hard to criticize – it is, after all, a seat that one lounges on. And if it is an error, it's an old one. I've found examples in American literature going back into the 1850s. In the issue of *Scribners Monthly* for April 1876 appears this sentence, which suggests the confusion had by then become common enough to need noting: 'This particular *chaise longue*, or lounge, is said to be the one on which George Fox slept.'

Cheap at half the price

On the face of it, this saying is self-evidently true, since if you buy a thing at half the price it's going to be cheaper than paying full whack. But it's one of those sayings that cause people to think it over and then shake their heads in bemusement. It seems from digging around that a lot of people are puzzled by it. As a result, there are two contradictory meanings for it in circulation.

I was sure there was a single obvious sense until I looked into Eric Partridge's *A Dictionary of Catch Phrases*, as revised by Paul Beale in 1985. If something is cheap at half the price, it is argued there, then the price being asked must be reasonable, fair value. A glossary of Australian slang online gives much the same explanation, saying that it is 'an expression of satisfaction over the cost of something'. Other sites online that use the phrase also seem to think it refers to a good thing.

I don't. I was sure even before I started investigating that it's a deliberate and humorous inversion of an old street trader's cry. He might shout 'cheap at twice the price', so informing prospective customers that something he was selling was twice as cheap and therefore extremely good value. If it were cheap at half the price, on the other hand, it suggests that the price actually being charged is excessive. That was certainly the way my late father used it in London in the 1940s – to him, it was a sarcastic and dismissive comment on an item that was over-priced. 'Wouldn't touch it with a bargepole', he might well have added.

I find to my mild relief that my view equates exactly with that of the late Kingsley Amis, who wrote about it in the *Observer* in 1977 and who said firmly that it meant something was 'bloody expensive'. The online *Notes and Queries* column of the *Guardian* newspaper has two replies by British readers to just this question and they also agree with me (or I with them, or all of us with Sir Kingsley).

The entry in *A Dictionary of Catch Phrases* remarks rather sadly, having gone into the matter, that this is a question that must be settled by leaving it unsettled. I disagree. However, as it stands it's most certainly thoroughly confusing to anyone who might stumble across it.

My guess is that, once the phrase moved away from its London street-trader roots, it became less easy to understand, and people who have tried to analyse it have come up with exactly the wrong idea. As a result, it's best avoided unless you spell out exactly what you mean by it, but of course if you do that it loses most of its force.

Cheque

The name for the printed form on which we tell the bank to pay someone money from our account (Americans prefer to spell it *check*) comes from Arabic. But the process is a tortuous one and writers sometimes muddle the history of the word in curious ways. One version appeared in *Newsweek* in October 2002: 'Arab currency was held from Scandinavia to China, and a draft order signed against an account in Damascus would be honored in Canton. These were known in Arabic as *sek*, from which the English "check" is derived.'

Alas, not so. The sense of a money draft developed in English, not in Arabic, and is actually surprisingly recent, dating only from the latter part of the eighteenth century.

The origin of all the senses is the game of *chess*, whose name can be traced back through Old French *echès* via Old Persian to Sanskrit. The Old French word is also the source of *check*, which was at first likewise a chess term with the same meaning as it has now – the act of threatening the king. The Old Persian source of both was *shah*, a king, a word we still recognize in reference to the former rulers of Iran. (*Checkmate* is from Old Persian *shah mat*, meaning roughly that the king is left helpless.)

From the chess sense a number of others evolved, first that of an attack, then a rebuke, then some reversal of fortune, then a sudden stoppage, then a restraint of action by some superior authority. This last sense led to the idea of checks being made on the accounts of an organization, and also to the check mark that is placed against an account item that has been considered and approved. In the sixteenth century, officials in the royal household were called *clerks of the check*, whose job was part auditor, part supervisor; by the following century the same term was being used in the royal ports and dockyards for men with similar responsibilities. By the end of the eighteenth century, a check could be a written token of some sort (a usage that survives in the American *hat check* and also *check* for a restaurant bill).

Our bank draft sense of *check* grew out of its application to counterfoils that were attached to bills of payment from the early eighteenth century onwards, whose purpose was to counter the risk of forgery and so to provide a check on the bill's veracity. The term later became applied to any form that had a counterfoil and by the end of the eighteenth century had taken on the modern meaning because bank drafts always had them.

The British spelling *cheque*, by the way, came from *exchequer*, the ancient royal department in charge of finances, whose name originally referred to a table covered with a cloth divided into squares, on which accounts were kept by means of counters. This name, too, comes from the Old French word for a chessboard.

Chew the fat

When we say this today, we mean that people are chatting, gossiping, or passing the time in idle conversation to no very deep purpose.

Some wonderfully literal-minded stories have been invented to explain its origin, especially in the USA, where it has been linked to native peoples – American Indians or Inuit in the north of Canada – who would chew hides to soften them, an activity

carried out in their spare time. Another suggestion is that Elizabethan farmers in Britain would keep a haunch of smoked pork
hanging by their kitchen hearths. On days when no fieldwork
could be done, the family and visitors would sit around the hearth
talking, and would slice off slivers of pork to *chew the fat*.

The evidence suggests it might have originally come from the
Indian Army. At least, our first reference to it is in a book by
J. Brunlees Patterson, *Life in the Ranks of the British Army in India, and on
board a Troopship*, dated 1885. He suggested it was a term for the
kind of generalized grumbling, the bending of the ears of junior
officers as a way of staving off boredom that is an immemorial
part of army life. The next examples are actually American, dating
from the early part of the twentieth century, but then it gradually
becomes more common on both sides of the Atlantic.

Mr Patterson also records the phrase *chew the rag*, which at one
point he uses in the same sentence as *chew the fat* and which he
obviously considers to be synonymous. This is actually a little
older – an example is recorded in the *Random House Historical Dictionary
of American Slang* from 1875: 'Gents, I could chew the rag hours on
end, just spilling out the words and never know no more than a
billy-goat what I'd been saying.'

It would seem there are some unanswered questions about
how the expression got from British India to America (or back).
But we don't need to invoke any literal interpretations: it's enough
to compare the steady chomping of the jaws in chewing with
the mouth movements of conversation to see where the phrase
came from.

Chunder

This is common Australian slang for the action of vomiting. A story told in that country is that the word is an abbreviated form of 'watch under', supposedly shouted out by upper-deck passengers on emigrant ships just before being sick over the rails to the peril of those below.

The word is closely associated with Barry Humphries, who popularized it but didn't invent it. (The first recorded use is actually in the 1950 novel *A Town Like Alice*, by Nevil Shute.) The 'watch under' story was mentioned in an article in the *Times Literary Supplement* in 1965 in connection with Barry Humphries' Barry McKenzie comic strip in *Private Eye*. The writer of the piece accepted the story, but I have to tell Australians that it is a classic bit of folk etymological storytelling and they mustn't believe a word of it.

The writer of the *TLS* article recorded that he remembered it as being common in the mid-1950s in 'Victoria's more expensive public schools'. Others have suggested that it was actually Second World War military slang.

The most erudite explanation is persuasive, though it is a little tentative because it is based on anecdotal associations rather than hard evidence and there is a big gap in the evidence. It is said that it comes from a series of advertisements for Blyth and Platt's Cobra boot polish. These appeared in the *Bulletin* newspaper in Sydney from 1909 on, originally drawn by the well-known Australian artist Norman Lindsay. The ads featured a character named Chunder Loo of Akim Foo and were popular enough for Norman's brother, Lionel Lindsay, to write and illustrate *The Adventures of Chunder Loo* for Blyth and Platt in 1916. The character's name became a nickname in the First World War (sometimes abbreviated to *Chunder*), which is where the idea of a military link may have come from.

Alternatively, it's suggested that the term is rhyming slang

(*Chunder Loo = spew*) and that it first appeared as public school slang, perhaps in the 1950s, as the TLS's writer thought. It moved into surfing slang in the 1960s, which was where Barry Humphries found it. Because he used it in *Private Eye* in the 1960s (along with inventions like 'point Percy at the porcelain' and 'technicolor yawn'), the word became widely known in Britain almost before it did so in Australia.

Cock a snook

The gesture of derision this phrase encapsulates is that of putting one's thumb to one's nose and extending the fingers. Waggling them is optional but improves the effectiveness of the insult. The gesture is widespread but names for it vary: *cocking a snook* is the usual name for what Americans, I am told, sometimes describe as a *five-fingered salute*.

Because *snook* isn't now known in standard English, folk etymology has turned the phrase into *cock a snoot*, since *snoot* is a slang name for the nose. The fourth edition of the *American Heritage Dictionary* of 2000, for example, gives *cock a snoot* as the standard form and other American dictionaries mention it as an alternative.

Cock here is a verb that refers to sticking something out stiffly, often in an attitude of defiance, as the cockerel's neck, crest or tail is erect when he crows. So we have expressions like *to cock the nose*, to turn one's nose up in contempt or indifference. A *cocked hat* is one whose brim has been turned up; a *cocked gun* is one whose hammer has been raised, ready for firing. And so on.

So far so good. *Snook* is not so easily explainable. The word is well known as a name for various species of fish, but that comes from the Dutch *snoek* for a pike and is unconnected. (British readers with long memories may remember the tins of *snoek* that were imported from South Africa in the years of austerity following the

Second World War. That name came from Dutch into Afrikaans and was given to a fish found in southern oceans that's also called the barracuda or barracouta.)

Another sense, long obsolete, is recorded from medieval times in Scots and northern dialect for a promontory or projecting point of land. We have no idea of its origin, though some suggest it might be connected with *nook*. That word might easily be transferred to the nose. There might also be a link with the surviving Scottish dialect word *snoke*, meaning to sniff about or nose out. It might be a variant form of *snout*, as *snoot* certainly is.

The earliest example of *cock a snook* is dated 1794, but the phrase didn't become widely recorded until the last years of the nineteenth century. By the end of the following century, the loss of *snook* as an active word in the language had caused the expression to change in a way that is almost certainly irreversible.

Cockroach

Not only does this pestiferous insect infest so many kitchens worldwide, but it's sneaky enough to do so under an alias, one that has been created through the traditional English disdain for foreign-sounding words.

It seems the English had too little exposure to cockroaches to name them until the seventeenth century, though Drake is reputed to have encountered them as an infestation on a captured Spanish ship in the 1580s. Indeed, it was the Spanish from whom we get the name. Today, they call it *cucaracha*, though an older form seems to have been *cacarucha* (the syllables became inverted through a process called metathesis). Either way, it's from *cuco*, a sort of caterpillar.

We owe the first recorded mention in English to Captain John Smith, whose book *The Generall Historie of Virginia, New-England and the*

Summer Isles of 1624 gives as good a description of the pest as one could want: 'A certaine India Bug, called by the Spaniards a Cacarootch, the which creeping into Chests they eat and defile with their ill-sented dung'. (*India* here is the old name for the Americas, based on Columbus's false belief that he had found that country.)

General dislike of Spain and the Spanish, plus ignorance and suspicion of all things foreign, augmented people's desire to turn this odd word into something that sounded more familiar. So they borrowed the English words *cock* and *roach* to create an amalgamated term to describe something that is neither fish nor fowl. It was nineteenth-century American ladies, ultra-sensitive to anything that smacked of sexual slang, who abbreviated its name to *roach* to avoid that distressing first syllable, but who by doing so helped to confirm the false construction.

Cocktail

Almost everything that has been written about the origin of the name for this great American institution is spurious. H. L. Mencken wrote in 1946 that he had found forty supposed etymologies, and a quick look at a few current books on drinks (and also, alas, etymology) show that many of them are healthy and still going the rounds.

The problem is that the word *cocktail* suddenly appears in print in 1806, with no antecedents that would enable us to decide its provenance. It's as though some alien had suddenly put it into men's minds in that year. The result has been a vast outpouring of speculation, most of it way out in 'here be dragons' territory:

- Several stories link the word to Betsy (or Betty) Flannigan, an innkeeper of Pennsylvania (sometimes Virginia). She is sometimes said to have used the tail feathers of cocks as swizzle sticks when serving drinks to soldiers during the American Revolution. Or the same lady served a soldier a mixed drink containing all the colours of a cock's tail, to which he gave the name. Or she roasted a rooster stolen from a supporter of the English and in triumph decorated the accompanying drinks with the cock's feathers.

- It is said to derive from a meal of bread fortified with mixed spirits, named *cock-ale*, that was given to fighting cocks before a contest, and which was later taken up by humans and renamed. An associated story points instead to the practice of toasting the victor in a cockfight, the one that had most feathers left in its tail, by drinks that had feathers to that number inserted into them.

- *Cock-ale* was an old English drink made from a new cask of ale by putting into it a sack containing an old rooster, mashed to a pulp, plus raisins and spices, and letting the mixture infuse for a week or so. There really was such a drink, though not made quite like that.

- Some point to an old French recipe of mixed wines, called *coquetel*, which was perhaps carried to America by General Lafayette in 1777.

- It comes from the *tailings*, the dregs of casks of spirits, which would be drained out through their *cocks* or spigots, mixed together, and sold as a cheap drink under the name of *cock tailings*.

- A *cock-tailed horse* in the same period was one that was not thoroughbred, so of mixed blood and the name was transferred to the drink, which was also a mixture and subsequently abbreviated.

- It comes from a West African word *kaketal* for a scorpion, which was transferred to the drink because of its figurative sting.

- The drink *cocked your tail* like a crowing rooster.

- A Louisiana apothecary in New Orleans named Antoine Peychaud (who also invented Peychaud bitters) is said in the 1790s to have served drinks to his guests that were compounded of brandy, sugar, and water plus his crucial new ingredient of bitters. He served them in a sort of double eggcup, whose name in French was *coquetier*, in time corrupted to *cocktail*.

If you hunt around you can find wild elaborations of many of these stories, plus others. There's no evidence that supports any one in particular, though some are clearly more silly than others. The New Orleans story is especially attractive, because it names dates, people and places and seems therefore to be more plausible; however, it has been discovered recently that the Antoine Peychaud who opened the apothecary's shop at 123 Royal Street, New Orleans, did so in 1838, too late for him to have been the source of the term. The confusion arose because it was a relative of the same name who arrived in 1795.

One intriguing point about the cocktail is that the first reference to it says that it is 'a stimulating liquor, composed of spirits of any kind, sugar, water, and bitters'. Charles Dickens wrote in *Martin Chuzzlewit* in 1844: 'He could . . . smoke more tobacco, drink more rum-toddy, mint-julep, gin-sling, and cocktail, than any private gentleman of his acquaintance.' Later still, Thomas Hughes wrote 'Here, Bill, drink some cocktail' in his *Tom Brown's Schooldays* of 1857. These and other early examples suggest that the original cocktail was a specific drink, one made from spirits and bitters, not a generic name for a type of drink. From the description in the 1806 example, it sounds as though it was something like the cocktail now called an *old-fashioned*, a name that is possibly significant.

The liquor itself is certainly stimulating, but so also is the speculation of those who seek its fountainhead with more ingenuity than accuracy.

Cold shoulder

To *give somebody the cold shoulder or show somebody the cold shoulder* is to treat them with disdain, a marked coldness, or a deliberate and obvious show of indifference.

I know of at least two supposedly reputable books of word histories that give detailed stories about the origin of this phrase based on the presumption that unwelcome guests in olden times were given cold shoulder of mutton as an unappetizing dish that indicated to the visitor that it was time to leave. A variation on this is that the least favourite guests were seated the furthest from the fire, so giving them literal cold shoulders. All such stories create complexity where none exists.

Let me give you the facts. The first recorded use of the phrase is in a novel by Sir Walter Scott, *The Antiquary*, in 1816: 'The Countess's dislike didna gang farther at first than just showing o' the cauld shouther.' (If you find the Scots dialect hard going, you may prefer this, from another of his works, *St Ronan's Well* of 1824: 'I must tip him the cold shoulder, or he will be pestering me eternally.')

Within a decade or two of that date it was being seen all over the place in Britain – it appears in works by Charlotte and Emily Brontë, Charles Dickens and Anthony Trollope, among others. The first reference I can find in American works is in a book of 1844; later it became at least as common there as in Britain and can be found, for example, in works by Louisa May Alcott and Mark Twain.

The sudden popularity of the phrase from the 1820s on, and its complete absence in literature before Sir Walter Scott used it, suggests strongly that he either invented it or popularized a saying that beforehand had been uncommon. As he takes the trouble to define it in a glossary in The Antiquary, it's clear that he expected his readers not to understand it. The phrase just might have been an existing Scots expression that he happened to find useful, though I can discover no trace of it. It's difficult nowadays, when Scott's novels are hardly read, to remember how popular and successful he was and how influential his writings were. It is entirely possible that those two uses I've quoted were enough to establish cold shoulder in the public mind.

The phrase almost certainly never referred to meat. It is much more probable that the cold shoulder in question was a dismissive jerk of one side of the upper body to indicate a studied rejection or indifference. Scott's use of 'tip the cold shoulder' and 'show the cold shoulder' suggest this is so.

The Oxford English Dictionary points out that there were many puns created around the phrase in the nineteenth century. One of these was cold shoulder of mutton, but the move is undoubtedly from the shorter phrase to the longer, not the other way about. But the existence of that version gave unwarranted support to people thinking it had something to do with offhand and perfunctory hospitality.

Come a cropper

I won't embarrass the famous British industrial museum by identifying it, but a guide there told me an inventive story about the origin of this phrase for falling heavily. He said that a cropper was a printing machine for trimming (or cropping) paper; it was fed by hand and it wasn't uncommon for a printer to get his hand caught in it while it was working, so suffering a serious injury. I have also heard a serious suggestion that it refers to a horse, lagging badly in a race, which its jockey has to encourage by liberal applications of the crop; if it comes to the line as a loser, it will come as a cropper.

The only merit of the second story is that it connects the phrase with horses. Though the exact derivation is not totally clear, it does derive from hunting, where it originally meant a heavy fall from a horse. Its first appearance was in 1858, in a late and undistinguished work called *Ask Mamma* by that well-known Victorian writer on hunting, R. S. Surtees, best known for *Jorrock's Jaunts and Jollities*: '[He] rode at an impracticable fence, and got a cropper for his pains.'

The earliest easily traceable source of *cropper* is the Old Norse word *kropp* for a swelling or round lump. This is closely related to the Old English word for the rounded head or seed body of a plant, from which we get our modern word *crop* for the produce of a cultivated plant. In the sense of a lump, it was applied first to the *crop* of a bird but then extended to other bodily protuberances. This is where things get complicated: the same word travelled from a Germanic ancestor through Vulgar Latin and Old French back into English as *croup* for the rump of a horse. From this we also get *crupper*, the strap on a horse's harness that passes back from the saddle under the tail.

At the end of the eighteenth century English developed a phrase *neck and crop*, with the sense of 'completely'. This is first recorded in a poem by Lady Carolina Nairne:

> The startish beast took fright, and flop
> The mad-brain'd rider tumbled, neck and crop!

(You may not know her name, but she's best remembered for writing, among others, the songs 'Will you no come back again?' and 'Charlie is my darling'.)

Now, *neck and crop* is a rather odd expression, and we're not sure how it came to be. It could be that *crop* is a variant of *croup*, suggesting that a horse that fell *neck and crop* collapsed all of a heap, with both head and backside hitting the ground together. Or perhaps *crop* had its then normal meaning of a bird's crop, so the expression was an intensified version of *neck*, perhaps linked to an older expression *neck and heels* that's similar to *head over heels*.

It's thought that *come a cropper* derives from *neck and crop*, with *cropper* in the role of an agent noun, referring to something done in a *neck-and-crop* manner, and that the phrase developed from there.

Condom

Though this word for a prophylactic sheath has been good English – in various spellings – since the beginning of the eighteenth century, until recently it was surrounded by the taboos that have accompanied everything sexual. A researcher, James Dixon, wrote to the editor of the *Oxford English Dictionary* in 1888 concerning his finding of the first known usage: 'I suppose it will be too utterly obscene for the Dictionary.' He was right; it didn't appear in that work until a supplement of 1972. This was typical of dictionaries of the period, however, few of which included it until the end of the 1950s or even later. It took the arrival of HIV/AIDS to make it a word that could be uttered in polite, non-medical society. We may have lost some of the embarrassment, but stories about its supposed origins are still making the rounds.

No doubt taking the view that all things sexual must be French, a story that was common at one time connected it to the town of Condom in southern France. Other proposals linked it to the Latin *condus*, that which preserves, and to the Persian *kondu*, a vessel for holding grain. However, the most common ones suggest that it derives from the name of the doctor who either invented it or introduced it. A Dr Condon or Conton, or perhaps Quondam, or even Gondom, supposedly doctor to the libidinous English monarch Charles II, is often mentioned. Alternatively, a Colonel Cundum, a courtier to Charles II, is said to have introduced the device into Britain.

The word is first recorded in 1706 in reference to the fear that such engines of protection might be brought north from England to Scotland as a result of the impending union of the two countries and encourage immorality. Beyond that, little is known of its early history. Every attempt to trace the source of these eponymous attributions has come to nothing. The most comprehensive is recorded in a monograph, *Looking for Dr Condom*, by William Kruck of the University of North Carolina, published in 1981; he found no trace of anybody with a similar name associated with the half century before the word's first appearance in print; partly as a result, current dictionaries usually quote the eponymous origin only in order to deny it.

It is certain in any case that the device itself goes back further than the seventeenth century. The first known reference is in a medical treatise of 1564 by the Italian anatomist Gabriello Fallopio, who claimed to have created one from moistened linen. However, medical writers suggest that an innovation took place around the Restoration in which animal caecum replaced the linen.

It's most probable that there never was a single inventor, but that the device evolved over time. But how it became known as a *condom* remains hidden in the mists of etymological history.

Cop

Half a dozen explanations at least have been put forward for this one, including an acronym from 'constable on patrol' or 'constabulary of police', which are reminiscent of the story behind POSH and quite certainly just as spurious. Some say it comes from the copper badges carried by New York City's first police sergeants (patrolmen were alleged to have had brass ones and senior officers silver). It is almost as often said to refer to the supposedly copper buttons of the first London police force of the 1820s. All these stories are about equally unlikely.

The most probable explanation is that it comes from the slang verb *cop*, meaning to seize, originally a dialect term of northern England which by the beginning of the nineteenth century was known throughout the country. This can be followed back through the French *caper* to the Latin *capere*, 'to seize, take', from which we also get our *capture*.

The situation is complicated because there are – or have been – a large number of other slang meanings for *cop*, including 'to give somebody a blow', and the phrase *cop out*, as an escape or retreat. Both of these may come from the Latin *capere*. But it's suggested that another sense of *cop*, 'to steal', could come from the Dutch *kapen*, 'to take or steal'. There's also 'to beware, take care', an Anglo-Indian term from the Portuguese *coprador*, and phrases like 'you'll cop it!' ('you'll be punished, you'll get into trouble'), which could come from the idea of seizing or catching, but may instead be a variant form of the word *catch*.

But an origin for the police sense in the idea of capturing someone is the most plausible. A *copper* is someone who seizes malefactors, a usage first recorded in Britain in 1846. It looks very much as though *cop*, noun and verb, is a back-formation from this, first appearing in the 1850s.

The old children's rhyme incorporates the old and new senses:

He that cops what isn't his'n,
Will be copped and put to prison.

Policemen are therefore those who catch or apprehend criminals, who cop them, a worthy occupation, and one which led to the apocryphal response by the essentially fair-minded criminal when fingered by the fuzz: 'It's a fair cop, guv.'

Copacetic

It's possible this word, which means 'extremely satisfactory', has created more column inches of speculation in the USA than any other apart from OK or JAZZ. It's rare to the point of invisibility outside North America. People mostly became aware of it in the 1960s as a result of the US space programme – it's very much a *Right Stuff* kind of word. But even in the USA it doesn't have the circulation it did thirty years ago.

We know that its first recorded appearance in print was in 1919, in Irving Bacheller's novel based on the life of Abraham Lincoln, *A Man for the Ages*: ' "As to looks I'd call him, as ye might say, real copasetic". Mrs Lukins expressed this opinion solemnly. Its last word stood for nothing more than an indefinite depth of meaning.' Dictionaries are cautious about attributing a source for it, reasonably so, as there are at least five competing explanations, with no conclusive evidence for any of them.

A story that's given much credence is that it derives from one of two Hebrew expressions, either kol b'seder, 'all is in order', or an unrecorded phrase kol b'tzedek, meaning 'all with justice', which were supposedly introduced into the USA by Jewish immigrants. Other accounts say it derives from a Chinook jargon word copasenee, 'everything is satisfactory', once used on the waterways of Washington State, or from the French coupersetique, from couper, 'to strike', or from a supposed Italian word *copacetti*. If you don't like these, you can strain at comprehending the idea that it might come from *the cop is on the settee*, supposedly a hoodlum term used for a policeman who was not actively watching out for crime.

The problem with all of these is that it seems pretty definitely to have originally been a word of African-Americans in the USA, especially those associated with jazz in the early part of the twentieth century. The name of Bill 'Bojangles' Robinson, a famous black tap-dancer, singer and actor of the period, is often linked to it. Indeed, he claimed to have invented it when he was a shoeshine boy in Richmond. But other blacks, especially southerners, said that they had heard it from parents and grandparents, which would put its origin in the late nineteenth century.

The origin does seem to be in the American South, which puts the kibosh on all these various suggestions, especially the Hebrew ones, as the chances of southern blacks hearing enough Hebrew to borrow a word from it are small. It has been suggested, however, that it actually appeared in Black English not in the south but in Brooklyn, a city with a large Jewish population, which would make cross-fertilization from Hebrew more likely.

It just has to be tagged for the moment as 'origin unknown'.

Crap

It is often said that *crap*, for defecation, and *crapper*, for the place where one does it, derive from the name of the late Mr Thomas Crapper, plumber. This is a seductive thesis, given additional life by sparse information about the early history of these items of mildly coarse slang. However, though he achieved a great deal in his lifetime, Mr Crapper was neither the inventor of the flush toilet (as some insist he was), nor is there any evidence that his name is connected with these words other than by an odd coincidence.

Crap is actually Middle English. It seems to be a mixture of two older words – one thread comes from Dutch *krappen*, to pluck off, cut off, or separate; the other may be from Old French *crappe*, siftings or waste or rejected matter, from medieval Latin *crappa*, chaff. The first sense in English was indeed that of chaff, and was also used in some places as the name for weeds that infested cereal crops, such as darnel, ryegrass or charlock. Later (we're talking about the end of the fifteenth century) it took on an extra meaning of the waste residue that was left after rendering fat.

Its application to the bodily function appeared in the 1840s. There's an example in the *Oxford English Dictionary* from 1846 that refers to a *crapping ken*, a privy, where *ken* is an old slang term for a house. This seems to be where the sense came from, but it doesn't derive directly from the word *crap* already mentioned. Older examples show that this term for a privy was originally *croppin ken*. Its source may be a dialect English word meaning a tail, which developed from the obvious anal associations.

What seems to have happened is that *croppin ken* changed to *crapping ken* around the middle of the nineteenth century under the influence of the idea of *crap* as smelly rubbish. Crap, noun and verb, later came from *crapping* by a process called back-formation, in which speakers think a word is a compound, and mistakenly derive a previously non-existent root term from it, in this case by leaving off what looks like an -ing ending.

As Thomas Crapper wasn't born until 1836, didn't start his business until 1861, didn't invent the flush toilet, and didn't become well known until much later, it's clear his name had no influence on the development of the word *crap*. A lot of the confusion about Crapper the man is due to a tongue-in-cheek book of 1969 by Wallace Reyburn, *Flushed with Pride: The Story of*

Thomas Crapper, which told a lot of falsehoods about him, and even led some people to conclude that he had never existed. Another popular mistake is to assume that he was knighted as Sir Thomas Crapper. Though he did act as sanitary engineer for members of the royal family and worked for a while by royal appointment, he never received an honour.

He was, however, a successful businessman and salesman who did invent and patent improvements to the flush toilet. He sold great numbers of items of sanitary ware from his base at Marlboro Works in Chelsea, London. Examples of toilet fittings with his name on them may still be seen even now in older establishments, or for example on the occasional manhole cover.

Crapper is American slang that dates from the 1920s, and is an obvious extension of the older noun and verb. The common story that American servicemen stationed in London in the First World War saw Mr Crapper's name on sanitary ware and borrowed it is unsupported by evidence (though it doesn't seem implausible and the coincidence would have tickled the fancy of anybody encountering it).

Crayfish

Any biologist will tell you that a *crayfish* (American *crawfish*) isn't a fish, but a crustacean. The ancient people who named it knew that very well: the word comes from the Old High German *krebiz*, from which modern German gets its word for a crab, *Krebs*. Old French took its word, *crevise*, from the same source and transmitted it to Middle English as *crevis* or *crevish*. The word was at various times applied to any edible crustacean – such as the crab or the lobster – and it was only in the fifteenth century that it was applied specifically to the fresh-water animal. In the sixteenth century the folk etymologists got at it, assuming that because it lived in water the last part of this word was really fish, and changed its name accordingly. The American form, *crawfish*, derives from a variant Middle English form *cravis*.

Curry favour

It's an odd phrase. Why should *curry* have anything to do with winning the favour of somebody or ingratiating oneself with him? It becomes even weirder when you discover that the phrase really means 'stroke a fawn-coloured horse'.

Its origin lies in a French medieval poem called the *Roman de Fauvel*, written by Gervais de Bus in the early 1300s. Fauvel was a horse, a conniving stallion, and the poem is a satire on the corruption of social life. There are several layers of meaning in his name: *fauve* is French for a colour that is variously translated as chestnut, reddish-yellow or fawn. A close English equivalent is the rather rare *fallow*, as in *fallow deer*, an animal which has a brownish coat (it may be that uncultivated ground is also said to be fallow because it looks vaguely that colour; we're not sure). In addition, *fauve* can be the collective name for a class of wild animals whose coats are at least partly brown, such as lions and tigers (the *fauverie* in a French zoo is the section devoted to the big cats). In the poem, the name Fauvel is also an anagram of the initial letters of the French names of six sins: flattery, avarice, depravity, fickleness, envy and cowardice. And his colour evokes the old medieval proverbial belief that a fallow horse was the symbol of dishonesty.

The poem was well known among educated people in Britain, who started to refer to *Fauvel*, variously spelled, as the symbol of cunning and depravity. That quickly became *curry Favel*. *Curry* here has nothing to do with Indian food (that word arrived in the language from Tamil via Portuguese much later, at the end of the sixteenth century), but is the term for rubbing down or combing a horse. The idea behind currying Favel is that the horse in the poem was susceptible to flattery, figuratively a kind of stroking.

Among people who didn't know the poem – then, as now, that was nearly everybody – Fauvel or Favel meant nothing at all. Favour seemed much more sensible a word; by the early part of the sixteenth century popular etymology had changed it to that and so it has remained ever since.

Cut and dried

Something that is cut and dried (sometimes cut and dry) is prearranged or inflexible, completely decided in advance, so it lacks freshness, originality or spontaneity. So much is widely known, but the expression itself often exercises the ingenuity of people who try to find a rationale for it.

A common American story, harking back to frontier days, is that it comes from meat that has been turned into jerky by cutting it into strips and drying it in the sun so that it will keep on long journeys. An alternative story is that it refers to timber that has been cut and left to season by drying. In either case, the resulting product is standard and unremarkable.

The problem with the second story is that timber was tradition- ally seasoned in the round and cut afterwards, so that if the expression came from that source, it would be more likely to be dried and cut. The problem with the first is simply that of date and place, since the expression is known from the early eighteenth century in Britain and has no known connection with situations in which dried meat might be encountered.

The true story is likely to be as prosaic as the expression itself. Though we can't prove it, the saying is more likely to come from the cutting and drying of herbs for sale and use in herbalists' shops. Such dried herbs would lack freshness.

The first known use of the expression is in a letter to a clergyman in 1710 in which the writer commented that a sermon was *ready cut and dried*, meaning that it had been prepared in advance, so lacking freshness and spontaneity. The next known use is in a poem by Jonathan Swift in 1730 which speaks of 'Sets of Phrases, cut and dry, Evermore thy Tongue supply' – clichés, in other words.

Cut the mustard

As much speculation and as many well-meaning attempts to find its origin are connected with this phrase as to any other in the language. It means to come up to expectations, to reach the required standard, to perform as expected, more generally to succeed at what you are attempting.

But why *cut*? And, especially, why *mustard*? Theories abound. Perhaps the most common one is that it's really a mishearing of *cut the muster*. A *muster* is a military parade, one called to check that everyone is present and correct, hence the idiom *to pass muster*, to pass the inspection of one's officers, which has something of the same sense as *cut the mustard*. This similarity of sense and form has led people to equate the two. There's a big problem with this rather neat story, though: there is no known example of *cut the muster* anywhere in English literature (heaven knows, enough people have looked). And if you 'cut a muster', *cut* here must surely mean you absent yourself; but if you aren't present to be inspected, you fail, the exact opposite of the sense we're looking for.

People who know mustard principally as the little shoots that come in mustard and cress salad might assume that it is hardly hard to cut. But farmers who have done it by hand tell me that mustard plants cultivated for their seed grow tall, have to be cut down to harvest them, and that their stems are hard enough to make the process arduous. So it might be that the ability to *cut the mustard* is a literal reference to the physical prowess needed to harvest this crop. However, none of the early usages have anything agricultural about them, and there's no example known of the phrase being applied to a mustard harvest, as there ought to be if it had grown out of that activity.

Another suggestion is that it refers to the practice of adding vinegar to ground-up mustard seed to reduce its bitter taste, where *cut* here is used in its sense of reducing the strength of something. There's no evidence for this in old cookery books or anywhere else.

Time to look at what evidence does exist. The phrase is of early twentieth-century US origin. The first recorded use is in 1907, in a story by O. Henry called *The Heart of the West*: 'By nature and doctrines I am addicted to the habit of discovering choice places wherein to feed. So I looked around and found a proposition that exactly *cut the mustard*. I found a restaurant tent just opened up by an outfit that had drifted in on the tail of the boom.'

It's much more likely that the expression is a development of the long-established use of *mustard* as a superlative, based on the pungency of the spice, as in phrases such as *keen as mustard*, which goes back to the seventeenth century. Around the beginning of the twentieth century, Americans used it for something that added zest to a situation: *the proper mustard* was the genuine article; a person who was *all to the mustard* was sharp-witted or keen.

Every one of these forms was used by O. Henry, among the most famous writers in America at the time. He used the word in the sense of 'something excellent' in *Cabbages and Kings* in 1904: 'I'm not headlined in the bills, but I'm the mustard in the salad dressing just the same', a sentence which clearly points to where all these forms are coming from. He must be given the credit for popularizing, perhaps even inventing, *cut the mustard*.

The more recent slang term *cut it*, to accomplish or perform something, seems to be an elliptical form of *cut the mustard*.

Davy Jones's locker

Davy Jones is the old-time sailor's devil. The first clear reference to him is by Tobias Smollett, who wrote in *The Adventures of Peregrine Pickle* in 1751: 'This same Davy Jones, according to the mythology of sailors, is the fiend that presides over all the evil spirits of the deep, and is often seen in various shapes, perching among the rigging on the eve of hurricanes, ship-wrecks, and other disasters to which sea-faring life is exposed, warning the devoted wretch of death and woe.' Davy Jones's locker is the sea-devil's storage place at the bottom of the sea, the place to which all sailors who die at sea are transported.

So much for facts. There are various stories about the origin of the term, usually attempting to identify a real David Jones. One of this name was said to run a pub in London, with a neat sideline – a sort of privatized press gang – of drugging unwary patrons and storing them in his ale lockers at the back of the pub until they could be taken on board some ship. Another story tries to identify him with Jonah of the Old Testament, who – you will recall – spent three days and three nights in the belly of a great fish; but Jonah survived, which makes the story irrelevant to the sense, since no sailor ever returns from Davy Jones's locker. A third theory says that Davy Jones was a fearsome pirate, who loved to make his captives walk the plank, so they ended up at the bottom of the sea; but nobody, so far as I know, has identified this alarming but stereotypical outlaw. Others have suggested that *Davy* was inspired by St David, the patron saint of Wales, who was often invoked by Welsh sailors; *Jones*, once again, is a corruption of the Biblical Jonah.

Yet another theory, dating at the latest from the 1898 edition of *Brewer's Dictionary of Phrase and Fable*, has it that the name derives from *duppy*, a spirit in West Indian mythology that seizes souls, a name which one writer has tried to link with the Hebrew *dybbuk*, but which presumably comes via the slave trade from a West African language. This was presumably coupled with the name of Jonah to make *Duffy Jonah*, which was later corrupted to *Davy Jones*. Stranger things have happened, but it sounds far-fetched, and there's no evidence for it.

The true source remains unfathomed.

Dead as a doornail

The expression is ancient: we have a reference to it dating back to 1350, and it also appears in the fourteenth-century work *The Vision of Piers Plowman* and in Shakespeare's *Henry IV*. Another version, of rather later date, is *as dead as a herring*, because most people only saw herrings after they had been preserved by salting and were rock-hard and obviously lifeless. There are other similes with the same meaning, such as *dead as mutton*, or *dead as a stone*.

But why particularly a doornail, rather than just any old nail? Could it be because of the repetition of sounds, and the much better rhythm of the phrase compared with the version without *door*? Almost certainly the euphony has caused the phrase to survive longer than the alternatives I've quoted. But could there be something special about a doornail?

The usual reason given is that a *doornail* was one of the heavy studded nails on the outside of a medieval door, or possibly that the phrase refers to the metal plate on which the knocker rested. A doornail, because of its size and probable antiquity, would seem dead enough for any proverb; the plate on which the knocker sat might be thought particularly dead because of the number of times it had been knocked on the head or because of the muffled noise it made when struck.

But William and Mary Morris, in *The Morris Dictionary of Word and Phrase Origins*, quote a correspondent who points out that it could come from a standard term in carpentry. If you hammer a nail through a piece of timber and then flatten the end over on the inside so it can't be removed again (a technique called *clinching*), the nail is said to be *dead*, because you can't use it again. Doornails would very probably have been subjected to this treatment to give extra strength in the years before screws were available. So they were dead because they'd been clinched. I hold no candle for this idea, but it's more plausible than the other stories.

The devil to pay

This usually appears as a warning that if some event happens *there'll be the devil to pay*, that serious trouble will ensue and will have to be dealt with. Joseph Conrad, for example, used it in his collection of short stories, *A Set of Six*, in 1908: 'If he happens to find the fellow making eyes at the lady there will be the devil to pay!'

The origin is often said to be from sailing-ship days, in which the *devil* is a seam that was difficult to reach and which needed a lot of tar to caulk, or *pay*. The same seam is also said to be the origin of BETWEEN THE DEVIL AND THE DEEP BLUE SEA. That word *pay* is a well-attested usage on board ship, first recorded in the seventeenth century, whose origin is the Latin *picare* for the process of tarring a seam – nothing to do with our more common sense of giving someone money. *Devil* as a name for a ship's seam is less well known, but it is usually said to refer to the long one along the side of the ship where the hull planking meets the deck. This was hard to get at and needed a lot of pitch to caulk. The full expression given in many books is there's the devil to pay and only half a bucket of pitch, or there's the devil to pay and no pitch hot.

Another explanation sometimes given is that London barristers once mixed work and pleasure in a public house called the Devil Tavern in Fleet Street. Their excuse for working was that they had to pay 'the Devil' for their after-hours enjoyment.

Neither of these stories is true.

The first appearance of the phrase was in The Journal to Stella by Jonathan Swift, dated 1711: 'The Earl of Strafford is to go soon to Holland, and let them know what we have been doing: and then there will be the devil and all to pay.' In the same book, Swift also uses 'the devil and all' in another way: 'So I went to the Court of Requests (we have had the Devil and all of rain by the bye) to pick up a dinner.' The phrase the devil and all was an idiom – recorded from the sixteenth century – which referred to everything or the whole lot, but especially everything that's bad or wrong.

The first usage of the devil to pay in the exact modern form is in a play by Sir John Vanbrugh and Colley Cibber dated 1728, The Provok'd Husband, or, a Journey to London. (The play was successful and may have been the impetus for the appearance three years later of a musical farce by Charles Coffey with the title The Devil to Pay.) It seems to have grown out of the earlier version. People may also have had in the backs of their minds a link to a Faustian bargain, a pact with Satan, and to the inevitable payment to be made to him in the end.

You can imagine sailors taking up the devil to pay once it had become well known, as a play on words around the existing shipboard meaning of pay. Once they started to do that, it is easy to imagine them applying the word devil to the most difficult seam to get at. The longer versions are fanciful later additions.

Dick's hatband

Nobody has ever got to the bottom of this odd saying. It was once commonly encountered in phrases like *as tight as Dick's hatband* or *as queer as Dick's hatband*. It means that something is absurd, perverse or peculiar.

There is a common story that it refers to Richard Cromwell, the son of Oliver Cromwell, who briefly took over as Lord Protector of England in 1658 after his father's death. He lasted only eight months before being deposed. The hatband was supposed to be a reference to the crown of England, something he found too tight to wear with comfort.

A neat story, but wrong in all its details. For example, Richard Cromwell never had the title of king, which was anathema to the Puritans of the time, and he certainly never wore a crown, nor would have had associations with one. Also, and even more tellingly, the expression first appears more than a century after these events – its earliest appearance in print is in the 1796 edition of Captain Francis Grose's *Dictionary of the Vulgar Tongue*.

From references in various dialect and local glossaries, it seems to have been widely known from the late eighteenth century onwards. It was noted in Cheshire in the form *as fine as Dick's hatband*, and elsewhere versions exist like *as false as Dick's hatband*, *as contrary as Dick's hatband*, *as cruikit as Dick's hatband*, and *as twisted as Dick's hatband*. An elaborated form was recorded in Newcastle in the 1850s: *as queer as Dick's hatband, that went nine times round and wouldn't meet*. It had by then been taken across the Atlantic, since it is included in 1848 in *A Dictionary of Americanisms* by John Russell Bartlett.

An intriguing suggestion I've seen is that *Dick* here was originally *Nick*, a reference to the devil. But why the hatband or what it was all about is a complete mystery. The first edition of the *Oxford English Dictionary* remarks rather dismissively that it may derive from 'some local character or half-wit, whose droll sayings were repeated', who would seem, if true, to have gained an international immortality second to none.

Mr Bartlett described it as 'one of those phrases which set philologists and antiquarians at defiance'. It may have done so then, but writers now are more inclined just to shake their heads and comment, as Jonathan Lighter does in the *Random House Historical Dictionary of American Slang*, that 'Despite speculation, the allusive origin is unknown and likely to remain so'.

Dinkum

Dinkum and its variant *fair dinkum* are possibly the most characteristically Australian terms of all. The word turns up first in Australian writing in 1888 in *Robbery Under Arms* by Rolf Boldrewood, in which it had the sense of work or exertion: 'It took us an hour's hard dinkum to get near the peak.' A little later it could also mean something honest, reliable or genuine, though this is actually first recorded in New Zealand, in 1905. *Fair dinkum* is recorded from 1890 in the sense of fair play, and it appears soon afterwards in the way that Australians and New Zealanders still use it – of something reliable or genuine, or which conforms to socially acceptable norms. There have been lots of related phrases since, like *dinkum oil* for an accurate report.

A report online of the 1998 Festival of Light in Sydney includes this: ' "The background to the words 'Fair Dinkum' can be traced to the gold rush days," said Mr Ruddock. "The Chinese word for gold sounded like 'Kum'. Real gold or a decent size find, sounded like 'Din-kum'. So now, when you hear people such as Pauline Hanson say 'Fair Dinkum', they're actually speaking Chinese!" '

There have been many similar statements in Australia in recent decades. The earliest I know is in a February 1984 issue of the *Sydney Morning Herald*. It's just another example, I'm afraid, of a well-meaning attempt to clarify the puzzling and elucidate the obscure. Like many such stories, there's an element of fact in it, in that the Cantonese words *ding kam* can mean 'top gold'. But there's no evidence at all that the Chinese words are actually the source, despite Chinese involvement in the Australian gold rushes of the nineteenth century.

Most dictionaries published outside Australia and New Zealand are unhelpful, just saying 'origin unknown'. But it seems very possible that it comes from an old English dialect term, which is recorded principally in Joseph Wright's *English Dialect Dictionary* of 1896–1905. He found several examples of *dinkum* in various parts of England in the sense of a fair or due share of work. He also encountered *fair dinkum* in Lincolnshire, used in the same way that people might once have exclaimed *fair dos!* as a request for fair dealing. But there's no clue where this word comes from, and dictionaries are cautious because it is not well recorded outside Wright's work.

For me, living about as far from Australia as it's possible to get on this planet, the word primarily brings to mind Robert Heinlein's *The Moon is a Harsh Mistress* of 1966, about a future penal colony on the moon in which everyone speaks a weird patois containing elements of Australian and Russian slang. The sentient computer at the centre of the story is described as 'a fair dinkum thinkum'. Go figure.

Dixie

A persistent story – which appears, for example, in the current edition of the *Encyclopaedia Britannica* – connects this name for the southern states of the USA with the Citizens' Bank of Louisiana. It is said that the Bank issued ten-dollar bills whose denominations, since Louisiana was a French-speaking area, were marked in

French as well as English: dix. These became known as dixies, and the name became transferred to the Confederacy at the time of the Civil War.

Like all the best stories, this one has a kernel of fact. The Bank existed and did issue such notes between 1845 and 1862. The problem is that nobody has found a reference to such notes by that name. A ten-dollar bill was a relatively large one by the standards of the time and it would seem that they didn't circulate widely enough for a nickname to be needed, or to become common if it existed. The story first appeared around 1912 in a brochure issued by the successor to the Citizens' Bank and it looks very much like a neat bit of PR puffery. If it is, it has been more successful than its inventor could have imagined or intended.

An early public appearance was in a famous song, 'Dixie's Land', later just 'Dixie', that was written by Daniel D. Emmett, a famous black-face minstrel of the period. He was performing in Jerry Bryant's minstrel show in the Mechanics Hall in New York in 1859 when he was asked at short notice to provide what was called a walk-around song, a final number in which the whole cast paraded around the stage, singing in chorus. There is some suspicion that he borrowed the tune from one already known in his native Ohio but added new words.

It became an instant hit. His creation was one of those fortunate ones that arrive on the world's stage at a critical moment, in this case just before the outbreak of the Civil War. Though also popular in the North, it was taken up as a marching song by the Confederate army and quickly became the unofficial anthem of the Confederacy (it was played at the inauguration of Jefferson Davis as President of the Confederate States of America on 18 February 1861).

There is no doubt that the song was the means by which the term Dixie for the southern states became widely known. The truth is also that we don't know for sure where Mr Emmett got the name from. Two other stories are widely given in attempts to explain it:

- It was named after a kindly slave owner named Johan Dixie or Dixy, who had a plantation on Manhattan Island but who was forced to take his slaves and move south because of anti-slavery sentiment, leaving his slaves yearning for the good old days in Dixie's Land. Alternatively, Mr Dixie was such a kind master that when he sold his slaves down south, they would think back nostalgically to the better times they had had on his plantation. This is too much of a muddle of historical periods and wishful thinking to be taken at all seriously.

- The term was a southern pronunciation of the name of Dixon in the Mason and Dixon Line, which had been surveyed between 1763 and 1767 as the boundary between Maryland and Pennsylvania and which had become the *de facto* boundary between the slave and free states. The land of Dixie was the part of the USA south of the line.

Daniel Emmett said in 1872 that the term had been known in the years before he composed the song. Hans Nathan quoted him in 1962 in his *Dan Emmett and the Rise of Early Negro Minstrelsy*: ' "Dixie's Land" is an old phrase applied to the Southern States . . . lying south of Mason and Dixon's line. In my traveling days amongst showmen [before 1859], when we would start for a winter's season south, while speaking of the change, they would invariably ejaculate [sic] the stereotyped saying: − "Wish I was in Dixie's Land," meaning the southern country.'

This seems to suggest that there really is some association with the Mason–Dixon Line. It was given as the origin by the Confederate propagandist Henry Hotze as early as 1861 in his *Three Months in the Confederate Army*, an extract of which Richard Harwell reproduced in *The Confederate Reader: How the South Saw the War* (1957):

'Years before I heard the tune I have heard negroes in the North use the word "Dixie" in that sense.' (Hotze commented of the tune that 'it now bids fair to become the musical symbol of a new nationality, and we shall be fortunate if it does not impose its very name on our country', which was prescient of him.)

There are some instances known of black-face characters using the name earlier (Hans Nathan found a character called *Dixie* in a skit of 1850 and thinks that the name may have been a generic one for a slave, similar to *Pompey*). It is most likely, though, that the source of all these is the surname of Jeremiah Dixon, the Englishman who helped to survey what turned out to be a key part of an infant country.

Dog *See* PUT ON DOG

Doozy

This American English word (also spelled *doozie*) refers to something that's extraordinary or outstanding of its kind: *that car's a real doozy.*

It has been suggested that *doozy* came from the name of the luxury Duesenberg car, which was named after the brothers Fred and August Duesenberg who developed it. I've also seen it suggested that the word might be from Polish *duz'y* or *duz'a*, meaning large, because the sense and spelling is similar and its date of first appearance is consistent with Polish immigration patterns to the USA.

Neither theory holds water once you start to look at the evidence. The first appearance of *doozy* in print is in 1903, some seventeen years before the first Duesenberg car was manufactured. The Polish story is yet another example of a type of folk etymology that seeks to find parallels across languages, parallels which are surprisingly easy to find but which are almost always false.

You might decide etymologists are slipping their mental gears once you learn that they think *doozy* probably comes from the flower named *daisy*. But *daisy* was once English slang, from the eighteenth century on, for something particularly appealing or excellent. It moved into North American English in the early nineteenth century and turns up, for example, in Thomas Chandler Haliburton's *The Clockmaker* of 1836: 'I raised a four year old colt once, half blood, a perfect picture of a horse, and a genuine clipper, could gallop like the wind; a real daisy, a perfect doll.'

The experts think that sense – still around at the end of the nineteenth century – was influenced by the name of the famous Italian actress Eleonora Duse, who first appeared in New York in 1893. Something *Dusey* was clearly excellent of its kind, and it is very likely that it and *daisy* became amalgamated in people's minds to create a new term.

Double-cross

A story connects this expression with Jonathan Wild, a crooked Londoner of the latter part of the seventeenth century. He employed thieves and kept a note of their names in a book, marking them with a cross when he had evidence of a crime. If the thief displeased him, Wild would earn a reward by shopping him to the authorities, marking his name with a second cross when he had done so. Hence *double-cross*.

It's a lovely story, all the better because it is grounded in fact. There really was a Jonathan Wild, who ran a neat little racket by acting as a receiver of stolen goods (in the early eighteenth century his activities led to this activity being made a crime) while representing himself as an honest broker to the real owners, being paid by them to get their property back. At one point he had three offices for the tracing of 'lost property' while running a network of gangs of thieves throughout London. He did often claim credit as a thief-taker by grassing on criminals in his employment. His crimes are described in *The Complete Newgate Calendar* and the *Dictionary of National Biography* and – somewhat fictionalized – in works by Daniel Defoe and Henry Fielding; he was also the inspiration for the character Mr Peachum in Gay's *The Beggar's Opera*. Wild ended his days on the scaffold at Tyburn on 24 May 1725.

However, none of this has anything to do with the phrase *double-cross*. It didn't exist in the language at the time, and is first recorded as the title of a poem by W. H. Ainsworth a century later, in 1834. The nearest it comes to the activities of Wild is that its origin is in thieves' slang.

Around 1800 *cross* came to refer to some transaction or practice that was dishonest – a joke on *square* or *straight*. Something done on *the cross* was crooked and goods obtained in this way were illicit. Crooks sometimes attempted to improve their chances by going back on an illegal deal, so crossing the crossers. It seems to have arisen first in horse racing or pugilism, in which a man who undertook to lose a race or a fight changed his mind, 'went straight' and won after all, so defrauding those who had bet on his losing. This was the double-cross. A classic reference appeared in the *Referee* in 1887: 'A double cross was brought off. Teemer promised to sell the match, and finished by selling those who calculated on his losing.'

These days, the phrase is often used for any transaction in which a person deceives or betrays another with whom he is supposedly co-operating. This is really only a single cross, but the name has stuck.

Drag

There's much uncertainly about the origin of this term for dressing in the clothes of the opposite sex. A persistent story holds it to be an acronym for D*Ressed As a Girl*, a stage direction from the Elizabethan period, when the female parts were played by men and boys. As acronyms were unknown at this period, we may disregard this story.

However, to link the term with the theatre may be correct; several modern dictionaries of slang suggest that it did in fact arise there. The early history of the word is somewhat confused, though. It first appears in print in a British periodical, *Reynolds's Newspaper*, dated 29 May 1870: 'We shall come in drag, which means men wearing women's costumes.' This implies fancy dress rather than any link either to the theatre or to homosexuality, a sense which most authorities assume arose only in the 1920s.

The 1873 edition of John Camden Hotten's *Dictionary of Modern Slang, Cant, and Vulgar Words* confirms it had only recently appeared: 'Drag, Feminine attire worn by men. A recent notorious impersonation case led to the publication of the word in that sense.' This presumably refers to a court case three years earlier that followed the arrest in the Burlington Arcade of Frederick William Park and Ernest Boulton, two well-known homosexuals of the period, for wearing women's clothing. A pair of illustrations from another London publication, the *Day's Doings* of 20 May 1871, showed Park in both male and female attire. The two drawings were captioned 'Park in mufti' and 'Park in "drag"'. Note the quotation marks that indicate a word the writer felt to be not quite respectable. As a result, I suspect that the camp associations of *drag* were present pretty much from the start.

Its origin may be mundane. Early usages always refer to men wearing women's clothes rather than the reverse. It is likely that the unfamiliar sensation to men of long skirts dragging on the ground suggested the name.

Dressed to the nines

Somebody who is *dressed to the nines* or *dressed up to the nines* is dressed to perfection or superlatively dressed. Writers have run up a whole wardrobe-full of ideas about where the expression comes from, which indicates clearly enough that nobody really knows for sure.

One very persistent theory is that the British Army's 99th Regiment of Foot were renowned for their smartness, so much so that the other regiments based with them at Aldershot in the 1850s were constantly trying to emulate them – to equal 'the nines'.

The big problem with this is that the phrase *to the nines* is actually a good deal older – it's first recorded in the late eighteenth century in poems by Robert Burns. In its earlier days it wasn't even linked to high standards of dress, but to any superlative situation: people could refer to 'praising a man's farm to the nines', for example.

The Victorian philologist Walter Skeat suggested that it could originally have been *dressed to the eyes*, which in medieval English would have been *to then eyne*; the phrase could afterwards have mutated by what grammarians call metathesis, the same principle that caused *a norange* to change to *an orange*. That might have been a really convincing explanation, except that there's a gap of several hundred years between this supposed creation and its first appearance in print. No scholar now believes this is the origin.

Other attempts at explanation connect it with the nine Muses, or with the mystic number nine, or even perhaps reaching a standard of nine on a scale of one to ten – not perfect, but doing very well. These numerological theories seem to be the more likely ideas behind it, but we can't be sure.

Eat crow

This is mainly an American phrase, meaning to be humiliated by having to admit one's defeats or mistakes.

An article published in the *Atlanta Constitution* in 1888 claimed that, towards the end of the War of 1812, an American went hunting and by accident crossed behind the British lines, where he shot a crow. He was caught by a British officer, who, complimenting him on his fine shooting, persuaded him to hand over his gun. This officer then levelled his gun and said that as a punishment the American must take a bite of the crow. The American obeyed, but when the British officer returned his gun he took his revenge by making him eat the rest of the bird.

This is such an inventive novelization of the origin that it seems a shame to point out that the original expression is not recorded until the 1870s, and that its first form was *to eat boiled crow*, whereas the story makes no mention of boiling the bird.

The origin seems obvious – the meat of the crow, it being a carnivore, is rank and extremely distasteful. An old joke among American outdoorsmen – I am told – is that if you get lost in the woods without any food and manage to catch a crow, you should put it in a pot with one of your boots, boil it for a week, and then eat the boot. The experience is easily equated to the mental anguish of being forced to admit one's fallibility.

Eighty-six

This puzzling American slang expression now has a variety of meanings: as a verb it refers to stopping or disposing of something unwanted or undesirable ('eighty-six that rubbish'), or to eject somebody undesirable ('Do that again and I'll have you eighty-sixed from this bar'); as a noun, it can mean an item out of stock or a deadbeat customer.

One of the standard stories about it – which is given a seal of semi-approval by being mentioned in the fourth edition of the *American Heritage Dictionary* of 2000 – connects it with Chumley's bar and restaurant at 86 Bedford Street in Greenwich Village, New York City, in the 1920s. One such story explains that when a customer was forcefully ejected from the premises, he would find himself lying on the sidewalk looking up at the number 86 on the door.

Unfortunately, that story won't wash. The original sense of *eighty-six* was as a bit of jargon among waiters and kitchen staff to indicate that an item on a restaurant menu was no longer available ('Eighty-six the liver and bacon!'), or sometimes that a customer had changed his mind about what he wanted. The sense of chucking out a drunken or recalcitrant customer from a bar is not recorded until the 1940s.

There are several other explanations, so fanciful that I cringe a little even repeating them: that it derives from British merchant shipping, in which the standard crew was 85, so that the 86th man was left behind; that 86 was the number of the American law that forbade bartenders from serving anyone who was drunk (stories disagree about which state had enacted it); that bartenders substituted weaker drinks of 86 proof in place of those of the usual 100 proof when a customer was getting too tipsy for comfort; that a means of committing suicide at one time was to jump off the observation deck on the 86th floor of the Empire State Building; that an army pot of soup contained exactly 86 servings, so that to eighty-six it was to empty it; that in the days when news stories were sent by teletype, 86 was a code meaning 'last message sent in error'; that the 86th precinct of the New York Police Department was a notoriously rough one to which officers were assigned who had annoyed their superiors; that a fashionable New York restaurant only had 85 tables, so the eighty-sixth was the one you gave to somebody you didn't want to serve; or that a restaurant (usually said to be in New York) had an especially popular item as number 86 on the menu, so that it frequently ran out. I'd eighty-six all but the last of these out of hand.

More sensibly, it's suggested that the number is one of a large set that was created in the 1920s in soda fountains as a code between workers, partly to save time and partly to let them pass comments quietly between themselves. According to *The Morris Dictionary of Word and Phrase Origins*, on which I rely for this information, the manager was 99, the assistant manager was 98, and 97½ meant 'There's a good-looking girl out front!' Numbers for foods included 55 for root beer and 19 for a banana split. The jargon of soda fountains was as complicated and opaque as that of coffee shops today, so the idea isn't inherently implausible.

The *Oxford English Dictionary* suggests instead that it may have been rhyming slang for *nix*. Although it's often thought of as typically American, *nix* entered the language in the latter part of the eighteenth century in Britain, originally as underworld slang; it was borrowed from a colloquial version of the German *nichts*, nothing. But it is likely that *eighty-six* was created as rhyming slang in the USA. Though rhyming slang is most closely connected with the East End of London, Americans had a brief exposure to it in the early years of the twentieth century, after it arrived there the long way round via Australia. So it's a plausible suggestion, the one to which nearly all current dictionaries cautiously subscribe.

Elephant and Castle

As non-Brits may be puzzled by any reference to *Elephant and Castle*, let alone where the name came from, let me explain first that it's a district in south London, an important road junction since at least the eighteenth century. It is now notorious for its vast traffic circulatory system, a rather tatty shopping centre and some brutal-ist architecture that houses a government department. Its name derives from the sign of a public house in the area, which shows an elephant surmounted by a castle.

It's often asserted that the name is a corruption of *Infanta de Castile*, usually said to be a reference to Eleanor of Castile, the wife of Edward I (in Spain and Portugal, the *infanta* was the eldest daughter of the monarch without a claim to the throne). That would put *Elephant and Castle* in the same class of pub name as others that we know have become corrupted – as *Bacchanal*, for example, turned into *Bag o' Nails* and *George Canning* became the *George and Cannon* – but this seems not to be one of them. The story is extremely persistent, however, most probably because it is mildly exotic and allows its teller to seem extremely erudite.

Not the least of the problems is that Eleanor of Castile wasn't described as an *infanta*; the one *infanta* that the British have heard about from school history lessons is Maria, daughter of Philip III of Spain, whom Charles I once wanted to marry. The form *Infanta de Castile* seems to be a conflation of vague memories of two Iberian royal women separated by 300 years.

The *castle* here is actually a howdah on the back of the elephant, in India a seat traditionally used by hunters. The public house called the *Elephant and Castle* was converted about 1760 from a smithy that had had the same name and sign. This had connections with the Cutlers' Company, a London craft guild founded in the thirteenth century which represented workers who made knives, scissors, surgical instruments and the like. The guild used the same emblem. The link here is the Indian elephant ivory used for knife handles, in which the Cutlers' Company dealt.

We can't be absolutely sure this is the true story, even though it hangs together better than the one about the Infanta, because the direct evidence is missing. The symbol of the elephant and castle was not that uncommon in medieval times – some ancient chess sets have the piece variously called the rook or castle carved in this shape, and the image also appears on the civic crests of Coventry and Bolton.

The exception proves the rule

This expression has caused as much confusion as any other in the language and is often argued about. The misunderstanding has been amplified by well-meaning but incorrect attempts going back a century to explain it. It's a good example of a type of folk etymology that arises through the incorrect analysis of the meaning of a puzzling phrase.

These days it is often used sweepingly to justify an inconsistency. Those who use it seem to be saying that the existence of a case that doesn't follow a rule proves the rule applies in all other cases and so is generally correct, notwithstanding the exception. This is nonsense, because the logical implication of finding that something doesn't follow a rule is that there must be something wrong with the rule. As the old maxim has it, you need find only one white crow to disprove the rule that all crows are black.

It has often been suggested in reference works that prove here is really being used in the sense of 'test' (as it does in terms like proving ground or PROOF OF THE PUDDING, or in the printer's proof, which is a test page run off to check the typesetting is correct). It's said that the real idea behind the saying is that the presence of what looks like an exception tests whether a rule is really valid or not. If you can't reconcile the supposed exception with the rule, there must indeed be something wrong with the rule. The expression is indeed used in this sense, but that's not where it comes from nor what it strictly means.

The problem with that attempted explanation is that those

putting it forward have picked on the wrong word to challenge. It's not a false sense of *proof* that causes the problem, but *exception*. We think of it as meaning some case that doesn't follow the rule, but the original sense was of someone or something that is granted permission not to follow a rule that otherwise applies. The true origin of the phrase lies in a medieval Latin legal principle: *exceptio probat regulam in casibus non exceptis*, which may be translated as 'the exception confirms the rule in the cases not excepted'.

Let us say that you drive down a street somewhere and find a notice which says 'Parking prohibited on Sundays'. You may reasonably infer from this that parking is allowed on the other six days of the week. A sign on a museum door which says 'Entry free today' leads to the implication that entry is not free on other days (unless it's a marketing ploy like the never-ending sales that some stores have, but let's not get sidetracked). In *Modern English Usage* (1926), H. W. Fowler gave an example from his wartime experience: 'Special leave is given for men to be out of barracks tonight till 11 p.m.', which implies a rule that in other cases men must be back earlier. So, in its strict sense, the principle is arguing that the existence of an allowed exception to a rule reaffirms the existence of the rule.

Despite the number of reference books which carefully explain the origin and true meaning of the expression, it is unlikely that it will ever be restored to strict correctness. The usual rule in lexicography is that sayings progress towards corruption and decay, never the reverse. Unless this one proves to be an exception, of course.

Female

Some feminists dislike the word history, claiming that it places too great an emphasis on the role of men, and have coined herstory to replace it. It's a little surprising that they haven't also had a go at female, since it looks as though it contains male.

If they were to do so, they would be on firmer ground than with history, since the male ending of female is there, not because of an accidental formation, but because people changed an older form through folk etymology. The word appeared in English in the fourteenth century in various forms, such as femel and femele. It was borrowed from the Old French femelle, which derives from Latin femella, a diminutive of femina, a woman. Soon after its first appearance, certainly by the sixteenth century, the spelling had shifted to female, out of a mistaken idea that the word was similar in form to WOMAN.

Feverfew

This plant is widely found in British hedgerows and waysides. Other names for it are featherfew, from the shape of its leaves (which smell strongly of camphor when you crush them), and bachelor's buttons, from its little white flowers. It was introduced from eastern Europe in the Middle Ages and became a staple herb of physic. It was nothing less than the aspirin of its time, being widely pre-scribed for migraine headaches (recent careful research has proved its worth) and also to reduce fever. Its English name is therefore accurately descriptive. But it's folk etymology as well as folk medicine, since its Old English name was feferfuge, derived from Latin febrifuga (made up of febris, fever, plus fugare, to drive away, the root also of our medical English term febrifuge for a medicine used to reduce fever). The first part is just as valid as in Old English, but fuge seemed to make no sense, so it was turned into few, presumably on the grounds that eating the plant's leaves made sure that a person indeed did have few fevers.

Fiasco

Turning over the pages the other day of Charles Bombaugh's *Gleanings for the Curious from the Harvest-Fields of Literature* of 1874 (as one does), I found an ingenious explanation for the origin of this term. He said it came from the misplaced confidence of a German tourist in Italy who saw a glassblower at work and thought that the job looked easy. But after repeated attempts all he could produce were feeble little pear-shaped attempts that the glassblower politely referred to as *fiasco*, or little bottles. 'Hence arose', Mr Bombaugh said, 'the expression which we not infrequently have occasion to use when describing the result of our undertakings.'

That last point is true enough, and perhaps Mr Bombaugh had more cause to invent stories about *fiasco* than we do today, since he was writing in the latter part of the nineteenth century, only a few decades after this odd foreign word had appeared in the English language. But he was misinforming his readers about *fiasco*, since it's the Italian word for any bottle, not necessarily a small one (it comes from the same Latin source as our *flask*).

I've also come across stories that link the word with those Chianti bottles with rounded bottoms that have to be encased in a wicker sheath because they won't stand up by themselves, so perhaps implying something that has been poorly constructed or which, like trying to stand the bottle up, will surely fail.

An early appearance in English gives the clue to its associations. A tactful footnote in an American journal, *Littell's Living Age*, for 7 February 1846, says: 'Few of our readers can be unfamiliar with the meaning of *Fiasco*, a cant word used throughout Italy to designate a failure, especially in theatrical matters.' *Far fiasco*, to make a bottle, was Italian theatrical slang for the utter failure of a performance. It passed through French (*faire fiasco*) into English, at first as actors' slang but later in the wider language.

Where it comes from is obscure even to Italian etymologists, who have put forward various incidents in theatrical history to account for it, such as the dropping of a real bottle, vital to the plot, during a performance.

Mr Bombaugh is not alone in connecting it with glassblowing. The *Barnhart Dictionary of Etymology* (1988) says that 'one of many explanations refers to the alleged practice of Venetian glassmakers setting aside imperfect glass to make a common bottle or flask'. I'm suspicious about this story. Wouldn't the glassblower merely have thrown the glass back into the furnace to reheat and reuse it?

Foolscap

Few people now write on paper so named: in Britain, sheets of similar size are designated instead by the boringly abbreviated term *A4*. Although there has been much variation in size for different purposes, in office use *foolscap* usually referred to a sheet of paper 13 inches by 8 inches.

The name is usually said to come from a watermark of a fool's cap and bells, the symbol of a jester, that such paper once carried to mark its size.

An old story holds that at the time of the English Civil War, Parliamentary papers used to be impressed with the watermark of the royal coat of arms but that Cromwell and the Parliamentary forces showed their disdain for matters regal by substituting the cap and bells. More than a century ago this was being dismissed as nonsense by the editors of the first edition of the *Oxford English*

Dictionary, but it still turns up on occasion. One of the more significant objections is that the name isn't recorded until 1700, more than fifty years after this event is supposed to have taken place.

Another story has it that it was a type of paper made in Italy (known also as *Genoa foolscap*), which was at one time called *foglio capo*, literally a chief or full-sized sheet of paper. It has been suggested that the Italian term was imported with consignments of the paper and that the English *foolscap* is a corruption, with the watermark following the name. This was given as the true origin in some works at one time, but is considered now to be folk etymology.

It does indeed seem that the name comes from the watermark, which may have been introduced at some point from Germany, where it is known from the late fifteenth century. Now that metric sizes have replaced it, the name and its associations are slowly being forgotten.

Forlorn hope

A *forlorn hope* is a desperate one that is very unlikely to be fulfilled.

It hardly appears to be an expression that has arisen as the result of an error. We know of *forlorn* in several senses today, such as that of a person who is sorrowful or dejected, or a place that is deserted or abandoned, as well as some action that is useless, futile or doomed to failure. This last sense seems to fit the sense of the phrase exactly. Nevertheless, *forlorn hope* is a classic folk etymology, albeit one that arose in the middle of the sixteenth century and centuries ago became a settled part of the language.

The phrase is Dutch. A *verloren hoop* was a band of soldiers who were picked to head an attack, a vanguard. In the nature of pioneering efforts, the casualty rate in a group of this sort was high. *Verloren* is the Dutch word for 'lost', as it is in German. A *hoop* was a company or troop of soldiers. That word is quite closely related to our word *heap* and in modern Dutch the word has similar senses, a 'crowd, pile, multitude, mass or collection' as my dictionary comprehensively puts it (*te hoop lopen* means to gather in a crowd), though in English we don't usually apply it to people. So a *verloren hoop* was a lost troop, a company that the army was prepared to sacrifice to attain its objective.

The sense came over into English but the foreign words were quickly replaced by two that were more familiar and which seemed to make sense in the context.

Fritz *See* ON THE FRITZ

Frontispiece

There's nothing in *frontispiece* to suggest a piece, except what confused English speakers have put there. The original sense was of the façade of a building, the front part that was most clearly seen. It came from the French *frontispice* or the late Latin word *frontispicium*, both meaning 'façade'.

The Latin word was made up of *frons*, forehead, plus *specere*, to look at, and so originally meant a view of the forehead. You might think this referred to the forehead being a clearly visible part of a person's head, but it seems instead to have been connected with yet another of those weird methods of foretelling the future. Another name for it is *metoposcopy* (from two Greek words meaning 'observe the forehead') and it's the art of telling people's character or fortune from inspecting their foreheads. The association of ideas seems to be that the façade of a building is as expressive as a person's forehead.

The word was borrowed into English around the end of the sixteenth century in the French form *frontispice* but no later than 1607 was also being used for the title page of a book. This may seem a large shift in sense, but the link lies in the practice of engraving a highly illustrated title page with all sorts of architectural detailing, such as columns and pediments. And it was at the front of the book, which helped the idea.

By 1682 the word had taken on its modern sense of an illustration facing the title page of a book. And by then the folk etymologists had had their evil way with it, making a totally unwarranted association between *front* and *piece* and turning *frontispice* into *frontispiece*.

Fuck

This, the most-used item of vulgar slang in the language and still the one most capable of shocking even in these linguistically tolerant times, has always fascinated the know-alls of false etymology, especially those who see acronyms everywhere.

Jesse Sheidlower, in *The F-Word*, his magisterial examination of the word's origins and usage based on the researches of Jonathan Lighter, says that acronymic suggestions for its origin only began to appear in the 1960s, at about the time when the traditional taboos on printing it were beginning to decline. If you hunt about you will find quite a number, all variations on a theme:

- The origin was in the fifteenth century, when a married couple had to have permission from the king to procreate. Hence, *Fornication Under Consent of the King.*

- During the time of the Puritans, a person imprisoned in the stocks would have his or her crime displayed on the timbers. Because space was tight, when adultery was involved they used the acronym FUCK, which represented the words *For Unlawful Carnal Knowledge*.

- It originated as a medical diagnostic notation relating to soldiers in the British Imperial Army. When a soldier reported sick and was found to have VD, the abbreviation FUCK was stamped on his documents, short for *Found Under Carnal Knowledge*.

There are many variations. All are nonsense, of course, as is a story I've heard, told to a *World Wide Words* subscriber during his journalism training by a law lecturer, that *fuck* was commonly used in Chaucerian times in the sense of 'dibble'. A farmer would use his thumb to fuck or dibble the soil, to make a hole into which he then dropped a seed. There is, of course, not the slightest evidence that the word was ever used in this sense.

Fuck is often classed as one of the archetypal Anglo-Saxon four-letter words, but it isn't Anglo-Saxon – it isn't recorded until the fifteenth century. The first appearance is in a poem dated sometime before 1500 that satirizes the Carmelite friars of Cambridge. It includes the line *Non sunt in coeli, quia gxddbov xxkxzt pg ifmk*. The code can easily be broken to read *Non sunt in coeli, quia fvccant wivys of heli*. Being translated, this says 'They are not in heaven because they fuck wives of Ely'. *Fuccant* (in modern spelling) looks like Latin, but it's a humorous fake – fuck is actually Germanic, related to Middle Dutch *fokken*, Norwegian *fukka* and Swedish *focka*.

The word seems from the beginning to have been regarded as unacceptable in polite company. It remained literally unprintable until the 1960s other than in privately circulated material, though it has been in sustained and regular use in coarse speech. As late as 1948, the publishers of Norman Mailer's *The Naked and the Dead* forced him to bowdlerize it as *fug*, leading to the (surely apocryphal) story that Dorothy Parker remarked on meeting him, 'So you're the young man who can't spell fuck?'

Full Monty

Peter Cattaneo borrowed this phrase in 1997 for the title of his film. It had been in the spoken language for some decades but was still obviously unfamiliar to a lot of people. It means 'the whole thing; the lot; everything', though the film generated a subsidiary sense of 'naked'. Because it hadn't then appeared in many dictionaries, the reference vacuum resulted in masses of inventive suggestions.

The lexicographer at the *Oxford English Dictionary* who had the thankless task of writing its entry told me he had found sixteen distinct stories. It has been said – for example – that it's a corruption of 'the full amount'; a reference to bales full of wool imported from Montevideo; gamblers' jargon meaning the kitty or pot, deriving from the old US card game called *monte*; or from the name of the famous London theatrical outfitters Monty Burmans.

Tony Thorne goes for the gambling origin in his *Dictionary of Contemporary Slang* of 1997. He also reminds us that *monte* was once a common Australian and New Zealand horse-racing term for a good tip or certain bet. *Monte* is certainly long attested in both of these senses, but there's no firm evidence that *the full monty* has been derived from either of its senses, nor how it got from America or the Antipodes into British usage.

Easily the most common suggestion links it with Field Marshal Montgomery, General Montgomery as he was during his famous battles of the Second World War. He certainly had the nickname *Monty*, but the stories about Montgomery, alas, don't agree on which aspect of his life or character supposedly gave rise to the expression, though the majority refer to his liking for a good breakfast, even in the desert during the North Africa campaign. It's said that the phrase was taken up after the War, presumably by ex-servicemen, as a name for the traditional English breakfast of bacon, eggs, fried bread, tomato, mushrooms, toast and cup of tea. I have been told that it was in common use in transport cafés in the 1950s.

As with other expressions, we can get a feel for a possible origin by looking at the dates. The full monty became quite widely known in Britain during the 1990s: the Guardian had this in January 1995, for example: 'When conducting a funeral he wears the full monty: frock coat, top hat and a Victorian cane with metal tip.' Unfortunately, it first appears in print only in the middle of the 1980s. The first reference I've come across, dated 1986, is in a book entitled Street Talk: The Language of Coronation Street (Coronation Street being a long-running British television soap based on life in a northern town), though the OED has found one from the year before in the North West Sound Archive.

It must be older. My erratic memory is insistent that the phrase was around long before this; this impression is backed up by several correspondents to World Wide Words who say they heard it as far back as the 1950s, even apart from those who recall its use in transport cafés. Alas, nobody can provide any documentary evidence for these dates.

The origin that the experts point at, with due caution, is that monty here derives from the first name of Mr Montague Maurice Burton, a men's tailor. The expression does seems to have arisen in the north of England, where the firm began: Mr Burton's first shop was opened in Chesterfield in 1903, and by 1913 he had his headquarters in Sheffield. (By one of those odd coincidences this fits the Sheffield setting of the film.) The firm became huge, with more than 500 shops by 1929, and it made a quarter of British uniforms in the Second World War and a third of the demobilization suits. Someone who knew the business from before the Second World War told me that the firm used to offer a two-piece suit as the basic option, but that for a small extra amount you could also have a waistcoat and a spare pair of trousers. Paying the extra meant that you went for the full *Monty*.

My antennae suggest the Montague Burton origin is the right one. But that's just an educated guess, because we don't have enough evidence. The jury is still out on this one.

Gadget

A persistent story in the USA holds that this word comes from a Frenchman named Gaget who was involved with the construction of the Statue of Liberty, a gift from the people of France in 1886. He sold miniature bronze versions of it in New York, each with his name on the bottom. Everybody wanted one of these *Gagets* and a new word was invented.

Nice try. The name of Gaget is indeed associated with the construction of the statue, since the workshop in Paris that created the copper outer skin of the monument was that of Gaget, Gauthier & Cie. But, apart from this, the story is false, not least because *gadget* was not widely known until after the First World War.

Another story, somewhat more plausible, was told me several decades ago. As a callow young broadcaster, I was sent to a small village behind Brighton to talk to an old man who for many years had been Rudyard Kipling's chauffeur. Among many other things, but for no good reason that I can now recall, he told me with great emphasis that Kipling had invented the word *gadget* about the year 1904. His assertion isn't so wide of the truth, since Kipling did help to popularize it, in his *Traffics and Discoveries* of 1904: 'Steam gadgets always take him that way.' There's evidence, though, that the word had by then been around for many years, but exclusively among seafarers. Kipling may have picked it up during one of his journeys to India and back.

We now think of a gadget as being some small mechanical device, ill-defined perhaps, but certainly ingenious or novel. The evidence suggests that it was originally one of those hand-waving terms for something one temporarily can't remember the technical name for — a thingummy, a whatsit, a what's-his-name, a doohickey or dingus. There is anecdotal evidence, according to the *Oxford English Dictionary*, for this sense having been around since the 1850s. The origin is rather obscure, but a plausible suggestion is that it comes from French *gâchette*, a lock mechanism, or from the French dialect word *gagée*, a tool.

The writer who put *gadget* on the written map was one Robert Brown, whose *Spunyarn and Spindrift, A Sailor Boy's Log of a Voyage Out and Home in a China Tea-clipper* appeared in 1886. He wrote: 'Then the names of all the other things on board a ship! I don't know half of them yet; even the sailors forget at times, and if the exact name of anything they want happens to slip from their memory, they call it a chicken-fixing, or a gadjet, or a gill-guy, or a timmey-noggy, or a wim-wom — just *pro tem.*, you know.'

Gillyflower

It's not a name much known these days, but when it occurs *gillyflower* usually refers to the wallflower or stock. Traditionally, though, it's another name for the carnation or clove-pink (*Dianthus caryophyllus*), a connection that Chaucer and Shakespeare would have known. Whatever plant it names, it's certainly a flower, but that's not where it comes from.

It's the scent of cloves that ties the names together. The old name for a clove was *girofle*, introduced from French. This was a much modified version of the Latin *caryophyllum*, itself from Greek *karuophullon* (*karuon*, a nut, plus *phullon*, a leaf). So *sauce girofle* was clove sauce and a *clou de girofle* was a clove, literally a nail (French *clou*) from its shape. *Clou* changed into *clove* in English and the full phrase became *clove-girofle*, a name that became reserved for the clove-pink, whose scent reminded people of cloves (to the extent that it was often used to flavour drinks, which is why another name for it was *sops-in-wine*).

Folk etymology later changed *girofle* to gillyflower, and in various English dialects it lost all connection with the clove-pink and attached itself to other strongly scented flowers instead.

Glass slipper

Readers of the classic Cinderella fairy story have often been puzzled by the glass slippers which Cinders' fairy godmother gave her to wear at the ball. Such fragile, uncomfortable and potentially dangerous wear surely could not have been what was intended?

Succour for such doubters has been provided in the past century by writers who claimed that *glass slipper* was a mistranslation of the French story on which our modern versions are based. They say the slippers were really made of *vair*, a type of fur called minever in English, not of *verre*, glass. Explanations along these lines have appeared at various times in such standard works as *Brewer's Dictionary of Phrase and Fable*, the *Encyclopaedia Britannica* and the *Oxford English Dictionary*, as well as the Reverend A. Smythe Palmer's *Folk-Etymology* of 1882. All were relying on what seemed to be an impeccable authority, that of Honoré de Balzac, who wrote in 1836 that the slippers were 'without doubt of minever'.

Alas, this attempt to prove the story to be a folk etymology is itself a folk etymology. All modern authorities are certain that the slippers were indeed intended to be made of glass.

The story first appears in an accessible written form in Paris in 1697. It's one of eight folk tales in a delightful little book by Charles Perrault with the title *Histoires ou contes du temps passé* ('Tales of Times Past'). It was translated into English in 1729 by Robert Samber. Both French and English versions proved immensely popular. As well as the Cinderella story, it also included those of Babes in the Wood, Bluebeard, Puss in Boots, Tom Thumb, Little Red Riding Hood and Sleeping Beauty. Because the frontispiece shows an old woman sitting at a spinning wheel and telling stories, with the caption *Contes de ma mère l'Oye* ('Tales of Mother Goose'), children's fairy tales are often called Mother Goose stories.

As with the other stories in his collection, Charles Perrault was recording an oral folk tale current in France at the time, in this case one that folklore experts have traced back through hundreds of versions as far as China in the ninth century. Perrault actually wrote of the fairy godmother that *elle lui donna ensuite une paire de pantoufles de verre, les plus jolies du monde* ('she then gave her a pair of glass slippers, the prettiest in the world'), so Samber translated it correctly. Perrault was following a long tradition of giving Cinderella costly and impracticable footwear. The Brothers Grimm recorded a German version in 1812 that was closer in spirit to the darker and much more violent traditional rendering; in theirs the slippers were of gold.

Perrault seems to have invented the idea of making them of glass (as well as introducing the fairy godmother, also unique to his version). In doing so he had to leave out an important aspect of the traditional story, in which one ugly sister cut off her toes and the other her heel to try to fit their feet into the dainty slipper; they succeeded but both were found out and eventually blinded as a punishment. Their stratagems were discovered only later when blood was seen to stain their white stockings. Since the slipper was of glass in Perrault's version, their ghastly subterfuges would have been obvious at once.

One of the more important difficulties with giving Cinderella fur slippers is that they sound much too grandmotherly and everyday. A princess could not possibly wear anything so unfashionable. Gold slippers would certainly fit the bill, but the glass ones illustrate Cinderella's delicate nature especially well. She would have had to be physically light and dainty to be able to wear them without shattering them.

And, after all, this is a fairy story . . .

Go for a Burton

In informal British English, someone who has *gone for a Burton* is missing; a thing so described might be permanently broken, missing, ruined or destroyed. The original sense was to meet one's death, a slang term in the RAF in the Second World War for pilots who were killed in action (its first recorded appearance in print was in the *New Statesman* on 30 August 1941).

The list of supposed origins is long, but the stories are so inventive and wide-ranging that you may find them intriguing:

- A *Spanish Burton* was the Royal Navy name for a pulley arrangement that was so complex and rarely used that hardly anyone could remember what it was or what to do with it. Someone in authority who asked about a missing member of a working party might be told that he'd gone for a burton.

- The name of *burton* was given to a method of stowing wooden barrels across the ship's hold rather than fore and aft. Though they took up less space this way, it was dangerous because the entire stowage might collapse and kill somebody.

- The term *burnt'un* referred to an aircraft going down in flames.

- It refers to the inflatable *Brethon* lifejacket at one time issued by the RAF.

- It was a figurative reference to getting a suit made at the tailors Montague Burton, as one might say a person who had died had been fitted for a wooden overcoat, a coffin (compare FULL MONTY).

- The RAF was said to have used a number of billiard halls, always over Burton shops, for various purposes, such as medical centres or Morse aptitude tests (one in Blackpool is especially mentioned in the latter context). To *go for a Burton* was then to have gone for a test of some sort, but to have failed.

- It was rhyming slang: *Burton-on-Trent* (a famous British brewing town in the Midlands), meaning 'went', as in *went west*.

- A pilot who crashed in the sea was said to have ended up *in the drink*; to *go for a Burton* was to get a drink of beer, in reference to Burton-on-Trent. So the phrase was an allusive reference to crashing in the sea, later extended to all crashes.

- It is said that there was a series of advertisements for beer in the inter-war years, each of which featured a group of people with one obviously missing (a football team with a gap in the line-up, a dinner party with one chair empty). The tagline suggested the missing person had just popped out for a beer – had *gone for a Burton*. The slogan was then taken up by RAF pilots for one of their number missing in action as a typical example of wartime sick humour.

There's little we can do to choose one of these over the others. If the advertisements really did run before the Second World War they would be the most obvious source (there is doubt about this, as none have been traced and the obvious candidate, the Burton Brewery Co. Ltd., closed in 1935 and was hardly well known even before then). Whatever the truth, and knowing a little about wartime pilots, my bet would be on some association with beer.

Golf

One of those e-mails that circulate eternally online, being passed from person to person in an endless chain, says this about the origin of the name: 'In Scotland, a new game was invented. It was entitled Gentlemen Only Ladies Forbidden, and thus the word *golf* entered into the English language.'

Don't believe a word of it. Claims that words originate in acronyms are almost always spurious (see COP, FUCK, POSH, SHIT and TIP for some other examples). It's easy to refute such suggestions by consulting a dictionary, though in this case the process may not enlighten you much, since the true origin of *golf* is unknown.

There is a Scots word *gowf* for a blow or slap, but the experts think this probably comes from the game, rather than being its source. The name of the game may be related to a Dutch word *kolf* for a club or bat, though likewise this isn't recorded until after the Scots word first appeared in writing in 1457.

Gossip

An ingeniously preposterous story has been making the rounds, claiming that *gossip* derives from an early form of opinion sampling. Before the days of telephones and the mass media, the story goes, the only way politicians had of judging what people thought was to sit in pubs and listen to their conversations. So politicians would instruct minions to 'go sip some ale' and pick up information. Over time, 'go sip' turned into *gossip*. You've got to laugh, haven't you?

Surprisingly, in view of its modern meaning, the origins of *gossip* are religious. The word appeared first in Old English as *godsib*, a person who was a sponsor at a baptism, for example a godfather or godmother. It literally meant somebody who was related to you in God – it's a compound of *God* with *sib*, a relative, the latter now more narrowly defined in our *sibling* for a brother or sister.

The word evolved so that by the fourteenth century it meant a close friend, at the time either male or female, one with whom you would discuss all the events of the day. By the time of Shakespeare it had taken on a specific sense of a close female friend that a woman would invite to be present at the birth of her child, so focusing on women rather than men. It could also already be used in its modern sense of 'a woman of light and trifling nature, especially one who delights in idle talk', to quote the *Oxford English Dictionary*'s entry. It added the sense of the idle talk itself in the early nineteenth century.

Grapefruit

To show you once again that there's nothing new about folk etymologies, when this strange word first began to appear, writers immediately jumped to the wrong conclusion. John Lunan, in whose botanical work of 1814 about Jamaica, *Hortus Jamaicensis*, the word first appeared, said of it: 'There is a variety known by the name of grape-fruit, on account of its resemblance in flavour to the grape; this fruit is not near so large as the shaddock.' Mr Lunan had either never tasted one, or the grapefruit of the period were a lot sweeter than they are now, or he was suffering from sour grapes.

The grapefuit is botanically rather an interesting plant; it appeared in the eighteenth century in the West Indies as a natural cross between the pummelo and the orange. The pummelo, also called by its Dutch name of *pompelmoose*, is the same fruit as Mr Lunan's shaddock, the latter name being from a Captain Shaddock of the East India Company who brought it to the West Indies from the Malay archipelago late in the seventeenth century. The grapefruit was first described in Barbados in 1750 by the Reverend Griffith Hughes and was then and often afterwards called the *forbidden fruit*, because it was seized upon by those searching for the identity of the original tree of good and evil in the Garden of Eden (the banana had previously been a candidate).

It turns out that the grapefruit was given that name because it grows in small bunches that to a vivid imagination when unripe and green look a bit like those of grapes. To add another layer of confusion, the pummelo is at times, but not always, the same as the *pomelo*, a name sometimes reserved for the grapefruit.

Grass widow

The usual meaning given in British dictionaries is of a woman whose husband is temporarily away, say on business. This sense is known in other English-speaking communities such as Australia. It has long been used in the USA in the rather different sense of 'a woman who is separated, divorced, or lives apart from her husband', as the *Random House Webster's Unabridged Dictionary* of 1999 has it.

Some writers have suggested that it's actually a corruption of *grace-widow*. But etymologists are quite sure this isn't correct, because the phrase has always been recorded with *grass* and not *grace*. In support, its Dutch and German equivalents may be translated as 'straw widow'.

The phrase itself is ancient. Its first recorded use is by Sir Thomas More in his *Dialogue* of 1528. Then it meant something rather different: either an abandoned mistress or an unmarried woman who had cohabited with several men. It might have expressed the idea that the abandoned lover had been 'put out to grass'. But it could conceivably have come from the same type of origin as *bastard*; this is from the Latin *bastum* for a packsaddle, suggesting a child who had been born after a brief encounter on an improvised bed, such as a packsaddle, whose owner had gone by morning. Could the grass in *grass widow* refer to surreptitious love-making in the fields rather than indoors, or the straw in a barn used for an illicit tryst?

Another theory is that its modern sense derives from slang, of the period of the British Raj in India, for wives sent away during the hot summer to the cooler (and greener) hill stations while their husbands remained on duty in the plains. We can trace this back to the famous Anglo-Indian dictionary *Hobson-Jobson* of 1886. It says that the term is applied 'with a shade of malignancy', a tantalizingly opaque comment. Our modern sense appears in the 1840s and some early examples do have Anglo-Indian connections. It's possible that the term in its older meaning was indeed applied derisively to Anglo-Indian wives sent away for the summer (there were well-known opportunities for hanky-panky in the hill stations, as Rudyard Kipling recorded rather later). That could explain the 'shade of malignancy' comment in *Hobson-Jobson*, though it says tactfully about the older senses of the word that 'no such opprobrious meanings attach to the Indian use'. Its meaning could well then have softened over time to refer only to wives being temporarily separated from husbands.

Another possibility is hinted at in the 1811 edition of Captain Francis Grose's *Dictionary of the Vulgar Tongue*. Under the heading of *widow's weeds*, he notes that the term is applied to a grass widow, but also says 'a woman whose husband is abroad, and said, but not certainly known, to be dead'. Could this be the source of the transition from the older to the current senses, both British and

American? Given the uncertain nature of ship travel and difficulties of communication, a woman whose husband had been abroad a long time may well have considered him dead and taken another partner.

Graveyard shift

An anonymous online inventor of etymological tall tales has been arguing that this comes from Victorian burial practices. He suggests that people were so afraid of being buried alive that undertakers installed devices inside coffins that would enable the mistakenly inhumed person to attract attention by ringing a bell. Somebody was assigned the mildly unpleasant job of sitting in the cemetery all night to listen for the bell. Hence *graveyard shift*.

I love such stories, complete and utter hogwash though they are, not least for the light they cast on the ability of people to believe any narratively satisfying story, no matter how crazy.

This one at least has the merit of building its edifice of invention upon a firm base, since fear of premature burial was indeed rife in the nineteenth century. Edgar Allan Poe, in his short story *The Premature Burial*, said: 'To be buried while alive is, beyond question, the most terrific of these extremes which has ever fallen to the lot of mere mortality', and recounted several tragic stories of this supposedly happening.

Many ingenious devices were patented to relieve the minds of those about to expire. The first in the USA was in 1868 and two were patented as late as the 1980s. A British example from 1940 proposed a method by which a toxic gas such as hydrogen cyanide might be released inside the coffin after it was sealed 'to prevent any return to consciousness of the occupant of the coffin', a macabre and drastic – albeit satisfactorily permanent – solution to the problem.

In truth, *graveyard shift* is an evocative term for the night shift between about midnight and eight in the morning, when – no matter how often you've worked it – your skin is clammy, there's sand behind your eyeballs, and the world is creepily silent, like the graveyard. Sailors similarly know the *graveyard watch*, the midnight to four a.m. stint.

The phrase is American, and dates from the early years of the twentieth century. Another American name for it is the *lobster shift*, for reasons that are entirely obscure.

Great Scott

The exclamation of surprise and astonishment is frequently said to be a corruption of the German greeting *Grüß Gott!* You can be sure that German immigrants to the USA, say from Bavaria or Austria, brought with them their usual greeting, though it isn't easy to work out how it could have been converted to *Great Scott*, since the German greeting is usually half swallowed and doesn't sound anything like it. On the other hand, it is clear that *Great Scott!* does indeed contain a euphemism for God, and so belongs in the same set as interjections like *Great jumpin' Jehoshaphat!* and *Great Caesar!*

There's some confusion about this one, with various possibilities being put forward for the Scott in question – sometimes a generic archetypal Scot is suggested and even Sir Walter Scott has been mentioned (this last one isn't as daft as you might think, as I've found several examples in nineteenth-century writings of 'the great Scott' in reference to him).

Let's look at the facts. Until recently the earliest known example, in the *Oxford English Dictionary*, was from F. Anstey's *Tinted Venus* of 1885: 'Great Scott! I must be bad!' But the digitizing of electronic texts and the recent publication of the diary of an American Civil War veteran have moved the saying back in stages to the time of that conflict. The diary is published as *Eye of the Storm: A Civil War Odyssey* (2000), written and illustrated by Private Robert Knox Sneden. He says in his diary entry of 3 May 1864: '"Great Scott," who would have thought that this would be the destiny of the Union Volunteer in 1861–2 while marching down Broadway to the tune of "John Brown's Body".'

So it's almost certainly American, of Civil War era at the latest. Two later examples that I recently found suggest that it may have referred to a real person. One is from *Galaxy* magazine of July 1871: '"Great–Scott!" he gasped in his stupefaction, using the name of the then commander-in-chief for an oath, as officers sometimes did in those days.' The other is from a book of 1872, *Americanisms; the English of the New World* by the excellently named Maximilian Schele De Vere: '"Scott, Great!" a curious euphemistic oath, in which the name of a well-known general is substituted for the original word, probably merely because of its monosyllabic form.' Another electronic search, by Fred Shapiro of Yale Law School, turned up an earlier example from a May 1861 issue of *The New York Times*: 'These gathering hosts of loyal freemen, under the command of the great SCOTT.'

There was a famous American general named Scott, who did have the title of commander-in-chief of the US Army at the time of the outbreak of the Civil War, though he is best known as one of the two American heroes of the Mexican War of 1846–8. This was General Winfield Scott, known to his troops as Old Fuss and Feathers. It seems plausible that he is the source being pointed to, especially as in his later years he weighed 300 pounds (21 stone or 136 kg), was too fat to ride a horse and was certainly a great Scott in a very literal sense.

There's nothing new in this attribution, however. Winfield Scott has previously been fingered as the origin by several writers, among them Eric Partridge. And we still can't be absolutely sure that he was the Scott being alluded to. But the combination of dates and the references written so soon after the event point to him quite strongly.

Gridiron

This humble cooking utensil is rarely encountered in our kitchens these days but has moved outdoors to be a component of the barbecue.

Its most famous illustration must be in *The Martyrdom of St Lawrence* by Titian, in which Lawrence is reclining on a gridiron while his executioners busily stoke the fire underneath to a red heat that, strangely, doesn't seem to be grilling the saint's body. It is just a coincidence, of course, that in the northern hemisphere his saint's day of 10 August falls in the barbecue season. It's also no more than an oddity of word history that the earliest example of the word in English refers not to cooking but to torture (as does the first appearance of its close relative *griddle*).

Though historically the gridiron was a grid made of iron, etymologically speaking there's no metal in it. The original Old English form was *gredile* (the ancestor of *griddle*), ultimately from Latin *craticulum*, a diminutive of *cratis*, wickerwork or a hurdle. Old English borrowed the idea of interwoven wicker to refer to the net-like form of the griddle. *Gredile* is early on spelled as *gredire*, perhaps because the Old English word for iron, *ire* or *iren*, was linked to the ending of *gridile* out of folk etymology. By the end of the fourteenth century that word had been transformed into our modern gridiron. It became abbreviated to *grid* in the nineteenth century.

Americans most often associate *gridiron* with the pattern of white lines at five-yard intervals on an American football pitch. This slang sense came into the language at the end of the nineteenth century, replacing an older one dating from no later than 1812 that referred to the Stars and Stripes. This arose, of course, from the red and white horizontal bars on the flag and seems to have started its life as naval slang.

Grindstone *See* KEEP ONE'S NOSE TO THE GRINDSTONE·

Gringo

This mildly derogatory Spanish term for a white person from an English-speaking country has had some weird folklore attached to it.

The most usual story is that it comes from the war between the USA and Mexico between 1846–8, in which Mexicans heard American soldiers singing 'Green Grow the Rushes, O' (or, in a variation, 'Green Grow the Lilacs') around the campfire and dubbed them *green grows*, later modified to *gringos*. If you're unhappy with this suggestion, you might prefer to associate the singing with Irish volunteers serving in Simon Bolivar's army in the early nineteenth century, or with American troops attempting to track down Pancho Villa in Mexico in 1916–17, all of whom were supposedly singing from the same song sheet (the last of these often mentions Black Jack Pershing, since to attach a famous name to a story improves its credibility no end). Finally, there are the stories that link the term with the green uniforms (hence *green coats*) worn by American troops of the period, who might have been urged by the locals 'green go home'.

The real story is actually rather more interesting, since it takes us to two continents and involves four languages. A medieval Latin proverb referred to something unintelligible: 'Graecum est; non potest legi' ('It is Greek; it cannot be read'). Shakespeare borrowed it in *Julius Caesar*: 'Those that understood him smiled at one another and shook their heads; but for mine own part, it was Greek to me.' It's the origin of our modern saying it's *all Greek to me*.

The Spanish version of this Latin proverb was 'hablar en griego', literally to talk in Greek, and hence to speak unintelligibly. This was known in Spain no later than the last decades of the eighteenth century. Esteban de Terreros explained in his dictionary of 1787, *El Diccionario Castellano*, that 'gringos llaman en Málaga a los estranjeros, que tienen cierta especie de acento, que los priva de una locución fácil y natural castellana; y en Madrid dan el mismo, y por la misma causa con particularidad a los Irlandeses' ('Foreigners in Malaga are called gringos, who have certain kinds of accent that prevent them from speaking Spanish with an easy and natural locution; and in Madrid they give this name to the Irish in particular for the same reason'). He explained that *gringo* was a simple phonetic alteration of *griego*.

The first recorded use of the word in English is in 1849, which does rather suggest it was the Mexican War that brought it to the attention of Americans. It appears in the diary of John Woodhouse Audubon, the son of the wildlife illustrator, who recorded on 13 June in that year that 'We were hooted and shouted at as we passed through, and called "Gringoes"'. As his diary wasn't published until 1906, public notice of the word in America probably came about through a book by one Lieutenant Wise of the US Navy that appeared in January 1850: *Los Gringos; or, an inside View of Mexico and California, with Wanderings in Peru, Chili, and Polynesia*.

Gry

Nobody seems to be absolutely sure how it started, but quite suddenly in the mid-1990s everybody concerned with language in North America, from librarians to newspaper columnists to dictionary makers to experts on word history were deluged with enquiries along the lines of: 'There are three words in English ending in -gry. I only know *hungry* and *angry*. Please tell me what the third one is. I'm going mad trying to find the answer.' The craze for trying to solve this curious conundrum even crossed the Atlantic to Britain. In the years since, there have been further sporadic outbreaks, like a plague that has mainly run its course but occasionally flares up.

The reason why so many people were tearing their hair out is that there is no third common word in English ending in -gry, though there are several rare or obsolete ones. So why were so many people desperate to find something that didn't exist?

It seems that the question had been taken from some old book of puzzles, had been given publicity, perhaps on a radio programme (Richard Lederer says it was on the Bob Grant radio talk show on WMCA in New York City in 1975), had taken the fancy of large numbers of people, and had been passed by word of mouth across North America, becoming corrupted on the way, until later hearers only received the bastardized version I've already quoted. I've seen various versions of the supposed original form of the riddle. It may have been something like:

> There are two words that end with 'gry'.
> Angry is one and hungry is another.
> What is the third word.
> Everyone uses it every day and
> Everyone knows what it means.
> If you have been listening,
> I have already told you what the word is.

One of the first mistakes in transmission appears to have been the inclusion of a question mark at the end of the third line. This turned a simple bit of verbal trickery, whose answer is *what*, into a fruitless exercise in lexicographical detection. Another version is:

> Think of words ending in 'gry'.
> Angry and hungry are two of them.
> There are only three words in the English language.
> What is the third word?
> The word is something that everyone uses every day.
> If you have listened carefully,
> I have already told you what it is . . .

and in this case the answer must surely be *language* (the third word in 'the English language').

Yet a third version claiming to be the original was published in the US magazine *Parade* in March 1997, in a letter from Charles Wiedemann of New Jersey, who was responding to an article on the mystery by Marilyn Vos Savant. His version is:

> There are at least three words
> in the English language that end in g or y.
> One of them is 'hungry', and another one is 'angry'.
> There is a third word, a short one,
> which you probably say every day.
> If you are listening carefully to everything I say,
> you just heard me say it three times.
> What is it?

which relies on verbal trickery to confuse the quickly said *g* or *y* with *gry*. The answer is actually *say*.

So a corrupted riddle has been the source of vast anguish to puzzled seekers after truth and a lot of trouble to inoffensive writers on etymology. We all pray that some misguided newspaper columnist or broadcaster doesn't resurrect the whole matter some day.

Guinea pig

There are several puzzles about this inoffensive little animal, not least that it isn't a pig and it doesn't come from Guinea. It's actually a rodent from central South America, though the variety that children have as pets doesn't occur in the wild.

Why it should have that name is a mystery; the *Oxford English Dictionary* guesses that it might have been confused with the Guinea hog, a hardy species of pig from the Guinea coast of Africa, which was taken to the USA as part of the slave trade and was at one time a common homestead animal in rural America. The problem with this, as the *OED*'s editors surely knew, is that *guinea pig* is actually about a century older as a term in English than *guinea hog*, being known from 1664. The guinea pig was early on also called the *Spanish coney* (*coney* being the old name for a rabbit, which was applied by sailors and explorers to several small, furry, vaguely rabbit-like animals that they encountered; Spanish because it came from the Spanish colonies in South America); it has been suggested that *coney* became corrupted to *guinea*, which seems only marginally probable.

Yet a third story suggests that it was first brought to Britain in Guineamen, vessels that made the triangular voyage to Guinea and the New World as part of the slave trade, but similar problems about dating crop up here. A story, widely held, says that the first sailors who brought them to Britain sold them for an English guinea (£1.05), though this seems a large sum, even for an exotic rarity, at a time when a household servant earned £5 a year, and I've found no evidence that they ever actually did so.

Whatever the origin, it may have ended up being called a pig because it does squeal a bit like one. The animal was domesticated three centuries ago and became widely distributed in Europe and America.

In the nineteenth century the phrase was also a dismissive term applied to midshipmen in the ships of the East India Company, possibly because they paid their dues to the captain in guineas. It was also a deeply sarcastic expression for men ('of more rank than means' as one writer put it) who took on notional duties as directors of companies, lending out their names for a good dinner and a guinea fee.

Guinea pig was first used by George Bernard Shaw in 1913 to refer to a human who was being experimented upon and this sense has if anything become more common than the literal one. Quite where he got it from is a mystery. The guinea pig was used for medical experimentation in the nineteenth century – there are many examples mentioned in the literature going back at least as far as the 1850s. But it has proved impossible to connect these experiments to the expression or to say why they should have so caught the imagination that the term was taken up as a metaphor.

My suspicion – I can hardly rate it better than that – is that it was the famous experiments of Louis Pasteur in Paris on infectious diseases, rabies in particular, in the 1880s and 1890s that brought the guinea pig to wide general attention in this context. I've been able to establish that he did in fact test vaccines on them and that this became widely known at the time. But, as so often, key links in the chain of evidence are missing.

Ham

A *ham* or *ham actor* is one who struts his piece upon the stage to little effect, a fifth-rate artiste of the sort that P. G. Wodehouse said 'couldn't play the pin in *Pinafore*'. He may fail because he is an unskilled amateur, though the word is often applied to a thespian who overacts in a theatrical or ranting manner to compensate for his poor grasp of the techniques of his profession or to upstage his fellow actors.

The term is American and dates from the nineteenth century. Where it comes from has been the subject of more folk etymologies than you can shake a stick at. It is said to derive from Hamlet's advice to the actors ('O, it offends me to the soul to hear a robustious periwig-pated fellow tear a passion to tatters, to very rags, to split the ears of the groundlings'), though why it had to wait 300 years to appear is not explained (a subsidiary suggestion is that the word comes from the title of the play, which is one that amateurs frequently perform badly). Others argue it's from a Cockney pronunciation of 'amateur', *hamateur*, but that's to put the origin on the wrong continent. A troupe of actors managed by one Hamish McCullough was said to have toured the west after the Civil War and to have become known as *Ham's actors*, with the epithet gaining its slang sense because they were so bad, but nobody seems to have good knowledge of this troupe.

To the evidence, then, before this tide of falsity overwhelms us.

Around the 1860s the word *ham* began to appear in America for somebody who was stupid, clumsy or worthless, such as an untalented prize fighter. This might suggest an origin in *ham-handed* or *ham-fisted*, except that both these terms are later creations, of the First and Second World Wars respectively, in reference to inept pilots; there's an elaboration of the term, for inept boxers in particular: *ham-and-egger*, but this dates from around 1910 and seems to be derived from *ham* rather than the other way around. About 1880 *ham* began to be applied to performers in variety, who were looked down on by 'legitimate' actors. In this sense *ham* is usually considered to be an abbreviation of the slightly older *hamfatter* for an inept performer. A related term was *hambone* for a poor performer, especially a musician.

This is as far as the evidence takes us, leaving several questions without answers. Does the earlier, often sporting, sense of *ham* have anything to do with the performing one, and where does it come from? And why should the theatrical hams be linked to ham fat?

There's no good explanation that I know of for the first question. The second is often answered by saying that low-paid performers had to make do with ham fat to clean off their heavy make-up after a performance rather than a proper cream. There was also a minstrel song, 'The Ham Fat Man', which had been written by a man named Jones and published in Cincinnati in 1863; this was popular and may have been part of the source of the term, perhaps because it was often performed by fifth-rate minstrel groups – certainly there's nothing in the words of the song itself that might have prompted a link. Neither explanation is altogether convincing, but it's the best we have.

Hangnail

We associate this word with a bit of torn skin at the root or side of a fingernail, so the name seems eminently reasonable – it's something hanging from a fingernail.

Surprisingly, the original of this word in Old English meant a corn on the foot. It later came to mean any painful swelling on a finger or toe (much like a whitlow). Only in the eighteenth century did it take on its current sense and spelling. The changes resulted from folk etymology.

The Old English word was a compound of *ange*, something that is painful or troublesome, with *nayle*, so making *agnayle*. However, the second element didn't refer to a finger or toe nail, but to the sort made of iron. The idea behind it was that the corn was round-headed and hard, like a nail.

By the sixteenth century this distinction had been lost and

people came to assume that it referred to the other sort of nail. By then, *ange* had long since become obsolete and it may be that speakers confused the word – by then usually written as *agnail* – with a French or Latin word that meant a sore. The final step, around the 1740s, was to change the meaning and shift the spelling to *hangnail*, on the grounds that both made more sense.

Happy as a clam

Americans know this proverbial phrase as a way of saying that someone is perfectly content. Few stop to wonder why a clam should be marked out as the epitome of happiness. Even the most pleasantly situated can hardly be called the life and soul of the party. All they can expect is a watery existence, likely at any moment to be rudely interrupted by a man with a spade, followed by conveyance to a very hot place. In the late 1840s John G. Saxe put it better, at any rate more poetically, in his 'Sonnet to a Clam':

> Inglorious friend! most confident I am
> Thy life is one of very little ease;
> Albeit men mock thee with their similes,
> And prate of being 'happy as a clam!'
> What though thy shell protects thy fragile head
> From the sharp bailiffs of the briny sea?
> Thy valves are, sure, no safety-valves to thee,
> While rakes are free to desecrate thy bed,
> And bear thee off, – as foemen take their spoil,
> Far from thy friends and family to roam;
> Forced, like a Hessian, from thy native home,
> To meet destruction in a foreign broil!
> Though thou art tender, yet thy humble bard
> Declares, O clam! thy case is shocking hard!

The saying is very definitely American, hardly known elsewhere. In its short form it is first recorded in the 1830s, though it is almost certainly a lot older; by 1848 the *Southern Literary Messenger* of Richmond, Virginia could say that the expression *happy as a clam* 'is familiar to every one'.

The fact is, we have lost its second half, which makes everything clear. The full expression is actually *happy as a clam at high tide*, or sometimes *happy as a clam at high water*. An example appears in *Cap'n Warren's Wards* by Joseph Lincoln in 1912: 'So, when I went to sea as a cabin boy, a tow-headed snub-nosed little chap of fourteen, I was as happy as a clam at highwater 'cause I was goin' in the ship he was mate of.'

Clam digging has to be done at low tide, when you stand a chance of finding them and extracting them. At high water, clams are comfortably covered in water and so able to feed, free of the risk that some hunter will rip them untimely from their sandy berths. I suspect that's a good enough definition of *happy*, at least for a clam.

Harebrained

Or is it *hairbrained*? It's easy to find lots of examples of each form, not only in unedited text online but also in books and newspapers.

It would be easy to say that the right answer is *harebrained*, because that's the first form recorded and the reference is pretty clearly to the apparently stupidly senseless behaviour of hares in the mating season: approach the term through *mad March hares* and you will get the idea.

So it would be equally easy to say that *hairbrained* is wrong, a folk etymology based on inadequate knowledge. But even a superficial look at the historical evidence stops one. The first example in the *Oxford English Dictionary* is dated 1548, and that has *hare*. But the second is from 1581, and that has *hair*. The editor who compiled the OED entry seems to have deliberately alternated examples in the two forms, since there's roughly one of each cited from every century since.

The reason for this, at least to start with, was that *hair* was at the time an alternate way of spelling *hare*. That spelling was preserved in Scotland into the eighteenth century. When Sir Walter Scott used it in *The Monastery* in 1820 ('If hairbrained courage, and an outrageous spirit of gallantry, can make good his pretensions to the high lineage he claims, these qualities have never been denied him'), he may have been perpetuating the Scots spelling. As a result of the two spellings coexisting for so long, it's impossible to tell when people began to write *hairbrained* instead of *harebrained* in the belief that it referred to somebody who had a brain made of hair, or perhaps the size of a hair.

There are many examples of the *hair* spelling from both Britain and the USA throughout the nineteenth century and down to the present day. So it's not enough to say that one is an error and the other not. At the very least, it's an error of such antiquity that the patina of age has done something to soften our objections to it.

The current status of *hairbrained* is disputed: some style guides say that it should not be used, as the fourth edition of the *American Heritage Dictionary* does: 'While hairbrained continues to be used and confused, it should be avoided in favor of harebrained which has been established as the correct spelling.' Robert Burchfield's third edition of *Fowler's Modern English Usage* (1996) describes it as an erroneous form 'which is still occasionally found' (rather more often than that, as my research shows). Other guides disagree, a case in point being *Merriam-Webster's Dictionary of English Usage* which says: 'Our opinion based on the evidence is that it is established.'

Harlot

This archaic word for a prostitute or promiscuous woman has had a varied career and its origin was first subject to the whims of etymythology as early as the sixteenth century. Around 1570 William Lambarde suggested that the word was actually an eponym, taken from the name Arlette or Herleva, the unmarried mother of William the Conqueror.

Lambarde's theory was completely up the creek, though a lot of people who should have known better retold it in later centuries. In 1656, Thomas Blount included it in his *Glossographia* thus: 'From *Arlotta* and *Harlotha*, Concubine to *Robert* Duke of Normandy, on whom he begat *William* the Bastard, Conqueror, and King of *England*; in spite to whom, and disgrace to his Mother, the English called all Whores Harlots.' As the *Oxford English Dictionary* remarks rather sharply, only somebody who lived at a time when the earlier senses of the word had been forgotten could have put forward such a theory.

What defeats Lambarde and his followers at the first step is that the English word at first referred to a male person. It actually derives from Old French *harlot* or *herlot*, a knave or vagabond. The first English sense – in the thirteenth century – was, as the OED so comprehensively puts it, a 'vagabond, beggar, rogue, rascal, villain, low fellow, knave'. (A court record of the period refers to a *naughty harlot*, meaning a wicked rogue.) Within a century or so it had moved somewhat to mean a jester or buffoon, or an all-round good fellow, which is what Chaucer meant when he referred to the Summoner in his *Canterbury Tales*:

He was a gentil harlot and a kynde,
A bettre felawe sholde men noght fynde.

However, Chaucer also uses the word in the same book for a male servant and in the old sense of a vagabond, showing that its sense

was shifting about. It was a century or so later, in the 1480s, that
harlot changed sex, first to refer to a female juggler (the female
equivalent of the jester, perhaps) or an actress. Actresses have had
a steamy reputation at most periods, so the shift to 'prostitute'
was just a step. Its wide popularity was partly due to various
fifteenth-century translations of the Bible, and in particular to the
1611 King James Version, which used it as a slightly softer term
in place of the older *whore*.

Head over heels

We are so conditioned by our knowledge of idioms that we rarely
stop to think about what they really mean. This example is more
than a little weird when you do so – what's so strange about
having one's head over one's heels? We do, after all, spend most
of our waking lives in that position.

To be *head over heels* almost always means that one has fallen
madly in love in an impetuous and unconstrained way. But by
itself it can also refer to one's state while turning a somersault or
cartwheel.

It looks so odd because during its history it got turned upside
down, just like the idea it represents. When it first appeared, back
in the fourteenth century, it was written as *heels over head*, which
makes perfect sense. It meant – quite logically – to be upside
down, or, as *to turn heels over head*, to turn a somersault. It became
inverted around the end of the eighteenth century, it seems as the
result of a series of mistakes by authors who didn't stop to think
about the conventional phrase they were writing, or who found
the stress pattern of *head over heels* more persuasive than the older
form.

The two forms lived alongside each other for most of the next
century – the famous Davy Crockett was an early user of the

modern form in 1834: 'I soon found myself head over heels in love with this girl.' As late as the early years of the twentieth century L. Frank Baum consistently used the older form in his Oz books: 'But suddenly he came flying from the nearest mountain and tumbled heels over head beside them.' And Lucy Maud Montgomery stayed with it in her *Anne of Windy Poplars*, published as late as 1936: 'Gerald's pole, which he had stuck rather deep in the mud, came away with unexpected ease at his third tug and Gerald promptly shot heels over head backward into the water.'

Some people deliberately use *heels over head* for the sake of effect. However, if you do so on the grounds that it makes more sense and was the original form, you are open to accusations of perpetrating an etymological fallacy. For better or worse, we're now stuck with the inverted form.

Helicopter

There's nothing wrong with this evocative word for what is more generically called a rotating-wing aircraft, since it derives – via French – from the Greek words *helix*, a spiral, plus *pteron*, a wing. It's what people have done with it that puts it into the class of false etymology.

Understandably enough, the correct division of the word into its elements *helico-* and *-pter* doesn't occur to anyone, a split into *heli-* plus *-copter* being preferred. Unfortunately, there's no other common word in English containing the *helico-* form that might provide a corrective, though it does occur in a few specialist words like *helicorubin*, a form of haemoglobin found in snails.

As a result, a number of compounds have been created that use *heli-* to refer to helicopter, as in *helipad*, *heliport* and *heliskiing*. This misapprehension is now much too firmly fixed in the language for even the most die-hard of pedants to contemplate countering.

Helpmate

Few weirder examples exist of the way that phrases can become distorted through oral transmission. *Helpmate* doesn't appear in the language in that spelling before 1715, but there is an older form, *helpmeet*, which has remained in use alongside it down to the present day.

We can pinpoint its origin exactly, to the King James Version of the Bible, published in 1611. The phrase *help meet* appears twice in chapter 2 of the Book of Genesis. The first reads: 'And the Lord God said, It is not good that the man should be alone; I will make him an help meet for him.' When this was read out in church, the two words ran together in listeners' heads. But what the text is actually saying is 'I will make help suitable for him', where *meet* is an adjective with the sense of someone or something fit or proper for its purpose. That help turned out to be Eve, of course, and in the modern usage of the word she was indeed his *helpmate*.

Early appearances of the noun were hyphenated, as here in the first recorded use, in the then Poet Laureate John Dryden's *Marriage à la Mode* of 1673: 'If ever woman was a help-meet for man, my Spouse is so', which echoes the form of the scriptural passage.

There is some small doubt whether *helpmate* evolved from *helpmeet*, but in view of the dates it seems highly probable that English speakers piled folk etymology on top of the original error. Having mistakenly turned *meet* into a noun, they then became puzzled over its meaning and decided that it must instead be *mate*, a highly suitable word for the situation.

Early on, educated people were aware of the error and this led to a long delay in its acceptance: it doesn't appear in Dr Johnson's famous dictionary of 1755, for example, or even in some later ones. It only started to be listed in the nineteenth century.

Hobo

Though many people would equate *hobo* and *tramp*, these rootless migrants made a careful distinction among themselves: a hobo travelled to find work while a tramp travelled to avoid it. (A bum was worse than either, since he stayed in one place and existed on handouts or begging.)

The word in its modern form was first recorded in the north-western USA. The first known example appeared in November 1889 in the *Ellensburgh Capital* in Washington State: 'The tramp has changed his name, or rather had it changed for him, and now he is a "Hobo".' Note the initial capital letter, which also turns up in other early examples, and which has led some writers to conclude that it was a proper name, or at least the hoboes' own name for themselves.

As to where it came from, there is no clear evidence, and as a result there are many conflicting theories:

- Possible parallels have been suggested with the English dialect words *hawbuck* and *hawbaw* for a coarse or clumsy fellow.
- It is named after Hoboken, New Jersey.
- It comes from the Japanese *houbou*, 'to wander about', or from the Irish Gaelic *ob*, to reject or shun.
- The French *Ho, beau!*, 'hey, handsome!' is said to have been a mocking cry by beggars in eighteenth-century France to get the attention of well-heeled passers-by.
- It might be an Anglicization of the Mexican-Spanish command ¡*jopo!*, meaning 'get out', but that word is not recorded.
- Similarly, a *hoe-boy* is a plausible-sounding name for a hoe-hand and is sometimes suggested, but nobody has found an example of it in print.

Nobody has ever provided any firm evidence that words from English dialect or foreign languages made their way into late nineteenth-century tramps' slang in the north-west of the USA. It also seems very unlikely that the name of an eastern US city like Hoboken would have given rise to a word that first appeared on the other side of the continent. The Mexican-Spanish origin would make sense of a report that appeared in the *New Orleans Picayune* in 19 August 1848: 'A year's bronzing and "ho-boying" about among the mountains of that charming country called Mexico, has given me a slight dash of the Spanish', but – as the *Random House Historical Dictionary of American Slang* carefully notes – the big gap between this and the next appearance of the word leaves a lot of questions unanswered, as is so often the case.

The last story in my list probably contains the germ of the idea. *Bo* as a term for a man or fellow is at least half a century older than the first appearance of *hobo*; it has been suggested that it comes from *Beau*, a common southern nickname, but is just as likely to be an abbreviation of *boy*. It's plausible that *hobo* might derive from the greeting 'Ho, Bo!' (or 'Ho, Beau!') of one migrant to another, or a challenge or greeting used by railway workers: 'Ho boy!'

A writer in the 1920s gave anecdotal evidence of just this origin in a call used by railway mail handlers on a line in Oregon in the 1880s. Another, in 1893, much nearer the word's origin, acknowledged a connection with the west coast and remarked: 'The origin of *Hobo*, the term now generally applied to the railway grader, is unknown, but is generally supposed to have come from the salutation of "Ho, boy!" which was shouted by one workman to another.'

That's as far as the evidence takes us. And we have to be cautious about anecdotal evidence. But an origin in 'ho, boy' looks highly plausible.

Honeymoon

Many invented stories exist about the origin of this word, mostly so sickly that I cringe at repeating them. One especially prevalent one suggests that at some time in some place there was a custom for newlyweds to drink mead (fermented honey) every day for the first month after the nuptials as an aphrodisiac. So *honeymonth* or *honeymoon*. For some reason, ancient Babylon keeps being mentioned in this connection, though sometimes ancient Persia gets a look in, and Attila the Hun is said to have choked to death on it at his wedding feast in AD 453. The story was given a boost in 2003 when the Royal Society of Chemistry in London advertised for newly married couples to imbibe draughts of a honey drink each night for a month and report on its effects. The press release uncritically reported the tale about the origin of the word but referred to the drink as *milheglin*, which is a misprint for *metheglin*, a spicy type of mead. That misspelling appears in Lillian Eichler's book *The Customs of Mankind*, published in New York in 1924, in which she told the tale. So we know where the Society (and many other people who tell the tale) got it from.

The big problem with the story, leaving aside its fanciful absurdity, is that the word only turns up in English in the middle of the sixteenth century, though the early examples suggest it is actually older. Let me quote you a passage from an early dictionary, Richard Huloet's *Abecedarium Anglico Latinum* of 1552 (I've modernized the spelling): 'Honeymoon, a term proverbially applied to such as be new married, which will not fall out at the first, but the one loveth the other at the beginning exceedingly, the likelihood of their exceeding love appearing to assuage, the which time the vulgar people call the honey moon.' A century later, Thomas Blount included an entry for the word in his *Glossographia, or a dictionary interpreting such hard words . . . as are now used*: 'Hony-moon, applied to those married persons that love well at first, and decline in affection afterwards; it is honey now, but it will change as the Moon.'

Putting it in modern English, the honeymoon was that charmed period when married love was at first as sweet as honey, but which waned like the moon and in roughly the same period of time. Cynical, I know, but don't blame etymology for that. There's no need to invoke mead or metheglin: we need look no further for the real origin of the word than human nature.

Hooker

A persistent story in the USA claims that this word for a prostitute derives from the name of Joseph 'Fighting Joe' Hooker, a major general in the Union forces at the time of the Civil War, who commanded the Army of the Potomac for five months in 1863.

General Hooker was not universally popular – one biographer calls him 'a conniver and carouser' – because he was quarrelsome, deeply disrespectful of his superiors, a womanizer, a drunkard and (worst of all) an unsuccessful soldier. Hooker's headquarters were described as a combination of bar and brothel into which no decent woman could go. It is also said that his men were an undisciplined lot who frequented prostitutes (a red-light area of Washington was said to have briefly been called Hooker's division for this reason). So it's not surprising that hooker is often assumed to derive from his short-lived command.

However, there's a fatal flaw: the word is recorded several times before the Civil War. It's listed in the second edition of John Russell Bartlett's Dictionary of Americanisms of 1859 and another example is known from North Carolina in 1845. An even earlier instance was turned up by George Thompson of New York University in the New York Transcript of 25 September 1835, which contains a whimsical report of a police court hearing in which a woman of no reputation at all is called a hooker because she 'hangs around the hook'. This obscure reference is to Corlear's Hook, an area of New York. Mr Bartlett suggests the same origin for the term, based on 'the number of houses of ill-fame frequented by sailors' in the area. Though this origin sounds plausible, it may well be that Mr Bartlett and others who made this connection were falling victim to an earlier version of folk etymology.

There is some evidence to suggest that it really comes from a much older British low slang term for a specialist thief who snatches items using a hook. In 1592, in a book on low-life called *The Art of Conny Catching*, Robert Greene says that such thieves 'pull out of a window any loose linen cloth, apparel, or else any other household stuff'. The implication is that the hooker catches her clients by similar, albeit less tangible, methods.

Hot dog

The usual story told about this comestible is that it was first sold by a food concessionaire named Harry Stevens at New York's Polo Grounds, the home of the New York Giants, in the early 1900s. It is said that the famous cartoonist T. A. Dorgan (Tad) recorded these odd new things in a cartoon in the *New York Journal*, drawing them as dachshunds in buns, and called them *hot dogs* because he couldn't spell *frankfurter*.

This tale is reproduced in almost every book on word histories I have on my shelves, and at many online sites, too. It seems to have come about as the result of the obituary of Harry Stevens that appeared in the New York *Herald Tribune* on 4 May 1934, in which these supposed events were recorded; the writer may have borrowed the story from an article in *Restaurant Man* in 1929. There are variations: the *Encyclopaedia Britannica* says the first stall selling them was at Coney Island in 1916; I've also seen the St Louis

World Fair of 1904 cited as the starting point, which takes us well away from the New York nexus of the majority view.

Hardly any of this is true.

Leonard Zwilling, of the *Dictionary of American Regional English*, has compiled a lexicon of Tad's language (he popularized a number of phrases, such as *malarkey*, *hard-boiled* and *kibitzer*, so he was worth the effort), and he did find a 1906 cartoon illustrating Harry Stevens' hot dogs, though it was at a six-day bicycle race in Madison Square Garden, not at the Polo Grounds. However, since the first recorded use of the phrase is way back in 1895, neither Tad nor Mr Stevens can claim inventor's rights in the name.

All this has been exhaustively researched by Barry Popik of the American Dialect Society, and a summary appears in *America in So Many Words* by David K. Barnhart and Allan A. Metcalf. The information here comes directly or indirectly from Mr Popik.

It seems that the link of *dog* with sausage actually goes back to the middle of the nineteenth century in the USA, expressing dark suspicions about the source of their meat content. Mr Popik has even found a popular song of 1860, of which you may know another version:

> Oh where oh where has my little dog gone?
> Oh where oh where can he be?
> Now sausage is good, baloney, of course.
> Oh where oh where can he be?
> They make them of dog, they make them of horse,
> I think they made them of he.

What seems to have happened is that near the end of the nineteenth century, around 1894–5, students at Yale University began to refer sarcastically to the wagons selling hot sausages in buns as *dog wagons*. One at Yale was even given the nickname of 'The Kennel Club'. It was only a short step from this campus use of *dog* to *hot dog* (the sausages were hot, even if the bun wasn't), and this fateful move was first recorded in a story in the issue of the *Yale Record* for 19 October 1895, which ended: 'They contentedly munched hot dogs during the whole service.' In 1900 the term was recorded in *Dialect Notes* and by then had turned up in US military slang.

By one of those coincidences that one can only suspect was part of some vast and subtle linguistic conspiracy, the term *hot dog* had been invented about a year earlier in another context, as a term for a well-dressed young man or a cockily proficient individual (in *Billy Baxter's Letters* of 1899 appears: 'A Messe de Mariage seems to be some kind of a wedding march, and a bishop who is a real hot dog won't issue a certificate unless the band plays the Messe'). That term has evolved, so that these days it suggests showing off, especially – as a verb – performing showy manoeuvres while surfing. This may have been borrowed from an older bit of American university slang, to PUT ON DOG.

The combination of the existing and new usages seems to have been a potent one in the air of the 1890s and within a few years *hot dog* became the most usual term (although *frankfurter* and *wiener* are both recorded from the early 1880s, they lost out somewhat in the popularity stakes to *hot dog*'s native charm).

There is enormous resilience in false but fascinating stories. I've added my two bits on the side of truth, and perhaps one day the real story of *hot dog* will be in all the books.

Hue and cry

This idiom, meaning a loud clamour or public outcry, contains the obsolete word *hue*, which people today know only as a slightly formal or technical word for a colour or shade. One result is that it often appears as *hew and cry*, perhaps with some idea behind it of hacking or chopping, but most probably because people who write unthinkingly or under pressure often put down words that sound right to their inner ears.

When it appears in journalists' copy, alert sub-editors usually manage to catch it, but one got through to the pages of the *Christian Science Monitor* in January 2002: 'Just the same, the Pentagon was neglectful in letting its allies in on this legal and moral reasoning, creating an international hew and cry that the US once again was being a unilateralist bully making up its own rules.'

Our modern meaning goes back to part of English common law in the years after the Norman Conquest. There wasn't an organized police force and the job of fighting crime fell mostly on ordinary people. If somebody robbed you, or you saw a murder or other crime of violence, it was up to you to raise the alarm, the *hue and cry*. Everybody in the neighbourhood was then obliged to drop what they were doing and help pursue and capture the supposed criminal. The person raising the hue and cry didn't need to be anybody in authority – any private citizen could do it (we retain a weakened survivor in the powers of citizen's arrest). If the criminal was caught with stolen goods on him, he was summarily convicted (he wasn't allowed to say anything in his defence, for example), while if he resisted arrest he could be killed. The same term was used for a proclamation relating to the capture of a criminal or the finding of stolen goods. The laws relating to hue and cry were repealed in Britain in 1827.

This mysterious word *hue* is from the Anglo-Norman French legal phrase *hu e cri*, which came from the Old French *hu* for an outcry, in turn from *huer*, to shout. The two words in this context are virtual synonyms, possibly part of an attempt to make legal phrases intelligible both to French and English speakers in the years after the Norman Conquest. It seems that *hue* could mean any cry, or even the sound of a horn or trumpet. The phrase *hu e cri* had a Latin equivalent, *hutesium et clamor*, 'with horn and with voice'.

The Old French *huer* survived in active use in Cornwall right down to the early part of the twentieth century: the lookouts on the cliffs who watched for the arrival of the pilchard shoals in early autumn were called *huers*, since they commonly alerted the fishermen waiting below by shouting through large speaking trumpets.

Humble pie

This one is an example of a shift in spelling of a word under the influence of another. In this case it's a portmanteau dish, since there also seems to be a joke involved.

The *umbles* were the innards of the deer: the liver, heart, entrails and other third-class bits. It was common practice in medieval times to serve a meat pie made of these parts of the animal to the servants and others who would be sitting at the lower tables in the lord's hall. Though this was definitely lower-class fare at the time, it seems to have gone up in the world later, at least to judge from Samuel Pepys, who mentions it in his diary for 8 July 1663: 'Mrs Turner came in and did bring us an umble pie hot out of her oven, extraordinarily good', and records a year earlier serving the same dish to the admiral Sir William Penn, hardly the action of an ambitious young civil servant if the dish was then as low-class as its origins suggest.

It was not until the nineteenth century that *eating humble pie* appeared in the sense we know now, of apologizing humbly, of submitting to humiliation as a result of error. It looks like a folk etymology, though some experts have reasoned that it arose as a deliberate play on words, an echo of the older expression *to eat one's words*. If so, it was a very small play.

The word *umbles* is a variant form of an old French term *noumbles* (originally from Latin *lumulus*, a diminutive of *lumbus*, from which we also get *loin* and *lumbar*); *umbles* is derived from *numbles* by the process called metanalysis which, for example, turned *a nadder* into *an adder*; *umbles* also sometimes appeared in medieval times and later in the form *humbles*. Contrariwise, the word *humble* (originally from the Latin *humilem* from which we also get *humility*) was frequently spelled and pronounced *umble* from medieval times right down to the nineteenth century.

So the figurative sense of *umble pie* could have appeared at almost any time since the medieval period; indeed, so close is the association that it is surprising that the *OED*'s first citation dates only from 1830. Charles Dickens turned it back to the older spelling in *David Copperfield* in 1850 as an indication of uneducated speech when he put these words into the mouth of the unctuous Uriah Heep: 'When I was quite a young boy . . . I got to know what umbleness did, and I took to it. I ate umble pie with an appetite.'

I could care less

This American expression has provoked a vast amount of comment and criticism in the past thirty years or so. Few people have had a kind word for it, and many have been vehemently opposed to it (William and Mary Morris, for example, in the *Harper Dictionary of Contemporary Usage*, back in 1975, called it 'an ignorant debasement of language', which seems too powerful a condemnation). Writers are less inclined to abuse it these days, perhaps because Americans have had time to get used to it.

A bit of history first: the original expression, of course, was *I couldn't care less*, meaning 'it is impossible for me to have less interest or concern in this matter, since I am already utterly indifferent'.

It's originally British. The first record of it in print I know of is in 1946, as the title of a book by Anthony Phelps that recorded his experiences in the Air Transport Auxiliary during the Second World War. By then it had clearly become sufficiently well known that he could rely on its being recognized. It seems to have reached the USA some time in the 1950s and to have become popular in the latter part of that decade. The inverted form I *could care less* was coined in the USA and is found only there. It may have begun to be used in the early 1960s, though it turns up in a written form only in 1966.

Why it lost its negative has been much discussed. It's clear that the process is different from the shift in meaning that took place with CHEAP AT HALF THE PRICE. In that case, the inversion was due to a mistaken interpretation of its meaning, as has happened, for example, with BEG THE QUESTION.

In these cases people have tried to apply logic, and it has failed them. Attempts to be logical about I *could care less* also fail. Taken literally, if one could care less, then one must care at least a little, which is obviously the opposite of what is meant. It is so clearly logical nonsense that to condemn it for being so (as some commentators have done) misses the point. The intent is obviously sarcastic – the speaker is really saying: 'As if there was something in the world that I care less about.'

However, this doesn't explain how it came about in the first place. Something caused the negative to vanish even while the original form of the expression was still very much in vogue and available for comparison. Steven Pinker, in *The Language Instinct* (1994), points out that the pattern of intonation in the two versions is very different.

There's a close link between the stress pattern of I *could care less* and the kind that appears in certain sarcastic or self-deprecatory phrases that are associated with the Yiddish heritage and (especially)

New York Jewish speech. Perhaps the best known is *I should be so lucky!*, in which the real sense is often 'I have no hope of being so lucky', a closely similar stress pattern with the same sarcastic inversion of meaning. No one is suggesting that *I could care less* came directly from Yiddish, but the similarity is suggestive. There are other American expressions that have a similar sarcastic inversion of apparent sense, such as *Tell me about it!*, which usually means 'Don't tell me about it, because I know it already'. These may come from similar sources.

So it's actually a very interesting linguistic development. But it is still regarded as slangy, and also has some social class stigma attached. And because it is hard to be sarcastic in writing, it loses its force when put on paper and just ends up looking stupid. In such cases, the older form, while still rather colloquial, at least will communicate your meaning – at least to those who really could care less.

In like Flynn

Reference books almost universally assert that this set phrase, an American expression meaning to be successful emphatically or quickly, especially in regard to sexual seduction, refers to the Australian-born actor Errol Flynn. His drinking, drug-taking and sexual exploits were renowned, even for Hollywood, but the phrase is said to have been coined following his acquittal in February 1943 for the statutory rape of a teenage girl. This seems to be supported by the date of the first example recorded, in *American Speech* in December 1946, which cited a 1945 use in the sense of something being done easily, though no sexual shenanigans are implied: 'In like Flynn. Everything is O.K. In other words, the pilot is having no more trouble than Errol Flynn has in his cinematic feats.'

The trouble with this explanation is that examples of obviously related expressions have now turned up from dates before Flynn's trial. Barry Popik of the American Dialect Society found an example from 1940, as well as this from the sports section of the *San Francisco Examiner* of 8 February 1942: 'Answer these questions correctly and your name is Flynn, meaning you're in, provided you have two left feet and the written consent of your parents.' To judge from a newspaper reference he turned up from early 1943, the phrase could by then also be shortened to *I'm Flynn*, meaning 'I'm in'.

It's suggested by some writers that the phrase really originated with another Flynn, Edward J. Flynn – 'Boss' Flynn – a campaign manager for the Democratic party during Roosevelt's presidency. Flynn's machine in the South Bronx in New York was so successful at winning elections that his candidates seemed to get into office automatically.

The existence of the examples found by Mr Popik certainly suggests the expression was at first unconnected with Errol Flynn, but that it shifted its association when he became such a notorious figure. Since then, it has altered again, because in 1967 a film, *In Like Flint*, a spy spoof starring James Coburn, took its title by wordplay from the older expression, and in turn caused many people to think that the phrase was really *in like Flint*.

Jazz

A mish-mash of colliding egos, conflicting claims and confused memories has led researchers down many false trails while searching for the origins of this American art form, not least where its name came from.

To pluck some examples from the many in the books: people have pointed to *Jasper*, the name of a dancing slave on a plantation near New Orleans in about 1825 whose nickname was *Jazz*; to a Mississippi drummer named *Chas* Washington in the late nineteenth century or to *Chas*, the nickname of Charles Alexander (of Alexander's Ragtime Band) about 1910; to a Chicago musician named *Jasbo* Brown; to a band conductor in New Orleans about 1904 called Mr *Razz*; to the French *chassé*, a gliding dancing step that had already been turned into the archetypically American verb *sashay* as long ago as the 1830s; to the French *jaser*, useless talk for the pleasure of hearing one's own voice; or the Arabic *jazib*, one who allures.

The intimate association of jazz with American black culture has led others to look for an origin in African languages, such as the Mandingo *jasi*, become unlike oneself, Tshiluba *jaja*, cause to dance, or Temne *yas*, be extremely lively or energetic.

One early jazz player, Garvin Bushell, was sure it had a fragrant origin. In his 1988 book *Jazz From the Beginning*, he remembers his early days in music, around 1916: 'The perfume industry was very big in New Orleans in those days, since the French had brought it over with them. They used jasmine – oil of jasmine – in all different odors to pep it up. It gave more force to the scent. So they would say, "let's jass it up a bit," when something was a little dead.' John Philip Sousa suggested in the 1920s that jazz slid into our vocabulary by way of the vaudeville stage, in which all the acts would come back on to the stage at the end of a performance to give a rousing, boisterous finale called a *jazzbo*, a type of low physical comedy. (This one looks plausible if you assume *jazzbo* is a corrupted form of the given name *Jasper*, as some suggest. However, *jazzbo* isn't recorded before 1917 and might be from jazz plus *bo*, an abbreviation of *boy*.)

If you weren't confused before, I suspect you are now. There are more folk etymologies around this word than almost any other, many of them vehemently held in defiance of the evidence.

What we do know, as the result of research by Gerald Cohen, is that the word suddenly starts to appear in the *San Francisco Bulletin* in March 1913 in a series of articles about baseball by E. T. 'Scoop' Gleeson (it's recently been found that an isolated example appeared about a year earlier in the *Los Angeles Times*, but this is also in a baseball context). Early examples had nothing to do with music but referred to an intangible quality possessed by baseball players, what another writer in the newspaper, Ernest Hopkins, described in April that year as 'life, vigor, energy, effervescence of spirit, joy, pep, magnetism, verve, virility, ebulliency, courage, happiness – oh, what's the use? – JAZZ. Nothing else can express it.' Gleeson later said that he had got it from another newsman, Spike Slattery, while they were at the training camp of the local baseball team, the San Francisco Seals. Slattery said he had heard it in a crap game.

Art Hickman, an unemployed local musician, was at the camp to make contacts among the newsmen but took on the job of organizing evening entertainments. Among these was a ragtime band he created from other out-of-work musicians, including a couple of banjo players. It was this band that developed a new sound that started to be described in the training camp as jazz. This name went with Hickman to engagements in San Francisco and later to New York, though his type of syncopated rag, later to be called sweet jazz, turned out to be a dead end musically.

By the following year, it seems that the word had spread to Chicago, most probably through the efforts of another bandleader, Bert Kelly. In 1916 it appeared there in a different spelling in the name of the New Orleans Jass Band. Despite this band's name, the word wasn't known in New Orleans until 1917, as early jazz musicians attested. It is said to have arrived through the medium of a letter from Freddie Keppard in Chicago to the cornet player

Joe Oliver. Oliver showed the letter to his protégé Louis Armstrong and the name soon became applied to the New Orleans style that became dominant and which was later called hot jazz to distinguish it from the Art Hickman sort.

The big question remains: where did those San Francisco crapshooters of 1913 get their word from? This is the point where we step off the path and run the risk of disappearing into an etymological quicksand. Scoop Gleeson said that when they rolled the dice players would call out 'Come on, the old jazz'. It looks as though they were using the word as an incantation, a call to Lady Luck to smile on them.

It's commonly said that the word had strong sexual associations, being a low slang term among blacks for copulation. This may be so, though it's odd that the worldly-wise journalists on the *San Francisco Bulletin* didn't realize it at the time. If they had, they would surely have stopped using it, at least in their newspaper columns. The first direct sexual associations date only from 1918, at a point by which the word's musical sense had become firmly established. We have no knowledge of the racial background of those crap-shooters in San Francisco, so there's even considerable doubt whether the word has any associations with black English at all.

The most plausible sexual origin is in the word jism, also known as jasm. This has a long history in American English, being known in print from 1842 and probably a lot earlier still in the spoken language. It could have the same sense of spirit, energy or strength later associated with jazz, but the primary idea seems to have been semen or sperm, the meaning jism still has, one that has obvious associations with vitality and virility. It may be relevant that one of the earlier examples, in the *Daily Californian* in February 1916, writes the word as jaz-m.

It doesn't seem too implausible to suggest that jasm lost its final letter, turned into jass and then into jazz. It's likely that Gleeson and his fellow newspapermen didn't connect their new word *jazz* with *jism*, not knowing about the intermediate steps.

Of course, that just takes the whole matter back another step in this never-ending dance of word history. The *English Dialect Dictionary* (1896–1903) records the eighteenth-century form *chissom*, to bud, sprout or germinate, which looks possible as the source of *jism*. Others have pointed to an origin, via black slaves, from words like Ki-Kongo *dinza*, the life force, or from other African languages. So at least some of those folk etymologies may be nearer the truth than one might have thought.

Jerry-built *and* jerry-rigged   *See* JURY-RIGGED

Jerusalem artichoke

This vegetable, you may not be surprised to hear, is not actually an artichoke, nor has it any connection with Jerusalem.

It's actually a species of sunflower from North America, well known to the early settlers in places like Virginia, who were told about it by the native American Indians. The settlers called it simply *artichoke*, because its tubers tasted a little like the more familiar vegetable of that name back home. The plant was pretty soon brought across to Europe and was cultivated in Italy. There it became known as *girasole articiocco*, the sunflower artichoke. (*Girasole* in Italian means 'turning to the sun', the exact equivalent of our *heliotrope*, an old name for the sunflower.) When the plant began to be cultivated in Britain, the second word of the Italian name was changed back easily enough to *artichoke*, a term already known. But the first word was misheard and became *Jerusalem*, perhaps because the plant seemed to originate from that general direction.

See also ARTICHOKE.

Jinx

This is an odd word and its origin is disputed. Explaining why is going to need a moment, since along the way we must take in the Ancient Greeks, the study of birds, witchcraft, nineteenth-century vaudeville and the history of baseball.

First, the firm facts. The word *jinx*, in the sense of a thing or person that brings bad luck, is first recorded as sports slang from the USA around 1910. Most of the early American citations relate to baseball – for example, *The Jinx: Stories of the Diamond* by Allen Sangree of 1910, and Christy Mathewson's *Pitching at a Pinch* of 1912 in which he says: 'A jinx is something which brings bad luck to a ball player.' From there it spread out into standard American English and later to other national varieties of the language.

Most dictionaries say with varying degrees of conviction that the word derives from the classical Greek word *iunx* for the bird that we in Britain call the wryneck. It's a member of the wood-pecker family, a species that breeds across Europe and Asia. It has a strange habit of twisting its neck right round when it's alarmed or when it's watchfully at rest, hence its English name; it has an odd courtship ritual, in which the male and female perch opposite one another, shaking their heads about, and gaping their mouths to show the pink inside. Such curious behaviour made people think the wryneck was uncanny, and from the time of the Greeks there were superstitions attached to it, with links to witchcraft, divination and magic. Its Greek name passed into Latin and then into English, either as *yunx* or *jynx*. So it's not surprising that dictionary writers often suggest that *jinx* comes from this bird of superstition.

But there are two big holes in this theory: the wryneck is not a North American bird and the word *jynx* for it was always a scholarly and uncommon one even in British English. Appropriate though it was, it would be surprising to learn that American sportsmen had seized upon it.

Another theory has been put forward by Barry Popik of the American Dialect Society. He suggested that it comes instead from a song, 'Captain Jinks of the Horse Marines'. Following his tip, I delved into its history. It was a humorous vaudeville song (the Horse Marines, for example, could not possibly exist, as cavalry on board ship are about as much use as a chocolate teapot). It was written and sung by William Lingard and first published in 1868. Captain Jinks was an unsuccessful soldier, who was eventually drummed out of the Army. The key verse is this:

> The first day I went out to drill
> The bugle sound made me quite ill,
> At the Balance step my hat it fell,
> And that wouldn't do for the Army.
> The officers they all did shout,
> They all cried out, they all did shout,
> The officers they all did shout,
> 'Oh, that's the curse of the Army.'

This became all the rage, almost immediately spawning another song by Will Hays about the captain's supposed wife: 'Mistress Jinks of Madison Square'. It grew to be a well-liked square dance tune, and a popular song of soldiers in the American Army in the decades after 1870 (its popularity has lasted, in fact, almost down to the present day). In 1901 the young Ethel Barrymore starred at the Garrick Theatre in New York in Clyde Fitch's melodrama of the 1870s which he called Captain Jinks of the Horse Marines; in 1902 Ernest Crosby, a friend of Mark Twain, wrote a satirical anti-imperialist novel about the Spanish-American War with the title Captain Jinks, Hero.

So, even thirty years after the song originally appeared it was still sufficiently well known for a playwright and author of the early 1900s to be able to refer to it separately in titles in the expectation that their audiences would understand them. These works appeared only a few years before the first recorded use of the word in its sense of a curse.

To support his theory, Mr Popik has found that some of the early sporting references spell the word *jinks*. However, it might have been spelled that way by analogy with the existing word *jink* in English (to change direction suddenly, to dodge), from which Captain Jinks' name was presumably borrowed and from which we also get *high jinks*.

Despite the authority of the ranks of dictionaries glowering at me from my shelves, I must say Mr Popik's theory is persuasive. What's missing, of course, is direct evidence that Captain Jinks, that curse of the army, was the inspiration for the term, or how it came to appear first in sports slang. That we may never discover.

Joystick

Though some authorities still consider it to be slang, *joystick* for the control column of an aircraft is now so widely used that it has almost, but not quite, achieved the status of standard English. (It has been borrowed for a method of controlling an image in computer games or computer-aided design and in that sense it is indeed standard.)

In a search for the source of the original aviation term some etymologists have been led up a blind alley. Several works on aviation history cite a man named Joyce as the inventor, so that the first form was presumably *Joyce stick*, later slurred and compressed into *joystick*. However, nobody who has looked into the matter has been able to find any evidence for the existence of this person (he is sometimes given as James Joyce, but that must be an unconscious transfer of his first name from the author).

The first known example of *joystick* is in a 1910 entry in the diary of the pioneering British aeronaut Robert Loraine (in that year he made the first radio transmission from an aeroplane and – less significantly, but as an example of the still primitive state of the art – became the first man to land an aeroplane on the Isle of Wight). He wrote: 'In order that he shall not blunder inadvertently into the air, the central lever – otherwise the *cloche*, or joy-stick is tied well forward.' (*Cloche* was the then usual French name for the same device, from the bell shape of some early types, especially in the Bleriot monoplane, to which all the control wires were fixed.)

I wonder if the insubstantial Mr Joyce was an attempt by writers to remove any suspicion that there was a sexual element in the choice of term. Some writers on word history have certainly claimed that the shape of the stick and its position between the (always male) pilot's legs led to the term. But as Mr Loraine's diary entry shows, the early joysticks were a different shape that may well not have suggested such a link. *Joystick* is indeed recorded as a slang term for the penis, but it appears in writing for the first time in 1916; this might suggest it was borrowed from the aviation term, not the other way round, though the dates of slang terms are notoriously unreliable.

On balance, it seems more likely that *joystick* derives from another sense of *joy* that was around at the time. The closest in time and space was *joyride*, which appeared in Britain around 1908 for an unauthorized trip in a vehicle; however, the early examples referred to motor vehicles, not aircraft (the latter were so rare and so hard to fly that the opportunity for an outsider to take one for a joyride, or the skill to do so, just didn't exist). The implication may have been that the aircraft's control column was the means to the exhilaration felt by an early pilot's journey into the air,

which was always an adventurous undertaking, not to say a hazard-
ous one.

Jury-rigged

It's increasingly likely you will see and hear this term – for a
temporary, makeshift or improvised contrivance – as *jerry-rigged*. It
has become common in recent decades and appears in almost
every newspaper from time to time, so perhaps it's invidious to
select an item in the *Ottawa Sun* of October 2002 as an example:
'Privacy is virtually unheard of, the bathrooms are mostly com-
munal, across hallways from most of the rooms and jerry-rigged
to accommodate wheelchairs or bathing slings.'

It has become so well known in that form that people have
created false explanations around it, in particular that it derives
from the nickname of the German soldier in the two World Wars,
Jerry (as in *jerrycan*), and has something to do with the Germans'
ability to keep equipment running in the field by patching it up.

That's inventive, but wrong. The term is much older than the
wars of the twentieth century. The oldest form was *jury mast*, a
makeshift mast erected on a sailing ship, perhaps because the
original had been lost or damaged in a storm or a battle. Nobody
knows for sure where it came from and this etymological vacuum
has drawn in its own folk etymology with the suggestion that it
was a short version of 'injury-rigged'. It's much more likely that
it comes from the Old French *ajurie*, 'aid, assistance'. *Jury-rigged*
came along much later, in the 1780s or thereabouts, to refer to a
ship so contrived.

Another source of confusion is the term *jerry-built*, for a house
that's been thrown up using unsatisfactory materials; this dates
from the middle of the nineteenth century and is sometimes said
to be from the name of a Liverpool firm of builders (one with a

reputation that has travelled, obviously) or possibly a contraction of Jericho (whose walls fell down, you will remember, at the blast of a trumpet). Neither has been substantiated, I'm sorry to say, and it is even possible that the confusion between jerry and jury is much older than we think and that jerry in jerry-built is actually a corruption of jury, in the modified sense of 'inadequate' rather than 'temporary'.

Whatever, the current shift from the correct jury-rigged to jerry-rigged is very understandable when jerry-built is also so common. In political circles, it looks very much as though another contribution to the shift is gerrymander, to manipulate the boundaries of an electoral district so as to favour one party or class.

Kangaroo

An oft-told tale has it that when Captain James Cook stopped to make repairs at Endeavour River in Queensland in 1770, he asked one of the natives for the name of the curious leaping animal he had encountered. The answer came back, 'kangaroo', and this was duly recorded as the indigenous name. Only later was it discovered that this meant 'I don't understand you' in the local language.

Similar stories are told about the experiences of other explorers. Yucatan is said to have come from a local having replied 'Tectatan', 'I don't know', to an enquiry by the Spanish explorer Francisco Hernandez about the name of the locality. The story goes that llama is from a repetition of the Spanish word llama by a South American Indian to a Spaniard's question '¿Como se llama?', 'What is its name?', so that the name of the llama is a word meaning 'name'. In each case, such stories are no more than sarcastic tales about the naivety and incomprehension of strangers in a strange land.

Actually, it was the naturalist of Cook's expedition, Joseph Banks, who first recorded the strange animal's name, in his diary for 14 July 1770: 'Kill Kangaru', though Cook noted it on 4 August the same year: 'The Animal which I have before mentioned called by the natives *Kangooroo* or *Kanguru*.'

There was a real puzzle at the root of the matter, though. Members of the First Fleet settling around Botany Bay were surprised to find that the natives they encountered didn't know the name and it was soon after claimed that nobody in Australia referred to the animal by any variant of it. So it was thought that Banks and Cook must somehow have got it wrong, a situation in which the false story could easily have grown up.

It is now much better understood that there were many Aboriginal languages at the time. Recent fieldwork has established that the language that the first expedition encountered was Guugu Yimidhirr, in which *ganjurru* was the name for one particular species of kangaroo, a large black or grey one, not a generic name for the type.

The confusion was such that the local Aborigines thought that *kangaroo* was actually the English word for any edible animal (they were recorded as asking whether the cattle being unloaded from the ships were also kangaroos). When Europeans settled along the Darling River, the word was taken over into the Baagandji language as the name for the introduced horse.

Kangaroo court

A *kangaroo court* is one that is illegal or not properly constituted or is manifestly unfair or unjust and in which the likelihood of the prisoner's being found guilty doesn't depend on the evidence.

You might reasonably assume that the term is Australian – only in that country, after all, does one find kangaroos. But the term is definitely American, with no known links to Australia apart from the animal's name. What's more, the early history of the term is almost totally opaque. Under such circumstances, folk etymology thrives.

It has been suggested that it comes from the habit of kangaroos out in the bush of staring fixedly at human intruders for minutes at a time, and that settlers might have connected this to the unwavering assessing stare of judge and jurors at a trial. Others argue that it might have come from a vicious streak which cornered kangaroos are reported to display. It has been seriously put forward that a prime characteristic of the first kangaroo courts was that they hopped unpredictably from place to place or that the prisoner was bounced from court to gallows. Or it might have been that kangaroo courts seem to defy the laws of nature, just as the kangaroo's appearance and hopping gait does.

Do I hear you calling for arbitration by way of facts? This is where the problem arises. The first example is recorded in a book by the pseudonymous Philip Paxton (whose real name was S. A. Hammett) in 1853 in *A Stray Yankee in Texas*: 'By a unanimous vote, Judge G— was elected to the bench and the "Mestang" or "Kangaroo Court" regularly organized.'

The kangaroo court in this case was an unofficial legal institution set up on the frontier at a time when the regular law didn't reach so far – much like the LYNCH LAW of the previous century on the other side of the continent. The association seems to be between the unruliness of the body and that of the kangaroo, since the mustang, a half-tamed horse, is also invoked. However, the next examples don't appear until the 1890s and most of those refer to mock courts organized by prisoners in jails to deprive new inmates of their money. The term seems not to have been widely applied even in Texas.

Many people like to see something in the closeness of the date of this first example to that of the gold rush in California in 1849. Many Australians came to seek their fortune there (it was easier for them to get to the American west coast by sea than it was for Americans coming from the east coast overland or around Cape Horn). It is suggested that informal courts were held in the gold diggings to control illegal prospectors, who were called *claim-jumpers*, and that the association of ideas between *jumping* and *kangaroos* was too strong to resist. But that might just be yet another popular etymology.

Keep one's nose to the grindstone

A curious explanation for this proverbial saying was given to me by a guide in California some years ago who was showing me around a traditional water-powered grist mill. The grindstones had to be set exactly the right distance apart: too big a gap and the corn didn't grind properly; too small and the grain overheated and began to burn. But the gap couldn't be judged by eye because the stones had to remain completely enclosed. So the miller had to use his nose: he would immediately be able to detect the slightest trace of burning by smell and adjust the gap before any harm was done. But to do this effectively meant the miller had to stay constantly close to the stones – hence, keep his nose to the grindstone.

Unfortunately, the standard reference works say that the grindstone of the saying is the smith's one for putting a sharp edge on a tool. And the story doesn't quite fit the modern sense of the phrase, which refers to keeping oneself continually engaged in hard and monotonous work. Nor does it fit the most ancient form of the expression, which was *to hold someone's nose to the grindstone* and meant to treat that person with harshness or severity, figuratively to grind him down.

The first example known is from John Frith's *a mirrour or glasse to know thyself* of 1533: 'This Text holdeth their noses so hard to the grindstone, that it clean disfigureth their faces', which quite clearly refers to sharpening tools, not to the miller's trade. And a famous cartoon of 1650 shows the future Charles II's nose being held to a grindstone by the Scots.

Kibosh

Many words in English have obscure origins, particularly those which may be said to have risen in the world from lowly origins in argot, cant or slang. None is more mysterious than this one, meaning 'ruin' or 'spoil', which is most often encountered in the phrase *to put the kibosh on something*.

This was a common enough expression in the London of my youth, sometimes in the impersonal form *That's put the kibosh on it!*, meaning 'that's stopped it', 'that's disposed of it', 'that's finished it off'. It was also used as a direct form to rebuke someone: *You've really put the kibosh on that, haven't you!*, meaning that the person being rebuked has terminally fouled something up, rendering it incapable of completion or execution.

But what is the origin of this strange word, which looks so very un-English? Down the years many writers have come up with a variety of explanations:

- It is from the Yiddish *Kabas* or *Kabbasten*, 'to suppress'.

- It refers to the number eighteen, perhaps from Hebrew *chai*. There was once a London slang term *kye* for one shilling and sixpence (18 pence, old money) and a nineteenth-century writer in *Notes & Queries* claimed that if at a small auction a bidder suddenly jumped his offer up to eighteen pence he was said to have *put the kibosh on* his fellow bidders. In the 1950s kibosh could refer to an 18-month prison sentence; however, it looks very much as though this derives from the older idea linking the word to the number.

- It comes from *caboshed*, which is the heraldic term for the emblem of an animal which is shown full-face, but cut off close to the ears so that no neck shows.

- It is related to, or influenced by, the slang term *bosh* for something that is untrue or nonsense, which is from a Turkish word meaning something empty or worthless.

- It's from the Irish phrase *caidhpín (an) bháis*, meaning 'cap of death', in reference to the black cap worn by a judge when he sentenced a prisoner to death.

If I am to be boring about it, the most likely answer is that none of these is really convincing and that nobody knows for sure: that's certainly the careful response of most dictionaries.

Whatever its origin, most authorities agree that the word is definitely English (not American, as H. L. Mencken once tried to claim), appearing in Britain in the early part of the nineteenth century. The first example recorded by the *Oxford English Dictionary* is in Charles Dickens's *Sketches by Boz* of 1836 in which he spells it in a way that reflects Cockney pronunciation: ' "Hoo-roar," ejaculates a pot-boy in a parenthesis, "put the kye-bosk on her, Mary".' It was soon taken to America and became naturalized there. Early written references varied a lot in spelling: in addition to Dickens's attempt, the London humorous magazine *Punch* used *cibosh* in an article in 1856. The modern form appeared first in *The Slang Dictionary* in 1869.

Someday perhaps, some earnest researcher will find an earlier citation for the word that ties down its origin to one of these explanations, or one nobody has yet thought of, which will really put the kibosh on all this speculation.

Kluge

Several reputable dictionaries say this was invented by Jackson W. Granholm in an article entitled 'How to Design a Kludge' in the February 1962 issue of the computer magazine *Datamation*. He defined it there as 'an ill-assorted collection of poorly-matching parts, forming a distressing whole'. It's used in computing and electronics for a hastily improvised solution to some fault or bug, especially one of dubious quality, but it doesn't seem to have moved much outside those fields, if at all. Mr Granholm borrowed it from German *klug*, smart or witty, presumably also being influenced by *bodge* and *fudge*. He says in the article: 'The building of a Kludge . . . is not work for amateurs. There is a certain indefinable, masochistic finesse that must go into true Kludge building.'

There is some disagreement over pronunciation and spelling. Eric Raymond, in *The New Hacker's Dictionary* (the 1991 printed version of the online Jargon File, the standard work for anyone interested in computer slang) argues that it ought to be spelled like its German original, *klug*; but, as we've seen, Mr Granholm spelled it with the inserted *d*, and that surely ought to be good enough for the rest of us. But having two spellings means we also have two pronunciations. The definitive American one rhymes with *stooge*, reflecting the vowel of the German word, but the more usual spelling results in it also being heard as rhyming with *nudge*, which is more common in British English.

Mr Raymond's argument for preferring *kluge* is that old-timers in the computer business have consistently reported that the word was around in the 1950s, always spelled *kluge* and originally used for bodged-up hardware repairs, not for programming (which was in its infancy then, anyway). Subscribers to my *World Wide Words* newsletter have also said they knew of it in that period. Mr Raymond cites a 1947 article reporting a shaggy-dog story current in the American armed forces, in which a *kluge* was 'a complex and puzzling artifact with a trivial function'. He has had reports that the word was Second World War US Navy slang for any piece of electronic equipment that worked well on shore but invariably failed at sea.

He has also had suggestions that the word may be from a device called a Kluge paper feeder, an adjunct to mechanical printing presses, originally designed in 1919. It has been described as a fiendishly complicated and clever device, which often broke down and was hard to repair, though it seems in reality to have been a relatively simple mechanism, leading to a suspicion that its complexity has been exaggerated in order to bolster a connection between the device and the word. (The name really comes from that of its inventor; *Kluge* is a common German surname.)

Others have said that the *kludge* spelling really derives from a Scots word for a toilet, *cludgie*, which was imported into America during the Second World War from British armed forces slang. However, Eric Partridge – who was well informed on services' slang – doesn't give it in any of his slang dictionaries, which he surely would have done if it had been at all current, so I'm strongly inclined to count this one a miss.

It seems pretty clear that the current spelling and sense were indeed Mr Granholm's invention, and that he should take the credit for popularizing it, but it looks as though he may have drawn on an existing jargon term. All this only goes to prove that linguistic truth is rarely pure and never simple and that there's no subject that investigation can't make more complicated.

Let the cat out of the bag

A theory that is sometimes bruited about is that this phrase refers to the removal of the infamous tool of punishment, the cat o' nine tails, from its canvas bag in preparation for shipboard punishment. But this doesn't fit the meaning of the phrase – to disclose some secret – as punishment was made as public as possible in order to deter others. On the other hand, it would be possible to imagine a situation in which an officer's discovering the truth behind some nefarious activity that would result in punishment could cause a sailor to remark, 'That's let the cat out of the bag.'

The usual explanation is that it comes from a sneaky trick of a stall keeper in a market of handing over a bag that supposedly contained a valuable piglet but which instead had in it only a useless cat (so it would be a version of selling a pig in a poke); *to let the cat out of the bag* was to expose the fraud. But anybody who has ever kept a live cat in a bag for more than a couple of seconds will know that even the most gullible purchaser would hardly mistake it for a piglet.

It may be that the phrase comes from the explosive exit of a cat from a bag when it's opened, so suggesting an original connection more with the shock and surprise of the event than of disclosure of the secret itself. But I suspect there's some other explanation that has now been lost. We do know, though, that it is first recorded in the eighteenth century.

Loo

There are many theories about this word, yet another term for what has been euphemistically described at various times and places as a restroom, bathroom, toilet, lavatory, water closet or jakes. There are few firm facts, however, and its origin is one of the more celebrated puzzles in word history.

The most common story, frequently told, is that it comes from the habit of the more caring Edinburgh housewives, in the days before plumbing, of warning passers-by on the street below with the cry 'Gardy loo!' before throwing the contents of their chamber pots out of upstairs bedroom windows. (It's said to be a corrupted form of French *gardez l'eau!* or 'watch out for the water!')

The one thing everybody does agree on is that it's French in origin, or at least a corruption of a French phrase. But we're fairly sure it's actually modern, with its origin having been traced back no further than the 1940s. So that throws the *gardy loo* story out of the window. And, equally, the late date refutes the idea that it comes from the French *bordalou*, a portable commode carried by eighteenth-century ladies in their muffs. It is also said that it's a British mispronunciation of the French *le lieu*, 'the place', a euphemism.

Another theory, a rather more plausible one, has it that it comes from the French *lieux d'aisances*, literally 'places of ease' (the French term is usually plural), once also an English euphemism, which could have been picked up by British servicemen in the First World War. But it's also suggested that it's a humorous abbreviation of *Waterloo*, a trade name for iron lavatory cisterns in the early part of the twentieth century, to which James Joyce may have been referring in *Ulysses* in 1922: 'O yes, mon loup. How much cost? Waterloo. Watercloset.'

Or it may be that several linguistic forces converged to create the new word. Nobody knows.

Love

Fifteen-love . . . thirty love . . . Every tennis player must wonder at some time or other why a word so irrelevant as *love* should have been adopted in the scoring system, though it does sound better than the tactless *zero* if you're the player losing points at every exchange.

A widespread theory, told to new players in tennis clubs worldwide, holds that the word was borrowed from French *l'œuf*, egg, with the same sense. There is collateral support for the theory in the American *goose egg* for a zero score, and in the English term *duck* for a score of nothing in cricket, which is an abbreviation of *duck's egg* (hence to move off zero is to *break one's duck*, originally to *break one's duck's egg*).

Unfortunately for proponents of the French egg theory, there is no evidence that the French ever used the expression. The word predates the modern game of tennis and indeed is first recorded in 1742 in *Whist*, a book on the card game by Edmond Hoyle, whose works became so famous as authorities that the expression *according to Hoyle* was coined for something that conformed to the strictest rules.

We can't be entirely sure where it comes from, since it seems to have appeared full-grown in the jargon of the card table (even as early as 1780 a writer in the *Gentleman's Magazine* was perplexed by the usage). The *Oxford English Dictionary* suggests that it derives from the phrase *for love*, without stakes, applied to the playing of a competitive game for pleasure alone, an idiom that is also found in *labour of love* and *neither for love nor money*. So it would seem that *love* came to be equated with nothing, later zero.

Lynch law

If you're ever in Galway, in the west of Ireland, you may hear of the sad story surrounding the origin of *lynch*, as in *lynch law*, the punishment of a person for some supposed crime without bothering with the niceties of a formal legal trial.

It is said that the son of James Lynch Fitzstephen, the Mayor and chief magistrate of Galway in 1493, stabbed a Spanish trader who was visiting the town because a local lady to whom he had taken a fancy was spending too much time with the visitor. Fitzstephen junior then confessed to his father, who insisted on trying him and condemning him to death. When no local person was prepared to carry out the execution, Fitzstephen did it himself from an upstairs window of his house.

In support of the story, local people can show you the window and a commemorative plaque recording this extreme example of unbending justice. However, an iconoclast reports that the wall and the window seem to be of much more recent date than the supposed happenings. The tale seems to have been invented by an enterprising local with an eye to the tourist trade sometime in the nineteenth century, after the word had become widely known.

As it happens, linguistic evidence alone is enough to scupper this emotional tale, since the term is not recorded until the nineteenth century and all the evidence points to its being American. For its origin we must look to Virginia in the 1780s, during the American Revolution. There is some doubt about which Lynch gave his name to the expression, since there were two: Captain William Lynch of Pittsylvania County and Colonel James Lynch of Bedford County. However, both were trying to bring order and justice to an area notoriously lacking both. William Lynch is the one usually pointed to in scholarly discussions, mainly it seems because documentary evidence survives of his efforts.

Though it is now taken to refer to execution, usually by hanging, and most commonly in the twentieth century to the killing of black Americans in the south by whites, early examples suggest it referred to punishments that were less terminal. The compact drawn up with his neighbours by William Lynch in 1780 said of the actions of the lawless men troubling the area: 'if they will not desist from their evil practices, we will inflict such corporeal punishment on him or them, as to us shall seem adequate to the crime committed or the damage sustained.' No mention of execution, you will note.

The first appearance in print of the term that I know of is in a humorous article in the *New-England Magazine* of October 1835 under the title of 'The Inconveniences of Being Lynched'; the storyteller suffers being tarred and feathered on suspicion of being an abolitionist. Similarly, a news item in the *New York Daily Express* in 1843 refers to a man 'lately taken from his house at night by some of his neighbors and severely lynched', which sounds as though a harsh punishment was inflicted but one short of death, since it is difficult to severely execute somebody.

Interestingly, some recent examples of the term in print have returned to this older sense.

Marmalade

Since writers on food are not always as expert in etymology as they are in the culinary arts, you may on occasion find a tale in a cookery book about the origin of the name for this fruit preserve. It is said that when Mary Queen of Scots was ill in captivity, her French cook made some to tempt her failing appetite; this breakfast delicacy became known as *Marie malade*, or 'sick Mary'. Mary's French connections would seem to have been enough to peg this extraordinary invention to her sad existence. This is yet another case of the way a good story can triumph over historical veracity.

As it happens, the real story is fascinating enough. The original foodstuff wasn't made from oranges, but from quinces. These were cooked with honey and in the process the unpromising bitter green quinces were transformed into a thick sweet pink paste, which was stiff enough to be cut with a knife and be served in slices as a kind of dessert. The first such preserves were made in Portugal and were given the Portuguese name for it, *marmelada*, from the name for the quince in that language, *marmelo* (it derives from Latin *melimelum*, from the Greek for honey apple, which seems to have been the name for a type of apple grafted on a quince rootstock).

The product kept well and was exported to Britain in wooden boxes. It was at first a luxury item (in the fifteenth century, customs duties were slapped on it, so it must have been worth taxing) but later on English cooks learned to make their own. The first name for it was *chardecoynes* or *chardequince*, the Old French term for a pulp made from quinces, but the Portuguese name was adopted in the early years of the sixteenth century. An early English recipe called for the quinces to be beaten to a pulp together with warden apples, boiled with honey until the mixture was thick and then spiced with a mixture of ginger, galingale and cinnamon.

The shift to oranges happened rather slowly and many other versions were made in the fifteenth and sixteenth centuries, including those from plums, dates, cherries and other fruits, all of which were called marmalades. Oranges were originally thought to have curative properties (they were often given to pregnant women, for example, which would indeed have been valuable because of the vitamin C they contain) and it was only in the seventeenth century that they began to permanently replace the quince as the principal ingredient. But the old name stuck.

Mind your beeswax

It's an odd expression to see or hear without warning, understand-ably a bit puzzling. One young person wrote asking whether this arose from the use of beeswax in the eighteenth century to fill small pox scars on the face, which required you not to sit too close to the fire or the wax would melt and run.

The questions people ask . . . and the stories people tell one another. This one was educational, speaking personally, since I had no idea that there was a slang expression *mind your own beeswax* until the question came in, though I've since discovered it is known both in Britain and the USA.

The supposed explanation is, of course, the product of a warped imagination. The phrase *mind your own beeswax* has the same sense as *mind your own business* – it's just a rather feeble attempt at creating a humorous alternative. It belongs to a group of such facetious inventions that includes the old-time Australian *mind your own fish* and the slightly more witty but also historical New Zealand version *mind your own pigeon* (*pigeon* here being derived from *pidgin*, business, as in Pidgin English).

Mind your Ps and Qs

These days this exhortation is mainly directed at young people and warns them to mind their manners, to behave properly. When it first appeared in the latter part of the eighteenth century it seems to have been more a warning to adults to be careful or prudent around other people and to watch out for their own interests – 'to be attentive to the main chance' as the 1811 edition of Captain Grose's *Dictionary of the Vulgar Tongue* put it. American books of slang also recorded a related sense in which *mind your Ps and Qs* was the same as *mind your own business*.

Charles Dickens used it in *Sketches by Boz* in 1835: 'To the unmarried girls among them she is constantly vaunting the virtues of her son, hinting that she will be a very happy person who wins him, but that they must mind their P's and Q's, for he is very particular, and terribly severe upon young ladies.' It appeared sometimes as *mind your peas and cues*, as here in *Annals of a Quiet Neighbourhood* by George MacDonald, dated 1867, which also suggests he was using it to mean formal manners and a desire not to intrude on the affairs of others: 'Well, I thought it wasn't a time to mind one's peas and cues exactly. And really it's wonderful how one gets on without them. I hate formality myself.'

We have no idea where it comes from. This makes it prime territory for those of agile mind who seek to make sense of it and many suggestions have been put forward at various times. These are the better-known ones:

- An abbreviation of *mind your pleases and thank-yous*, on the basis that it can be reanalysed as *p(l)eas(es) and (than)kyous*. This is seriously put forward by some dictionaries.

- Advice to a child learning its letters to be careful not to mix up the handwritten lower-case letters *p* and *q*, or similar advice to a printer's apprentice, for whom the backward-facing metal type letters would be especially confusing. But why should *p* and *q* be singled out for attention in handwriting, when similar problems occur with *b* and *d*?

- Jocular, or perhaps deadly serious, advice to a barman not to confuse the letters *p* and *q* on the tally slate, on which the letters stood for the *pints* and *quarts* consumed 'on tick' by the patrons. Men did once drink beer by the quart, but there's no evidence that any barman used the letters P and Q to mark them on a slate.

- Instructions from a French dancing master to mind their *pieds* and *queues* (*pied* being one's feet, so the dance steps; *queue* being one's wig, which would need care if it were not to be knocked off during the dance or fall off when bowing). We may disregard this daft story out of hand.

- An admonishment to sailors not to soil their navy *pea*-jackets with their tarred *queues*, that is, their pigtails.

There was a seventeenth-century colloquial expression *P and Q*, often written *pee and kew*, for 'prime quality'. This later became a dialect expression (the *English Dialect Dictionary* reports it in Victorian times from Shropshire and Herefordshire). The *Oxford English Dictionary* has a citation from Rowlands' *Knave of Harts* of 1612: 'Bring in a quart of Maligo, right true: And looke, you Rogue, that it be Pee and Kew.' This seems to be no more than coincidence and to have no connection with the other expression, though it has confused some writers.

The evidence we have doesn't permit us to tie the origin to any one of these stories, nor to dismiss them as inventions. If I had to make a choice, I would plump for the one about a child learning its letters.

Moot point

Moot point once had a firm and well-understood meaning, but no longer does.

It once referred only to a matter that was uncertain or unde-cided, open to debate. An example appeared in the *Guardian* in October 2002: 'An inquest heard yesterday that it was a moot point as to who owned the embalmed body of a tramp that was found hidden in the Plymouth studio of Robert Lenkiewicz after the portrait artist's death.' But since the 1960s it has steadily taken on a second meaning, of something that has no practical significance and which is of academic interest only. The *Denver*

Rocky Mountain News used it like this in November 2000: 'It was not clear whether she would be able to continue against Kim in the final. When Kim bowed out, it made the question moot.'

A large part of the reason why people are getting confused is that moot is now a relatively unusual word, rare enough that you sometimes see it spelled *mute*; there's an understandable tendency to convert the unknown into the known, and *mute point* seems to fit the new meaning rather better than does the odd-looking *moot point*.

It comes from the same source as *meet* and originally had the same meaning. In pre-Norman times in England it was often spelled *mot* or *mote* and referred specifically to an assembly of people, in particular one that had some sort of judicial function. There are references to the *witenagemot* (the assembly of the witan, the national council of Anglo-Saxon times), *hundred-mote* (a hundred was an Anglo-Saxon administrative area, part of a county or shire), and many others. So something that was *mooted* was put up for discussion and decision at a moot – by definition something not yet decided.

The problem arises because in more recent centuries another sense of moot has appeared – for a discussion forum (construed as a type of meeting) in which hypothetical cases are argued by law students for practice. Since there is no practical outcome of these sessions, and the cases are invented anyway, people seem to have assumed that a *moot point* means one of no importance. So we've seen a curious shift in which the sense of 'open to debate' has become 'not worth debating'.

Mushroom

English got mushroom from Middle French mousseron, which came in turn from the medieval Latin mussirionem, of uncertain origin (some say it's from a pre-Latin word, mussirio, known in northern France). Mousseron itself seems to have fallen victim to folk etymology in French, whereby the unconnected mousse (the word for moss) has been cited as the origin. (Though the usual modern French word for a mushroom is champignon, mousseron survives for some types of small edible mushrooms.)

English took over mousseron in the fifteenth century and had a lot of trouble with it, hacking it about to make forms like muscheron, mussetum, mushrump and mesrum in the following couple of hundred years. Though mushroom appears as a one-off in 1563, it doesn't become the standard spelling until the eighteenth century as the result of folk etymology, which converts the final part into something that looks English, though room has nothing to do with the matter.

Muskrat

This common rodent of North America spends much of its time in water. Many people think it's a relative of the beaver, because it swims so well and builds waterside lodges, but it's really a big field mouse that has taken to an aquatic existence. Its common name is the result of folk etymology.

The first English settlers in Virginia borrowed the Native American term mussascus from the local Powhatan dialect of the Algonquian language. Its first appearance in English is in Captain John Smith's book of 1624, *The Generall Historie of Virginia, New-England and the Summer Isles*: 'A Mussascus is a beast of the forme and nature of our water Rats, but many of them smell exceedingly strongly of Muske.' The native word meant 'it is red', from the colour of the animal's fur. A different name, *musquash*, appeared in New Hampshire, taken from another Algonquian dialect, Abnaki, in which the name *mòskwas* is said to have meant 'the one whose head bobs above the water'.

Because the animal has musk glands and it looks like a big rat, colonists very early on modified *musquash* into *muskrat*. Interestingly, *musquash* was long retained among fur trappers and is still the usual name in the fur trade for the skins.

Niggardly

Despite the similarity in spelling this word has no connection with *nigger*, the one word which it is almost impossible for white Americans to say or write publicly.

At the beginning of 1999, David Howard (the head of the Office of Public Advocate in Washington, DC) used it during a discussion with a black colleague in describing a budget allocation which he considered to be inadequate. He was reported as saying: 'I will have to be niggardly with this fund because it's not going to be a lot of money.' In large part the uproar came about because the word is not especially common: even Mr Howard said that he had learned it while studying, rather than by hearing it used. Misunderstandings and misapprehensions are much more likely under such circumstances.

The adjective *niggardly*, miserly or stingy, was formed in the sixteenth century from *niggard*, a miser or stingy person. In the Wycliffe Bible of 1384 it was spelled *nygard*; earlier still it can be found as *nigon*, and another form *nig* also existed. We are pretty sure this was borrowed from a Scandinavian source, because there are related words in several Germanic languages, for example, the

Old Norse *hnøgger*, meaning 'stingy'. So it has nothing to do with *nigger*, which comes via French *nègre* from Spanish *negro*, ultimately from Latin *niger*, meaning 'black'.

Huge sensitivities over a word that could just conceivably be intended as a racial slur led to a controversy that raged for weeks. It disproved the old adage that 'sticks and stones may break my bones, but words will never hurt me'. In reality, a number of black Americans found the word to be demeaning. Though newspapers and language writers (including this one) explained the true facts repeatedly, they did little to assuage the feeling of hurt. In such matters, perception is everything and etymology nowhere.

Mr Howard was shortly afterwards rehired in another post in the Mayor's office.

Nincompoop

It's a silly-sounding word for a 'fool, blockhead, simpleton, or ninny', as the *Oxford English Dictionary* describes it. Many writers have tried hard to find an origin for it.

The good Dr Johnson, in his famous *Dictionary* of 1755, thought it might be from Latin *non compos*, as in the legal and medical phrase *non compos mentis*, not mentally competent. As the OED commented 150 years later, the problem is that this origin doesn't explain the variations that were recorded in the seventeenth and early eighteenth centuries, such as *nincumpoop* and *nickumpoop*. The OED suggests it is just a nonsense word.

The late John Ciardi, in *A Browser's Dictionary* (1980), dismissively calls that 'a clerk's guess' and asserts that it comes instead from the Dutch words *nicht om poep*, meaning 'the female relative of a fool'. He comments: 'And if that does not work out . . . I will be a monkey's uncle.' Possibly not, but such a stretched derivation from a foreign language is typical of a type of folk etymology that turns up a lot.

Another intriguing idea connects it with the given name Nicodemus, especially the Pharisee of that name who questioned Christ so naively in the Gospel of John. This word does still exist in French as *nicodème*, a simpleton, and it might have been modified by the Dutch *poep* for a fool (which is said like the English *poop*).

No wonder most dictionaries play safe and list it as 'origin unknown'.

Nitty-gritty

African-Americans often claim this term is racist. It is said to refer to the noxious debris left in the bottom of slave ships once the slaves who survived the journey had been removed on arrival.

This belongs in the same line of folklore which holds that a PICNIC was a slave-lynching party. There is a slight link, in that nitty-gritty was indeed originally a black American English expression, and some people guess that nitty-gritty is a rhyming slang euphemism for *shitty*, which also suggests a relevance.

Jonathan Lighter, in the *Random House Historical Dictionary of American Slang*, records the first example from as late as 1956: 'You'll find nobody comes down to the nitty-gritty when it calls for namin' things for what they are.' As it is here fully formed, and has the now customary sense of the fundamental issues, the heart of the matter, or the most important aspects of some situation, it had by then probably already been in use for some while (I know of two people who claim to have come across it in the 1920s). But it is inconceivable that it should have been around since slave-ship days without somebody writing it down.

Its origins are elusive. One explanation is that it is a reduplication

– using the same mechanism that has given us *namby-pamby* and *itsy-bitsy* – of the standard English word *gritty*. This has the literal sense of containing or being covered with grit, but figuratively means showing courage and resolve, so the link is plausible, and, if it is not the direct origin, may have influenced it. It has also been suggested (in a 1974 issue of *American Speech*, the journal of the American Dialect Society) that *nits* refers to head lice and *grits* to the corn cereal.

None of these are supported by any firm evidence, and it's this lack of a clear origin that has contributed to the wide distribution of the slave-ship story.

Nose to the grindstone
See KEEP ONE'S NOSE TO THE GRINDSTONE

Off one's own bat
This expression often appears instead as *off one's own back*, which – if you don't know its real origins – seems a more sensible way to say that one is doing something unprompted or unaided, by one's own efforts.

A couple of recent British examples out of many – in the *Independent on Sunday* in January 2003: 'We both come from ordinary backgrounds, we've both been quite successful and we've done it off our own backs'; and from the *Daily Record* of April the previous year: 'The game itself was almost secondary to everything else, although Thistle did want to seal it off their own backs.' Somerset Maugham knew better in *Of Human Bondage* in 1915 when he had a character say 'I daresay one profits more by the mistakes one makes off one's own bat than by doing the right thing on somebody else's advice.'

For a sporting writer to get it wrong seems especially sad, since the term is certainly from cricket. It refers to a score made by a player's own hits, as opposed to those made by other members of his team, and so figuratively any result achieved solely by his own exertions. The Victorian cricket historian Henry Waghorn found a newspaper reference from 1742, which he included in his *Cricket Scores* of 1899: 'The bets on the Slendon man's head that he got 40 notches off his own bat were lost.'

The change has obviously been strongly influenced by *to get one's own back* and similar expressions. The English national game of cricket is so little known in the USA that expressions from the game mean little (though it might have been transferred to baseball, nobody seems to have made that link).

You might think that when Rudyard Kipling wrote, in *The Day's Work* in 1898: 'Once before in his life The Maltese Cat had heard that very same stroke played off his own back, and had profited by the confusion it wrought', that the author had fallen into the same error. But the Maltese Cat was a polo pony – the shot was literally played off his back.

OK

This is without doubt the best-known and widest-travelled Americanism, used and recognized everywhere even by people who hardly know another word of English. Running in parallel with its popularity have been many attempts to explain where it came from – amateur etymologists have been obsessed with OK and theories have bred unchecked for the past 150 years.

Suggestions abound of introductions from another language: from the Choctaw-Chickasaw *okah* meaning 'it is indeed'; from

Greek *olla kalla*, 'all good'; from a mishearing of the Scots *och aye!* (or perhaps Ulster Scots *Ough aye!*), 'yes, indeed!'; from West African languages like Mandingo (*O ke*, 'certainly') or Wolof (*waw kay*, 'yes indeed'); from Finnish *oikea*, 'correct, exact'; from French *au quais*, 'at the quay' (supposedly stencilled on Puerto Rican rum specially selected for export, or a place of assignation for French sailors in the Caribbean); or from French *Aux Cayes* (a port in Haiti famous for its superior rum). Such accidentally coincidental forms across languages are surprisingly common and all of these are quite certainly false. Many African-Americans would be delighted to have it proved that OK is actually from an African language brought to America by slaves, but the evidence is against them, as we shall shortly learn.

Some other theories I've seen mentioned: it comes from *Old Keokuk*, the name of a Native American Fox chief; from German *Oberst Kommandant*, 'Colonel in Command', because some German army officer fought on the colonists' side in the American Revolution (names such as General Schliessen or Baron von Steuben are mentioned but cannot be linked to real individuals); from the name of a freight agent, *Obadiah Kelly*, whose initials often appeared on bills of lading; an abbreviation for *Open Key*, popularized by early telegraphers; or from the initials of *Orrin Kendall* biscuits supplied to the Union Army during the Civil War. A particularly persistent and long-standing theory says that President Andrew Jackson used to write OK to abbreviate the illiterate 'ole korrek' on documents, a grievous calumny on a well-educated man. None of these theories can be supported with documented proof.

I could go on, but it would only strain your patience and fortitude as much as it would mine. The true story was researched by Professor Allen Walker Read in the 1960s. Let me give you the facts as he uncovered them through his assiduous reading of local newspapers.

He records that 'beginning in the summer of 1838, there developed in Boston a remarkable vogue of using abbreviations. It might well be called a craze.' He quotes many examples, including RTBS, 'Remains To Be Seen', GTDHD, 'Give The Devil His Due', OFM, 'Our First Men' (a satirical description of Boston's leading citizens) and SP, 'Small Potatoes' (for something considered to be of little importance).

Professor Read traced the earliest recorded use of OK to the Boston Morning Post of 23 March 1839, in a report about a 'frolicsome group' called the Anti-Bell Ringing Society (the ABRS), which campaigned to get a law banning the ringing of dinner bells rescinded. It seems to have been short for 'oll korrect', a fanciful way of writing 'all correct' that was itself part of another popular craze of the time for misspellings as a humorous device and which echoes the story about President Jackson from the previous decade.

What ensured that this one example survived out of many in a hugely popular but short-lived fashion was that it was picked up by the Democrats in New York. They created a body called the Democratic OK Club to support their candidate, Martin Van Buren, who was standing for re-election in the 1840 presidential election against William Henry Harrison. OK here actually stood for 'Old Kinderhook', Van Buren's nickname, taken from Kinderhook, his birthplace near Albany in New York State. The abbreviation became widely used during the campaign and survived Van Buren's losing the election.

However, its origins quickly became lost, as anything linked to yesterday's news usually does. Many earnest investigators have since tried to resolve the issue. Despite the fact that we have known the true story for the past forty years, people still keep coming up with ingenious but mistaken theories.

On tenterhooks

It's been so long since anyone has seen either a *tenter*, or the *hooks* on one, that the word and the idea behind it are now quite mysterious, so much so that it often appears as *on tenderhooks*, which sounds to its users as though it ought to make more sense. But at one time, the phrase *on tenterhooks* would have evoked an image that was immediately understandable.

It comes from one of the processes of making woollen cloth. After it had been woven the cloth still contained oil and dirt from the fleece. It was cleaned with soap and fuller's earth, but then it had to be dried carefully or it would shrink and crease. So the lengths of wet cloth were stretched on wooden frames, and left out in the open for some time. This allowed them to dry and straightened the weave. These frames were the *tenters*, and the *tenter hooks* were the metal hooks that were used to fix the cloth to the frame. At one time, it would have been common in manufacturing areas to see fields full of these frames (older English maps sometimes marked an area as a *tenter-field*). So it was not a huge leap of the imagination to think of somebody on tenterhooks as being in a state of anxious suspense, stretched like the cloth on the tenter. The tenters have gone, but the expression has survived.

Tenter comes from the Latin *tendere*, to stretch, via a French intermediate. The word has been in the language since the fourteenth century, and *on tenters* soon after became a phrase meaning painful anxiety. The exact phrase *on tenterhooks* seems first to have been used by Tobias Smollett in *Roderick Random* in 1748.

On the carpet

Some confusion has grown up about the origin of this useful little idiom for being closely questioned or reprimanded by some superior. The problem is that the expression has had two distinct meanings which have become muddled.

The older one is a translation of the French *sur le tapis*. *Tapis* originally referred to any cloth woven with designs in colour. This might have been used as a curtain, tablecloth, mat, carpet or wall covering, and in modern French is a rather broad term (for example, *tapis de souris* is a computer mouse mat and *tapis roulant* is a conveyor belt). Our word *tapestry* is a close relative, though the spelling changed in its passage from French. The phrase *sur le tapis* referred to something that was put on the table for discussion or consideration, as we might talk about tabling a motion in Parliament (confusingly, Americans mean by tabling that a subject has been set aside or postponed and so is not to be discussed). English borrowed the French word *tapis* in this specialized sense; its first recorded appearance was in 1690: 'Lord Churchill and Lord Godolphin went away, and gave no votes in the matter which was upon the tapis.'

Sur le tapis was translated at the beginning of the eighteenth century as *on the carpet*. This was a sensible move at the time, since the English word *carpet* could still have many of the senses of its French cousin. (In 1727 *Chambers Cyclopaedia* defined the word as 'a sort of covering . . . to be spread on a table, trunk, an estrade, or even a passage, or floor'. Note that 'even'; you can almost hear the compilers saying 'what a waste of a good carpet, to put it on the floor to be trodden on'. At that time, floor carpets were reserved for the private rooms of the well-to-do.) The English version of the French phrase turns up first in 1726: 'The great cry made for the people's powers in election . . . which is the case now upon the carpet.'

The reprimanding version is not found until rather more than a century later, at first as the simple verb *to carpet*. In 1840 it appeared in Henry Coxton's *The Life and Adventures of Valentine Vox, the Ventriloquist*: 'They had done nothing! Why were they carpeted?' *On the carpet* is recorded first in America, in *Scribners Magazine* in 1888: 'The mortification of being called into the superintendent's office to explain some dereliction of duty is disguised by referring to the episode as "dancing on the carpet".'

The etymological confusion comes from assuming that the verb *to carpet* and the phrase *on the carpet* come from the older sense of a matter for review, through the idea that calling a meeting supposedly for a discussion was in practice a euphemism for a telling off. There seems little justification for this, though that sense may have been a minor influence.

It is much more likely that it comes from the fact that at the time the term was created only the rooms of one's superiors were likely to contain a carpet, perhaps in front of the desk of your employer if you were working in a business, or in the parlour if you were a household servant. To be called to the carpet, or to be carpeted, was then to be hauled up in front of authority to be castigated.

On the fritz

The phrase is a common American expression meaning that some mechanism is malfunctioning or broken: 'The washing machine's on the fritz again' (the British and Australian equivalent would be *on the blink*). However, when it first appeared – about 1902 – it meant that something was in a bad way or a bad condition. Early examples refer to the poor state of some domestic affairs, the lack of success of a stage show, and an injured leg – not a machine or device in sight.

Some people, especially the late John Ciardi, the American poet and writer on words, have suggested it might be an imitation of the *pfzt* noise that a faulty connection in an electrical machine might make, or the sound of a fuse blowing, though he was extremely tentative about it. This theory falls down because none of the early examples is connected with electrical devices, and the phrase predates widespread use of electricity anyway (a fact he didn't know).

Others feel it must be connected with Fritz, the nickname for a German; in particular a German soldier, taken from a familiar version of Friedrich. (A related story connects it with supposedly poor-quality manufactured goods imported into the USA from Germany in the early years of the twentieth century.) This is a seductive idea. There's one big problem, though – the nickname didn't really start to appear until the First World War, about 1915, well after the saying had been coined (there's an isolated example of Fritz recorded from a letter in 1883, but otherwise examples are from the War period).

William and Mary Morris, in the *Morris Dictionary of Word and Phrase Origins*, suggest that it may nevertheless have come from someone called Fritz – in the comic strip called *The Katzenjammer Kids*. In this, two youngsters called Hans and Fritz got up to some frightful capers, fouling things up and definitely putting the plans of other members of the strip *on the Fritz*. The comic strip appeared in newspapers from 1897 onwards, so the dates fit rather nicely. But there's no evidence that confirms it, so far as I know. There's also the key question: why don't we talk instead about being *on the Hans*? And we also have to explain why some early examples appear as *on the fritzer*.

As so often, I've gone around the houses, considered this theory and that, but come to no very definite conclusion except that most of the stories told about the expression are false. But the truth is that nobody really knows, nor now is ever likely to.

On the wagon

A story has come my way arguing that this phrase for a person who is abstaining from alcohol derives from prisoners who were on their way to jail on the back of a wagon. They were allowed one last drink in the local pub before the enforced temperance inside. A variation refers to condemned prisoners on the way from Newgate Prison to be hanged at Tyburn being allowed to stop at a hostelry to have a last drink before being put back on the wagon for the final part of their journey to execution. Hardly so. A young American was a little nearer when he wrote: 'My teacher says it was during the temperance movement when men would parade around town on a wagon to show they've conquered their demons.'

Since the Salvation Army is very keen on temperance, it isn't surprising that the phrase has several times been attributed to them. An American Sally Army website says firmly: 'Former National Commander Evangeline Booth – founder William Booth's daughter – drove a hay wagon through the streets of New York to encourage alcoholics on board for a ride back to The Salvation Army. Hence, alcoholics in recovery were said to be "on the wagon".' The source seems impeccable, but the Sally Army is, alas, perpetrating another version of the same folk etymology.

However, the saying is indeed originally American and it is associated with wagons, of a sort. The original form, which dates from the early years of the twentieth century, was *to be on the water-wagon*, implying that the speaker was drinking water rather than alcohol and so was an abstainer, at least for the time being. The image of the horse-drawn water-wagon would have been an obvious one at the time – it was used to spray unpaved American streets in the dry summer months to dampen down dust thrown up by the traffic. A direct link with the temperance movement –

very active at the time – would seem probable, though I've not been able to establish this for certain.

One fell swoop

The phrase is one of those fixed expressions that we hardly think about most of the time. Because *fell* is not a word in most people's vocabulary, the saying often appears as *one foul swoop*. I've even seen *one fowl swoop*, which isn't so wide of the mark if you look into its history.

It means at one sudden descent, at a single blow or stroke. It's been around in the language for at least 400 years – Shakespeare is recorded as using it first, in *Macbeth*; when Macduff hears that his family has been murdered, he says in disbelief:

> All my pretty ones?
> Did you say all? O hell-kite! All?
> What, all my pretty chickens and their dam
> At one fell swoop?

You might guess that *fell* here has something to do with *fall*, but it hasn't. It actually means something of terrible evil or deadly ferocity. The image that Shakespeare's audience would have brought to mind at once was a falcon plummeting out of the sky to snatch its prey (as the kite does, for example, *kite* having been a bird of prey long before it became an aerial device). So a *fell* swoop was something sudden, deadly, unexpected and fatal.

We now never see *fell* outside this fixed phrase (or perhaps occasionally in poetic use) but once it was common in its own right. One of its relatives is still about: *felon*, which comes from the same Old French source, *fel*, evil. Originally, a felon was a cruel or wicked person; only later did the word evolve to mean a person who commits a serious crime.

There are actually four *fell* words in English; apart from this one, there is the verb meaning to cut something down, such as a tree (intimately linked with *fall*), the one meaning an animal skin (as in the obsolete trade of *fellmonger*), and the one meaning a hill (as in the fells of Cumbria). They all come from different source words.

Out of sorts

The most common story about this phrase – meaning that one is in low spirits, depressed, or ill – is that it refers to the printer's word *sorts* for the individual metal characters in his boxes of type, so called because they have been arranged, each into its own compartment, with all of one kind together. It would obviously be a substantial inconvenience if a printer were to run out of a sort during composition.

Though the word *sort* for a character is recorded from 1668, the figurative expression *out of sorts* is older still; the first recorded use of the phrase for printers' type in the *Oxford English Dictionary* is actually a good deal later, from the pen of Benjamin Franklin in 1784: 'The founts, too, must be very scanty, or strangely out of sorts.' It would seem he was attaching an already well-known idiom to the printer's trade, not the other way around.

A second idea is that it has something to do with playing cards. A pack that hasn't been shuffled is said to be *out of sort* and not suitable for playing with. The big problem with this is that the OED doesn't give any example of it being used in this connection, which it surely would if the expression had been common.

The Latin original of our word *sort* was applied to a piece of wood used for drawing lots. Later, still in Latin, it developed into the idea of one's fate, fortune or condition. This was the first meaning of *sort* in English, in the thirteenth century. It survived until shortly after Shakespeare's time, until about the point that *out of sorts* is first found. But *sort* soon evolved another meaning in English that related to rank, order or class. It was used to describe people, especially their qualities or standing. There were once phrases such as *of sort* that implied high quality or rank. Others that we still use today, such as *of your own sort*, *the right sort*, or *of all sorts*, evolved out of the same idea.

It would seem *out of sorts* developed from this idea of quality (lack of it in this case), perhaps influenced by the other meaning of fate or one's lot in life, so implying that fortune wasn't smiling on one, or that all wasn't well.

Pale *See* BEYOND THE PALE

Penthouse

Now regarded as the acme of domestic accommodations, the very peak of high living, a penthouse is a smart apartment at the top of a tall building, giving its occupants the feeling they are lords of all they survey. It will be galling for them to learn that the name derives from an old word for an open-sided shed or outhouse.

The origin was *pentis*. Etymologically speaking it's an appendage or appendix, since it's derived, through Old French, from the Latin root that has given us *appendix* in all its senses, something attached to another in a dependent state. It does occasionally appear as *appentis*, but the initial *a* seems to have been lost very early on. A *pentis* was a lean-to building attached to a larger one. It could also refer to a covered walkway between two buildings, occasionally to the dry corridor against a wall provided by the projecting eaves of a house, or even to a projecting awning in front of a shop.

The key element, so far as ordinary people were concerned, was that a *pentis* always had a sloping roof. This led to folk etymological confusion with the Middle French word *pente*, a slope. It was added to *house*, since a pentis was usually an enclosing structure of some kind, to generate *penthouse*, a spelling that was known from around 1530. In real tennis, the corridor with a sloping roof around three sides of the court is also called the penthouse.

The sense of a posh apartment is modern American: the first example dates from 1921: 'Two of the elevators were designed to run to the roof, where a pent-house . . . was being built.' The idea developed because a penthouse flat was a separate apartment constructed on the roof of a building, much as the older penthouse was an appendage to another structure.

Phat

It may be that the popularity of this hip-hop slang term for a sexy woman or cool music is already beginning to wane after its peak of popularity in the early 1990s. People are still scratching their heads about where it comes from and coming up with inventive but crudely sexual acronyms: 'PHysically ATtractive', 'Pretty Hips And Thighs', 'Pretty Hot And Tempting', 'Pussy, Hips, Ass and Tits', and 'Pretty Hole at All Times'. There are more, but you get the idea. Note that all of these refer to the first sense only. Perhaps invention failed where music was concerned.

It's a cool set of phrases, but they're later rationalizations, we're pretty sure (or just possibly ways to get a laugh out of teachers and parents not in the know). The word, in both senses, is almost certainly a playful respelling of *fat*, a word that has been around in black slang since the start of the twentieth century in the sense of something comfortable, fine or pleasant. *The Troubling of a Star* by Walt Sheldon, a novel about the US Air Force of 1951, has this definitive instance: 'If you played your cards right, you had it fat; you had it made brother, and in fact you never had it so good.'

The first example in print of the extended spelling is surprisingly early, from a piece on black slang in *Time* magazine of 2 August 1963: '*Mellow, phat, stone, boss.* General adjectives of approval.' This form was part of a 1960s craze of using amended spellings to mark membership of a counter-cultural crowd and which is echoed by more recent computer-related terms like *doodz* (dudes), *phreaking* (freaking: cracking the telephone network to make free long-distance calls) and *warez* (wares: illegal copies of copyright software).

Picnic

Stories circulating in the USA link *picnic* to black American subjugation. These are two of the versions that I've come across:

- *Picnic* was a shortening of *pick a nigger* and referred to an outdoor community gathering during which families ate from box lunches while a randomly chosen black man was hanged for the diners' entertainment.

- *Pick-a-nig* was a gathering for slave traders and their families in the seventeenth to eighteenth centuries. They would get together after slave trading and have a big party, called a *pick-a-nig*.

Though there's no truth in these stories from an etymological viewpoint, it is very understandable how they arose. Some of the historic photographs of lynchings show families with picnic baskets. This is evidence enough that a lynching was often a social occasion, but if you need further proof, you have only to look up how often the phrases *lynching bee* or *Negro barbecue* turn up in descriptions of such events.

Picnic is originally a French word, *picque-nique*, which appeared at the end of the seventeenth century. It later spread to Germany and other countries, but didn't become widely known in English until after 1800. It was at first a fashionable type of social entertainment – held indoors, incidentally; the association with an outdoor meal didn't appear until well into the nineteenth century – in which each person who attended brought a share of the food. The first part may be from the French *piquer*, from which we get *pick*. The *nique* part may just have been a reiteration (as in English words like *hoity-toity*), but could have echoed an obsolete word meaning 'a trifle', so the term could have meant something like 'each pick a bit'.

Poltroon

Claudius Salmasius, better known in his native France by his birth name of Claude de Saumaise, was an eminent classical scholar of the first half of the seventeenth century. Eminence and learning, alas, do not preclude mistaken conjectures about the origins of words.

He suggested that *poltroon*, an abject coward (in French *poltron*), derived from medieval military matters. At this time, longbowmen were crack troops whose skill with archery made their massed ranks the most formidable fighting force in Europe. Those who preferred not to risk their skins in combat had only to make themselves incapable of drawing a longbow. This, Salmasius said, they did by cutting off their right thumbs. In Latin, *pollice truncus* meant maimed or mutilated in the thumb and this, he claimed, had become corrupted into the French *poltron*.

No. The French word came from Italian *poltrone*, which could mean a coward, but could equally refer to somebody who was lazy – one possible origin is the Italian *poltro*, a bed or couch.

Salmasius's supposed etymology was widely believed in the seventeenth century and probably provoked another sense of *poltroon* that grew up in falconry, for a bird of prey whose hind toes were cut off to stop him flying at game.

Pom

This Australian term for British immigrants – also known in the longer forms *pommy* and *pommie* – has generated many stories for its origin: short for *Port Of Melbourne*, where the ships from England docked; from *POHM*, *Prisoner Of Her Majesty*, or from *POME*, *Prisoner Of Mother England*, since the first immigrants were convicts; an abbreviation for *Permit Of Migration*; derived from the common naval slang term for Portsmouth, *Pompey*; or from the French *pommes de terres* for potatoes. Please dismiss all these from your mind; their only virtue is ingenuity.

The term *pom* is actually not that old – its first appearance in writing was in Sydney in 1912. It is now generally believed that it derives from the word *pomegranate*.

That origin was explained by D. H. Lawrence in his Australian novel *Kangaroo* of 1923: 'Pomegranate, pronounced invariably pommygranate, is a near enough rhyme to immigrant, in a naturally rhyming country. Furthermore, immigrants are known in their first months, before their blood "thins down", by their round and ruddy cheeks. So we are told. Hence again, pomegranate, and hence Pommy. Let etymologists be appeased: it is the authorised derivation.' Part of the reason why this took so long to be accepted is that the usual educated English pronunciation of *pomegranate* early in the twentieth century had the first 'e' unstressed, so that the initial letters *pome* rhymed with *home*, which was why Lawrence had to explain how it was said.

There's a slight twist to take note of. H. J. Rumsey wrote about it in 1920 in the introduction to his book *The Pommies, or New Chums in Australia*. He suggested that the word began life among children around 1870 as a form of derisive rhyming slang. An immigrant was at first called a *Jimmy Grant* (a term known from 1859 in Australia but even earlier in New Zealand, from 1845), but over time this shifted to *Pommy Grant*, probably as a reference to *pomegranate*, because the new chums did burn in the sun and went a red colour that reminded people of the fruit. Later *pommy* became a word on its own and was frequently abbreviated still further.

Posh

Something *posh* is elegant or stylishly luxurious; in Britain it also means somebody or something typical of the upper classes.

The best-known and most widely believed story is that it comes from old-time ship travel from Britain to India on the packet boats run by the Peninsular and Oriental Steamship Company. It supposedly stood for 'Port Out, Starboard Home'. It is explained that somebody who had a cabin on the port side on the outward trip, and on the starboard side on the return trip, had the benefit of the sea breeze, and shelter from the sun, on the hottest part of the journey through the Suez Canal and the Red Sea. Such cabins were reserved for the most wealthy passengers, we are told, and the P&O company stamped their tickets with POSH to show their status.

The trouble is there's absolutely no evidence for it and P&O flatly denies any such term existed. It's just a legend, though a very persistent one. One argument against it is that *posh* is known from 1918, while the story of its origin first appears only decades later. Occasionally, somebody claims to have seen one of these tickets – William Safire quotes one in his book I Stand Corrected of 1984. But no dictionary editor is going to be swayed for a moment by such memories unless and until an actual ticket turns up.

The wide popularity of the ship-related story hasn't stopped people finding other possibilities. Some have pointed to The Diary of a Nobody of 1892, in which George and Weedon Grossmith introduce a character of that name: 'Frank called, but said he could not stop, as he had a friend waiting outside for him, named Murray Posh, adding he was quite a swell.' Others are intrigued by lines from Leaves of Grass (1860), by Walt Whitman: 'Cold dash of waves at the ferry-wharf, posh and ice in the river, half-frozen mud in the streets', but posh here is a dialect term for mud or slush (as in Yorkshire dialect one might say 'T' roads is all iv a posh'). Eric Partridge favoured an origin in an abbreviated form of polished or polish (an example of what's called grammatical syncopation, where a middle syllable has been left out).

The most probable solution – though unprovable because slang is so rarely written down – is that it comes from London street slang for money. This may well derive from Romany posh, half, originally applied to a halfpenny, then to any small sum of money, and then to money in general. It is recorded from as early as 1830 and was certainly still around in 1892 when Montagu Williams published his Down East and Up West, quoting in it a comment from a Londoner about a street singer who chatted up potential givers of money: 'That sort of patter I was just speaking of is the thing to get the posh, they'll tell you.' A shift in sense from 'money', to 'well off', and hence to 'upper-class', is not too hard to imagine.

There is a more direct London slang sense of 'dandy', known at least from the 1890s, which is probably where George and

Weedon Grossmith got the name of their character. This might be connected, or it might be a different word altogether.

Whatever its source, it looks from the evidence that posh in the modern sense was at first a military slang term of the First World War. Its first appearance is in the magazine Punch in September 1918, in which an RAF officer is saying to his mother, 'Oh, yes, Mater, we had a posh time of it down there'; the verbal phrase to posh up, to make oneself smart, is of the same period.

Proof of the pudding

It was the headline in an issue of the Society supplement to the Guardian in September 2002 that alerted me to a subtle change in this proverb: 'The proof is in the pudding.' It turns out to be a form that has been appearing with increasing frequency in books and newspapers for the last couple of decades, at first in the USA, so I ought not to single out the Guardian for censure. As another instance, the Washington Post had this in its issue of 28 April 2003: ' "The proof in the pudding is how many doctors are prescribing your medicine," Hadeed said, adding that the number tripled in 2002 after FDA approval.'

The principal trouble with the proof is in the pudding is that it makes no sense. What has happened is that writers half-remember the proverb as the proof of the pudding, which is also unintelligible unless you know the full form from which the tag was taken, and have modified it in an unsuccessful attempt to turn it into something sensible.

They wouldn't make this mistake if they knew two important facts. The full proverb is the proof of the pudding is in the eating and the word proof has the sense of 'test' (see also THE EXCEPTION PROVES THE RULE). The proverb literally says that you won't know whether food has been cooked properly until you try it. Or, putting it figuratively, don't assume that something is in order or believe what you are told, but judge the matter by testing it; it's much the same philosophy as in *seeing is believing* and *actions speak louder than words*.

The proverb is ancient – it has been traced back to 1300 and was popularized by Cervantes in his *Don Quixote* of 1605. It's sad that it has lasted so long only to be corrupted in modern times.

Ps and Qs *See* MIND YOUR PS AND QS

Put on dog

To *put on dog* or *put on the dog* is to be pretentious, to get all dressed up, to make an ostentatious display. P. G. Wodehouse borrowed it in his *Eggs, Beans & Crumpets* of 1940: 'An editor's unexampled opportunities for putting on dog and throwing his weight about.'

Individuals of too literal a turn of mind have suggested that this came from a practice of people in lowly stations of life, who would dress up and drape their dogs across their shoulders to emulate the fox furs of the rich. The image is risible enough, but the consequences of two individuals so dressed meeting in a crowded reception or theatre foyer is too awful to contemplate. Another, if possible even less likely origin, was suggested by a tourist guide who swore that at one time when the family dog died it was skinned and the hide turned into a pair of shoes, so that you literally put on dog. It has also been said, somewhat more plausibly, that it's from the tendency of rich old ladies to carry a lapdog everywhere with them.

It looks as though it was university slang of the 1860s or 1870s, since the first example recorded is in L. H. Bagg's *Four Years at Yale* of 1871: 'To put on dog is to make a flashy display, to cut a swell.'

Dog by itself meant style or good clothes. The origin is, alas, unclear.

See also HOT DOG.

Quiz

It is said that a Dublin theatre owner (or sometimes a pub landlord) named Daly (or perhaps Daley) had a bet with somebody (unspecified) that he could introduce a new word into the language within 24 (or 48) hours. He then hired a bunch of street urchins to go around Dublin chalking the nonsense word *quiz* on every wall so that by the next day everyone in the city was talking about it. This story is best viewed through the bottom of a glass of something Irish.

Just for once, we know where an anecdote comes from: it was told in a book of 1836 by Benjamin Stuart called *Walker Remodelled* (a revised edition of John Walker's 1791 *Critical Pronouncing Dictionary and Expositor of the English Language*). Though it was left out of the 1840 printing, it seems to have gathered an unstoppable momentum and is still with us.

Quiz, in our usual modern sense of a test of knowledge, only dates from the 1860s, and even then usually meant an informal examination of a student or class by a teacher. The competitive entertainment sense appeared as late as the 1940s. But the word is actually older than the exploits of the fictional Mr Daly. Its first known user was Fanny Burney, in 1782, who employed it to mean an odd or eccentric person: 'He's a droll quiz, and I rather like him.' Around the same time, it was also used for anything that looked odd, and was applied in particular to a French toy, also called a *bandalore*, a precursor of the yo-yo with a coiled spring inside. And to quiz somebody at this time was to make fun of them, to ridicule or mock them.

Where it comes from is open to some doubt. A plausible theory is that it's an abbreviated form of *inquisitive* (not of *quizzical*, which is actually a later derivation from *quiz*); others point to the Latin phrase 'Qui es?', meaning 'Who are you?', which was traditionally the first question asked in Latin oral exams in grammar schools. Though both of these could explain the later senses, they don't help greatly in penetrating to the source of the oldest ones.

Raining cats and dogs

This slightly outmoded expression for a heavy downpour has attracted many ingenious ideas about its origin.

It has been seriously suggested that the streets of old-time British towns were so poorly constructed that many cats and dogs would drown whenever there was a storm; people seeing the corpses floating by would think they had fallen from the sky, like proverbial rains of frogs. (If you believe this, I would suggest you are unobservant of the speed at which cats and dogs can move to get out of the weather.) A variation on this points to the lack of any sort of proper sanitation, suggesting that heavy rain would wash the corpses of cats and dogs from where they were lying into the street gutters.

Some other stories I've collected:

● It is said that cats were at one time thought to influence the weather, and that dogs were symbols of wind, often accompanying descriptions and images of the Norse storm god Thor. So when some particularly violent tempest appeared, people suggested it was caused by cats and dogs.

- In the days when houses had thatched roofs, these were a good place for small animals to live. When heavy rain came down the animals would sometimes be washed out of their comfortable hiding places, giving the illusion of a rain of cats and dogs.

- It comes from an unspecified Greek aphorism that was similar in sound and which meant 'an unlikely occurrence'.

- It's a corrupted version of a rare French word, *catadoupe*, meaning a waterfall.

The phrase first appears in its modern form in Jonathan Swift's *A Complete Collection of Polite and Ingenious Conversation* in 1738: 'I know Sir John will go, though he was sure it would rain cats and dogs.' Since that work is a satire on the use of clichés, it suggests the phrase is actually much older. A variant form is recorded in 1653 in *The City Wit*, a work of the English playwright Richard Brome, in which a character mistranslates a Latin sentence as 'It shall raine . . . Dogs and Polecats, and so forth'.

There are many other similes which employ falls of improbable objects as figurative ways of expressing the sensory overload of noise and confusion that can occur during a violent rainstorm; people have said that it's raining like *pitchforks* (first recorded in 1815 but common throughout that century), like *sluice-forks* (a tool for breaking up lumps in an American gold-miner's sluice-box), *hammer handles, old boots* and even *chicken coops*. A Welsh expression, *bwrw hen wragedd a ffin*, may be translated as 'raining old ladies and sticks'.

The version with cats and dogs fits neatly into this model, without needing to invoke supernatural beliefs or inadequate drainage.

Real McCoy

Something that is the *real McCoy* is the genuine article, the real thing. Its origin is unclear, which has opened the gates to admit an astonishing range of individuals bearing ideas, most of them owing much to ingenuity but little to hard fact. Was it perhaps from:

- Elijah McCoy, who invented a machine to lubricate the moving parts of a railway locomotive?
- The famous Hatfield–McCoy family feud that enlivened the West Virginia–Kentucky border in the 1880s?
- A Prohibition-era rum-runner named Bill McCoy?
- The *real Macao*, pure heroin imported from the Far East?
- From the name of the American boxer Norman Selby, known as Kid McCoy, who was welterweight champion from 1898 to 1900?

There is broad agreement among a lot of writers that this last one is the true origin. It is said that McCoy had so many imitators who took his name in boxing booths in small towns throughout the country that eventually he had to bill himself as Kid 'The Real' McCoy, and the phrase stuck. There's another anecdote in which a sceptical drunk who met the boxer in a bar denied he was the real article with such force that McCoy was forced to hit him. After recovering the drunk said, 'It's the real McCoy!' These stories, I have to tell you, are entirely apocryphal and there's no evidence whatsoever for the imitators or the drunk.

There's plenty of evidence, however, for suggesting that the original McCoy was actually a Mackay. The earliest example is from 1856, recorded in the *Scottish National Dictionary* (1931–76): 'A drappie [drop] o' the real MacKay.' The same work says that in 1870 the slogan was adopted by Messrs G. Mackay and Co., whisky distillers of Edinburgh. That would most likely explain the first instance of the expression in the *Oxford English Dictionary*, which records a letter written by the author Robert Louis Stevenson in 1883: 'He's the real Mackay.' Certainly early references are to a drop of the hard stuff.

And some other examples also point towards this Scottish origin. *A Rock in the Baltic*, by Robert Barr, dated 1906, has: 'I shouldn't have taken the liberty of introducing him to you as Prince Lermontoff if he were not, as we say in Scotland, a real Mackay – the genuine article.' And from Australia, Andrew 'Banjo' Paterson wrote in *An Outback Marriage*, also published in 1906: ' "We brought a drop o' rum," replied Charlie. "Ha! That'll do. That's the real Mackay," said the veteran, slouching along at a perceptibly quicker gait.'

It looks very much – without being able to say for sure – as though the term was originally *the real Mackay*, but became converted to *the real McCoy* in the USA, either under the influence of Kid McCoy or for some other reason.

Real tennis

This is a retronym, a term that has had to be created to distinguish an older form of something from a newer one. For example, we once just had guitars, then somebody invented the electric guitar; this made *guitar* ambiguous, so *acoustic guitar* was invented to describe the older type. Other examples of retronyms are *birth mother, black-and-white television, classic Coke, manual typewriter, natural turf, real cream, reel-to-reel tape recorder* and *regular coffee*.

The triggering event in this case was the development of lawn tennis in the 1870s, a game that was at first called *sphairistike*, from the Greek words for skill at playing at ball, but which was fortunately soon renamed. Until then there had just been one type of tennis, a game that required a sizeable and complex court, usually indoors. The aficionados of the older game, perhaps rather put out by this upstart contender to the game's historic title, naturally regarded their version as the true and original sort, and took to calling it *real tennis*, a term which is first recorded in 1880.

So far, so good. But then some people came to believe that *real* referred not to something actual and genuine, but was the now rather rare word meaning 'royal'. This comes from Latin *regalis*, through an Old French word that is also the source of both *royal* and *regal*. The history of the game rather supports this misapprehension, since in its heyday in the sixteenth and seventeenth centuries the game wasn't played by people much below the social level of monarch and there are several courts in Britain known to have been built by or played in by kings, including those at Hampton Court and the Falkland Royal Palace in Scotland.

A follow-up stage in this folk etymology is that people began to hypercorrect *real* into *royal* and so the term *royal tennis* came into being (it's the usual term for the game in Australia, for example; Americans prefer *court tennis*). This was helped along by the Hampton Court example being officially called the *Royal Tennis Court*, though this reflects its construction by Henry VIII in about 1530.

Rosemary

This aromatic evergreen shrub once had strong associations with weddings and was a symbol of fidelity in love. Rosemary is a lovely name, but the original Latin is even better: *ros marinus*, sea dew, perhaps because it grew in coastal margins.

That name was taken into English as *rosmarine* about the turn of the first millennium and survived until the seventeenth century (in 1654 it was written that 'Mr. Prynne and Mr. Burton were brought into London in great pomp and state, being conducted

Sirloin

One of the daftest examples of uncritical folk etymology extant (assiduous readers of this book will understand the magnitude of that claim) holds that the joint of beef called the *sirloin* got its name through being knighted by a British monarch, hence *Sir Loin*.

Those who hold it to be true, or who at least recount it unthinkingly for the amusement of the populace at large, do at least have the consolation that the story is half as old as Methuselah. The first rendering is in Thomas Fuller's *The Church-History of Britain* of 1655, in which he claimed the monarch was Henry VIII. Later writers attributed it to James I and Charles II.

The truth of the matter is, by comparison, prosaic. Sirloin comes from the Old French *surloigne*, from *sur*, above, plus *longe*, loin. So it was the cut of meat above or over the loin. The shift in spelling seems to have been under the influence of these stories, so the folk etymology became self-reinforcing.

Sixes and sevens *See* AT SIXES AND SEVENS

Sleep tight

This phrase, an injunction to have a good night's sleep, puzzles people and – as so often – leads to attempts at literal explanations.

It is often said, especially by tour guides in historical properties, that the phrase refers to old-time beds. These often consisted of a wooden frame with ropes threaded through side to side and top to bottom, on which the mattress was placed. The ropes sagged after a while and it was necessary to regularly tighten them. Hence the injunction – it is said – is along the lines of 'make sure your bed ropes are tight or you won't get a good night's sleep'. The story is quite certainly wrong. I'm not suggesting that beds of this type didn't exist, nor that they didn't need tightening (I've seen examples, and of the forked wooden tools used to tighten the ropes), just that the phrase has nothing to do with the matter.

One reason for arguing this is that the phrase doesn't turn up until about the middle of the nineteenth century and is quite rare in print even after that until the beginning of the twentieth. The first example I've found is in a diary by Susan Eppes, *Through Some Eventful Years*: 'May 2nd, 1866 – All is ready and we leave as soon as breakfast is over. Goodbye little Diary. ''Sleep tight and wake bright,'' for I will need you when I return.' I've not found another example until 1916, in L. Frank Baum's *Rinkitink in Oz*: 'Eat hearty, sleep tight, and pleasant dreams to you.'

The origin is pretty certainly the traditional children's rhyme:

Good night, sleep tight,
Wake up bright
In the morning light
To do what's right
With all your might . . .

which is the one that Susan Eppes seems to be quoting. (There's an optional interpolated second line, *Don't let the bedbugs bite*, which is even more recent and has given rise to some variations on the bed-tightening story, usually that to keep oneself tightly tucked in will discourage bed bugs, as if any self-respecting bug would have been constrained by such ploys.)

But why *sleep tight* in the first place? There are many examples of *tight* used figuratively – for somebody who is drunk, or who is mean (in full, *tight-fisted*), or in phrases like *tight corner*, *tight schedule*, *tight bargain*, or *tight ship* (one that is strictly run and well disciplined). The sense in these latter cases is that of 'soundly' or 'roundly'. It was applied to sleep from the end of the eighteenth century onwards, often in the form *tight asleep*. Inverting that to make the instruction *sleep tight* is a small step.

Sling one's hook

This idiom is a decidedly informal British one, not much known in the USA. Most dictionaries record it from the latter part of the nineteenth century, and note that it could occur also in the form *to take one's hook*. Both meant to leave, or go away, though it was often used as an urgent and impolite injunction to move on, often attached to a jerk of the thumb, as in this example from the *Daily News* of 1897: 'If you don't sling yer hook this minute, here goes a pewter pot at yer head.'

Now to the difficult bit – where it came from. There are at least two theories. One equates *hook* with a ship's anchor, so that to *sling one's hook* was to raise the anchor and sail away. The other says the hook is one on which a miner would hang his day clothes. When he finished his shift down the pit, he would change, collect his possessions from his hook, and leave. The second of these sounds much less convincing than the first, but the essential evidence isn't there to decide between them.

There's an earlier expression, *to sling one's daniel*, which had exactly the same meaning. What a *daniel* was nobody can say, except to suggest that it was rhyming slang for some form of pack, or perhaps a dialect word whose meaning is now lost.

Many agricultural workers had as a tool some sort of hooked implement, such as a *billhook*. *To take one's hook* makes sense, since it could refer to an itinerant worker who was moving on to his next task. It's also possible that *sling your hook* was an instruction to sling the implement over your shoulder in preparation for setting out to your next job.

As I say, nobody knows.

Smart Alec

Some writers, more versed in English comic writing than in the history of language, have asserted that this term comes from the fertile mind of the humorist J. B. Morton, who wrote the *Beachcomber* column in the *Daily Express* for more than fifty years. Several of Morton's characters were, at least for a while, more famous than their inventor, such as Captain Foulenough, Dr Strabismus (whom God preserve) of Utrecht and Mr Justice Cocklecarrot (most famously involved in the case of the twelve red-bearded dwarves). Another was Dr Smart-Allick, headmaster of the notorious public school Narkover.

Though it would be good to pin yet another medal for originality to the breast of this inventive and surrealistically comic writer, the phrase *Smart Alec* for an irritating, know-all person who always seems to have a smart answer for any question was already around well before Morton was born in 1893; he did no more than borrow it.

For many years, Smart Alec or Smart Aleck was thought to be no more than a generic character, first cousin to Clever Dick. For the truth, we are all indebted to Gerald Cohen, who has traced him to a real person (for the full story see G. L. Cohen, *Studies in Slang*, part 1, 1985). The original was Alex Hoag, a celebrated thief in New York in the 1840s, whose story is almost as weird as anything from the brain of Beachcomber.

Hoag worked with his wife Melinda and an accomplice called French Jack to fleece unwary visitors to the city who were looking for a little fun. It was common for prostitutes and their pimps to steal from customers once they had fallen asleep, so much so that the more worldly customers took the precaution of putting a chair under the door handle so they could not be surprised. Hoag invented a modification of the scam called the panel game, by which he could get into the prostitute's room through a hidden door at a suitable point in the proceedings. By the time that the mark had woken up and realized he had been the victim of a crime, Hoag and his associates were well away. It was the reputation that he gained for not getting caught that earned him the sobriquet *Smart Alex*.

Snob

It is frequently argued that this brief but expressive term is the shortened form of a Latin tag, *sine nobilitate*, 'without nobility'. One story is that Oxford and Cambridge undergraduates were required on admission to state whether they were nobly born or not; commoners were marked *snob*. Related stories apply the same idea to the more aristocratic sorts of gentlemen's clubs and to public schools.

The reference to the Latin tag is either mischievous or mistaken. The origin really lies in a dialect or colloquial term of the latter part of the eighteenth century for a cobbler. It seems that early usage implied a person of humble rank or status, as cobblers of course were. There is a link to the university story in that *snob* was used by some Cambridge undergraduates around the end of the eighteenth century for a townsman, somebody not a member of the university. By the 1830s the term had evolved a little further to mean somebody lacking in the required breeding or good taste to be accepted as a member of society. There's a hint in early examples that the close resemblance between *snob* and *nob* (a derogatory term for a person of wealth or high social position, from an old word for the head) may have played a part in its acceptance.

William Makepeace Thackeray pretty much invented our modern sense of a person of lowly origin who seeks to imitate or cultivate those of superior social standing or who slavishly admires them. He popularized it through his series of articles in Punch between 28 February 1846 and 27 February 1847 called The Snobs of England by One of Themselves, most of which were republished as The Book of Snobs in 1848. In this he dissected the character of various types of English snobs, such as the military snob and the country snob. Later, snob was also applied to a person who despised others whom he saw as being of lower rank.

As an antipodal aside, the Australian slang sense of snob for the last and most awkward sheep in the pen waiting to be shorn is a bit of double-derived wordplay, as the older term is cobbler, itself a joke on the phrase cobbler's last for the little anvil shoemakers use.

Sparrowgrass See ASPARAGUS

Spitting image

Some writers suggest that this phrase – for a person who is the exact double of another – is a corruption of spirit and image, suggesting that the two people are so similar to one another as to be identical in mind as well as body. You also see it as splitting image, perhaps because people think the expression refers to the cloven halves of one original.

Neither story is true, though there is some argument about the true origin. Several phrases have been used down the years to indicate that one person is the exact likeness of another: spitten image, spit and image, the very spit of, spit image, spitten picture, the very spit and fetch, dead spit for, and spit by itself.

The oldest of these is the very spit of, which was first recorded in 1825, though Eric Partridge claimed to find examples containing similar ideas much earlier. The evolution of the others is rather complicated, with variations turning up throughout the nineteenth century. The current *spitting image* is the last of them to appear, in 1901, and was at one time considered an error for *spit and image*, another form once seriously put forward as the original.

The core of all these variations is obviously *spit*. But why? One view is that it's the same as our usual meaning of liquid ejected from the mouth, perhaps suggesting that one person is as like the other as though he'd been spat out by him. The idea of some sort of exchange of body fluids is widely current in European languages (as in the French *C'est son père tout craché*, 'he is the very spit of his father'). Some writers suggest that *spit* is actually a euphemism, and make a link with seminal ejaculation, which may account for the phrase being used originally only of the son of a father.

Spud

For decades a persistent story has held that this name for the humble potato appeared not long after the vegetable had been introduced to Britain in the late sixteenth century. The potato, it is said, was regarded with suspicion by the English establishment, who thought that it would have a bad influence on the diet of the ordinary people. So they formed a society to advocate its rejection, the Society for the Prevention of an Unwholesome Diet, or SPUD.

Like all the better stories of its type, this one contains enough historical truth for it to sound reasonable. People in Europe did distrust the potato, often seeing it as fit only for animal fodder, not human consumption. Even when they did eat it, they often treated it as an exotic import, a speciality food that was on a level with the sweet potato. It took more than 200 years for it to be fully accepted. Only the Irish, for complicated reasons, took to it almost immediately and made it a staple of their diet.

The original *spud* wasn't the potato, but the implement that was used to dig it out of the ground. This word originally meant a short dagger or knife but is first recorded in the digging sense in the diary of Samuel Pepys in 1667. The word wasn't applied as a slang and dialect name for the potato until the middle of the nineteenth century. Where *spud* originally came from isn't clear; if there had been no earlier dagger sense one might think it was no more than a variation on *spade*. As with so many words, it has to be left as 'origin obscure'.

Incidentally, one of the reasons why the false story became popular is that it was recounted in 1949 in *The Story of Language*, by the eminent American linguist Mario Pei. It shows that you shouldn't believe experts just because of their reputations. Even Homer nods occasionally.

Square meal

This common term for a satisfying and filling repast leads many amateur etymologizers towards origins based on a literal reading of the words:

- Sailors used to eat off wooden boards; these were square in shape and were usually not filled with food. However, after a heavy watch the sailors were given a large meal which filled the board – a square meal.

- In Britain of yore, a dinner plate was a square piece of wood with a bowl carved out to hold your serving of the perpetual stew that was always cooking over the fire. You always took your 'square' with you when you went travelling, in hopes of a square meal.

- In former times in the US military, you were required to sit formally at meals, bolt upright with arms at right angles, so forming a square shape. So a meal in the mess was always a square meal.

Wonderful stuff. Rubbish, of course, but entertaining rubbish.

It's an interesting comment on the imagination of such storytellers that they haven't created similar stories about *square deal* or *fair and square*. Yet these also employ *square* for something that is fair, honest, honourable or straightforward. Older phrases of similar type include *the square thing* and *square play*. Several of them date to the seventeenth century and possibly even earlier. This figurative sense comes from the idea that something made with exact right angles has been properly constructed (*right* in *right angle* is another reference to the same idea).

We know that *square meal* was originally American. Early examples seem to have come out of miners' slang from the western side of the country. Mark Twain, in *The Innocents Abroad* of 1869, refers to it as a Californian expression. I found an article in *Harper's New Monthly Magazine* dated 1865 about the gold-mining town of Virginia City in Nevada, created to serve the famous Comstock lode: 'Says the proprietor of a small shanty, in letters that send a thrill of astonishment through your brain: "LOOK HERE! For fifty cents you CAN GET A GOOD SQUARE MEAL at the HOWLING WILDERNESS SALOON!"' The writer felt the need to explain this strange phrase: 'A square meal is not, as may be supposed, a meal placed upon the table in the form of a solid cubic block, but a substantial repast of pork and beans, onions, cabbage, and other articles of sustenance.'

Just so. Modern storytellers, please copy.

Square one

By saying that we are *back to square one* or *back in square one* we mean that some problem or error has lost us all the ground we have gained in some enterprise, so that we must go back to the beginning and start again. Richard Lewontin wrote in a review of

Stephen Jay Gould's *What Does It Mean to Be a Radical* in November 2002: 'To be radical is to consider things from their very root, to go back to square one, to try to reconstitute one's actions and ideas by building them from first principles.'

Its origins are open to dispute. We know it is a British expression, but it first appears out of the blue in *The Times* of London in May 1960: 'As far as building up a basis for profitable negotiations is concerned the two sides are back in square one.'

There is a persistent story that it is linked to the early days of radio in Britain. The first commentary on a football match was broadcast by the BBC on 22 January 1927. To help listeners visualize the pitch and where the players and ball were, the producer of that first broadcast, Lance Sieveking, worked out a scheme of dividing the pitch into eight numbered squares and had a diagram published in the BBC's listings guide, *Radio Times*. The commentator would then say that the ball was currently in square five, or square three, or whatever. Square one was to one side of one of the goals.

Ingenious though this suggestion is, it seems more than a little stretched, especially as it is hard to equate being at square one on the football field with having made no progress (though the teams change ends at half time, the commentator didn't invert the numbering to suit). The scheme was abandoned in the middle 1930s, and the long gap between then and 1960 may be further evidence that it isn't the source.

It's much more likely that it refers to a board game. Snakes and ladders is the obvious possibility, where landing on the wrong square can send a player down a snake right back to the beginning. However, in the current state of knowledge (or indeed the likely future state) it's impossible to prove.

Squaw

Americans often argue that *squaw* is an extremely derogatory term for a woman, derived from an Indian word for the vagina, and that as a result it has, to quote one website, 'the crudest sexual connotations'. The opposition to it has been so intense that many states have been lobbied to rename places that include it, such as Squaw Pond, Squaw Creek and Squaw Lake (all of which are in Minnesota), Squaw Gulch (in California) and Rugged Squaw Peak (in Arizona), plus about a thousand others. Many have now been changed.

It was actually settlers in New England who first came across the word in various Algonquian Indian dialects, for example as *squa*, a woman, in Massachusetts dialect, or its equivalent *squaws* in Narragansett. It is recorded in English as early as 1634, in a book by William Wood called *New England's Prospect*.

Although it started out in English with the same neutral sense as it had had in its Native Indian dialects, it quickly took on negative and mildly racist undertones, often appearing in humorous or disparaging contexts. That is the situation that prevailed until 1973, when Thomas Sanders and Walter Peek published an anthology called *Literature of the American Indian*, in which they said that it 'probably' came from a French corruption of the Iroquois word *otsiskwa*, female sexual parts, and suggested that it was therefore more insulting than anyone had previously thought. Their statement has been widely believed – despite that 'probably' – though the early English settlers had no contact with the Iroquois, who lived a long way away, and it is extremely unlikely that their word could have been clipped to make the English *squaw*, even via French, a route that is in any case improbable. The false derivation was given wide public airing on the Oprah Winfrey television show in 1992 and seems to have grown from there.

I hold no torch for the word – as commonly used it is indeed derogatory – but I suggest that attitudes to it ought to be based on evidence rather than misinformation.

Straight and narrow

We often use this phrase, in the sense of morally correct and law-abiding behaviour, as a clipped version of the full saying, variously the straight and narrow way or the straight and narrow path.

It is sometimes argued by writers on language that it's an error, at best a folk etymology, for strait and narrow. It is not hard to find examples of the latter spelling, as here in the Daily Telegraph of 1 April 2001: 'City firms already have huge compliance departments supposedly keeping them on the strait and narrow', or from the Guardian of 28 September 2000: 'Accounts of crime have always included anecdotes of the criminal's misspent youth and first deviation from the strait and narrow.'

Strait is now hardly used except in its sense of a narrow sea passage between two larger bodies of water, as in the Straits of Gibraltar. Its oldest sense is of something restricted or confined (it derives from Latin stringere, to bind tightly, which is also the root of our constrain and strict, among others), which is why that obsolete method of restraining lunatics, the straitjacket, is correctly so spelled. Its other extant meaning refers to a situation of difficulty, distress or need, but that usually appears only in the phrases dire straits, for a situation of extreme need or danger (a phrase known from the last decades of the nineteenth century but which is now a cliché), or straitened circumstances, living in poverty.

The folk-etymological confusion between straight and strait is widespread. Not only do we often see references to straightjackets, to the extent that this spelling is often given as an alternative in dictionaries, but the same form also appears in straight-laced, of someone who has very strict and unbending moral attitudes, a form which dictionaries also now allow. In the latter case, the original was certainly *strait-laced*, literally referring to stays or corsets that were tightly laced and confining, but which by the sixteenth century had already taken on the modern moralistic sense.

Strictly speaking, the form *strait and narrow* is a tautology, since both halves mean the same thing. It comes from the Gospel of Matthew (chapter 7, Verse 14) in the King James Version: 'Because strait is the gate, and narrow is the way which leadeth unto life, and few there be that find it.' The writer is here using *narrow* and *strait* in similar senses to reinforce each other in successive phrases, but writers who borrowed the image and the reference conflated them into a single phrase.

The first example I can find is from the *North American Review*, a long-defunct publication from Cedar Falls, Iowa, dated January 1834. In a review of Thomas Taylor's *The Life of William Cowper* appears: 'His zeal . . . could have no other effect than to attract them onward in the strait and narrow path of duty.'

As *strait* has become less common, *straight* has largely superseded it in this phrase, as it has in *straight-laced*. There is common sense behind *straight and narrow* that has helped its acceptance, since it can be said to contain the idea of a road which is direct and undeviating, the true path of virtue that leads us to our destination without succumbing to temptation along the way.

The *Oxford English Dictionary* notes that the first recorded use of the *straight and narrow* form is in J. E. Leeson's *Hymns and Scenes of Childhood* of 1842:

> Loving Shepherd, *ever near,*
> Teach Thy lamb Thy voice to hear;
> Suffer not my steps to stray
> From the straight and narrow way.

These days, it is by far the more common spelling, given as standard in dictionaries, so much so that it would be reasonable to regard *strait and narrow* either as an archaism or a pedantic hypercorrection.

Take the mickey

This British slang expression for teasing or ridiculing somebody is sometimes said to derive from *micturition*, an elevated word for urination, hence a learned variation on *take the piss* in the same sense.

It's a neat suggestion, the only thing wrong with it being that it's wrong. However, the connection with *take the piss* is extremely close, since it's from rhyming slang: *Mickey Bliss* = *take the piss*. As commonly happens, the first word was used on its own as a further level of obfuscation and was substituted for *piss* in the older expression. Though the first recorded use is in 1952, it seems from anecdotal evidence to date from the 1930s, roughly the same time that *take the piss* was invented.

Teetotal

The first element of this word seems to make no sense to us, and so some people have assumed that it is a misspelling, suggesting that those who abstained totally from alcohol turned instead to tea for their refreshment and so were *totally* reliant on *tea* (I've come across a curious idea held by at least one American, who thought it refers to somebody who carries, or TOTES, tea to drink on social occasions at which only alcohol was available). It has been argued as an alternative to the tea thesis that those who signed the pledge at temperance meetings had their names marked with the letter T to indicate their total abstention – Lansing, New York, is often quoted here, where it is said to have first happened in January 1827, but there's no contemporary evidence for it and the story only surfaces much later in the century.

However, this story is near the truth of the matter. It's accepted that the word, at least in the abstinence sense, was coined by Richard 'Dicky' Turner in a speech he gave to a temperance meeting in Preston, Lancashire, in September 1833. Turner was an illiterate working man, a hawker of fish, who had visited one of the early Preston temperance meetings in 1832 as a joke while half-drunk, but who came out of the meeting a convert. He was one of the founding Seven Men of Preston who signed the pledge and became a fervent advocate of that form of temperance that demanded total abstention from all forms of alcoholic drink, not just spirits as some more moderate reformers had been urging. There is no formal record of what he said at the meeting – one report had it that his words were 'nothing but the tee-total would do' but it is also claimed that he said in his strong local accent, 'I'll be reet down out-and-out t-t-total for ever and ever'.

Here's where it all gets a bit murky. Did Dicky Turner stutter, did he invent a new word by adding t as an intensifier to the front of *total*, or was he using one already known? We will probably never be entirely sure. What is certain, though, is that his new word caught on in the local temperance movement, was often quoted in its journal, the *Preston Temperance Advocate*, giving the credit to him as inventor, and soon became a standard word in the language. Richard Turner died in 1846 and is buried in St Peter's churchyard in Preston; he may be the only person in the world whose claim to have invented a new word is cited on his tombstone.

Confusing the issue is the fact that a related word, *teetotally*, already existed. That certainly did use t as an initial intensifier, so the first form would have been t-*totally*. It is first recorded in North America in 1832, the year before Dicky Turner's speech, and is common there throughout the following decades. The sense, though, is 'completely; utterly', with no link to alcohol. The Nova Scotian writer Thomas Chandler Haliburton put it into his book *The Clockmaker* of 1836: 'I hope I may be tee-totally ruinated, if I'd take eight hundred dollars for him.' There's a strong suspicion that this was an Irish dialect form that had been exported to North America some time earlier, since it also appears in British writing at the same period and with the same sense, and there is anecdotal evidence that it was known in Ireland much earlier. It appears, for example, in a story by Thomas de Quincey in 1839: 'An ugly little parenthesis between two still uglier clauses of a teetotally ugly sentence.' An Irish connection might be inferred from a late work by Anthony Trollope in 1872, *The Kellys and the O'Kellys*: 'Independent of the Kellys, is it, Mr Daly? Faix, thin, I'm teetotally indepindent of them this minute, and mane to continue so, glory be to God.'

However, no evidence has been put forward that *teetotally* was known at the time in the Lancashire dialect. If it were, Dicky Turner would hardly have been given the credit for *teetotal* that he received during his lifetime from Preston people. He does seem to have created the word anew.

Ten-gallon hat

You may accuse Texans of talking big or having swollen heads, but surely not to the extent of needing a hat that holds ten gallons of water. On the other hand, you will find books that tell you this is true. Their authors are dimensionally challenged.

The image of the wide-brimmed, high-crowned hats comes to us from the Tom Mix cowboy films of the 1920s (white ones for the heroes, black ones for the villains). These hats were often called Stetsons after a famous maker, though no real cowboy would have worn such an overblown and impractical virility symbol. Failing samples and a measuring device (a *stetsonometer*?), it's hard to be sure how big the crowns really were, but it's doubtful whether even the most extreme example could have held more than a couple of gallons or thereabouts.

The origin, as with so many cowboy terms, is in Spanish. *Galón* is braid (the English *galloon* for a type of close-woven ribbon is related). A *sombrero galoneado* was a wide-brimmed hat with braid on it. The word was borrowed into English and converted by folk etymology into *gallon*, so that people referred to a *gallon hat*. (Since *galón* in Spanish can also mean the liquid measure *gallon*, you may feel the confusion was inevitable, or at least excusable.)

It seems very likely that the idea of a *ten-gallon hat* was a joke on the size of the heroes' hats in early cowboy films. To show how divorced the term was even then from real range riders, the first example recorded in print is actually from an English newspaper, the *Daily Express*, of October 1928: 'She instinctively recognized that he was a cowboy, even though he did not wear a ten-gallon hat and a jacket embroidered with Mexican dollars.'

Some people will tell you that the term actually refers to the number of braids around the crown of the hat, since the most exuberant Mexicans had ten rows of braid, so making it a *ten galón hat*. Don't believe that either: it's just a later rationalization for the number.

Testify

One of the weirder bits of folk etymology currently extant holds that this word derives from a requirement of the Roman courts that men should swear to the truth of their statements on their testicles.

This would seem as good a moment as any to scotch the story. There really is a strong link between *testicle* and *testify* (as well as *intestate*, *attest*, *testament*, *contest* and other words) but those who swear by this belief have misunderstood the matter.

The Latin word for a witness was *testis*, which derives from an Indo-European word for the number three. That was because the Romans regarded a witness as what we would call a trusted third party, one who stands aside from the dispute and can tell it how it really was. The Romans did also use the word *testis* in a figurative way to mean testicle. The idea seems to have been that a testicle was a witness to a man's virility. And that's the whole story of the connection.

One reason for the confusion may be that swearing on the testicles is recorded in the Bible. The practice is mentioned in the Old Testament, though the King James Version bowdlerized the reference in Genesis to 'grasping the thigh'. But there is no evidence that the Romans – a long way away and in another era – used a similar method. In any case, the biblical reference implies that the man is swearing on the testicles of the king, not on his own.

Incidentally, *testis* sometimes appeared as the diminutive *testic-ulus*; this was converted into English at the end of the fourteenth century first as *testicule* and then as *testicle*. The Latin *testis*, with its plural *testes*, has continued in medical use to the present day.

Threshold

The story is told that in medieval houses that had earth floors, straw called thresh was strewn about to cover them and that a sill was put in the doorway to hold the thresh within the house. Hence *thresh hold*. Another story says that, since the threshing of corn was done outdoors, the threshold was a board put in the doorway to keep the straw and chaff out of the house. Neither story has any merit beyond misplaced ingenuity.

The mistake lies entirely in seeing *threshold* as a combination of two distinct words with clear meanings. It didn't start out that way. You can see that from the dozens of different spellings it has had down the centuries since it is first recorded in the ninth century, such as *þrescolde, þeorscwold, throschfold, threshal, thressald* and *threshwold*. The modern spelling didn't become at all common until the sixteenth century. It was created in the usual well-meaning attempt to make sense of an odd word. Presumably there was a second element to it in the ancient Germanic language from which English evolved, but nobody has a clue what that was or what it meant.

However, the first part of the word does seem to be associated with the Old English *thresh*, meaning to separate the grain from the husks. It comes from an old Germanic root meaning to stamp with the feet (perhaps from an even older word meaning to make a lot of noise, perhaps by stamping). Threshing was originally done by placing the stalks on the floor and treading on them, using the feet of men or oxen, and the word was transferred to the specific action. Another technique was to beat the stalks with a hinged wooden instrument called a flail, and this idea may have led to the creation of the variant form *thrash*.

It's probable that the threshold was linked to the sense of stamping through a link with stepping across it to enter or leave the house. It might have meant something like 'the tread stone', but don't quote me.

Tinker's damn

To say that something 'isn't worth a tinker's damn' is to express the idea that it's of no value at all, not worth even a moment's consideration. In the nineteenth century, writers on word histories – presumably offended by the mild swear word – attempted to bowdlerize it by showing that the phrase was really *tinker's dam*.

It was argued that when a tinker – an itinerant mender of pots and pans – was soldering the parts of a broken metal item together, he would make a small wall out of bread dough around the place he was to flood with solder in order to stop it from spreading. After he had finished, he would naturally throw the dough away as being of no further use, so that *a tinker's dam* was indeed something of no value.

A century ago, the compilers of the first edition of the *Oxford English Dictionary* were rightly scornful of this attempt to make a simple matter more complicated, though it is still to be found in some current works on phrase histories.

A more plausible theory points to the low social status of tinkers, and to their well-known tendency to include a swearword in every sentence. This theory is supported by variations such as *tinker's curse* and *tinker's cuss*.

Tip

An odd belief holds that this word, in the sense of a gratuity for a service rendered, is an acronym for the phrase *To Improve Performance* or *To Insure Promptness*. It's yet another example of the way that modern folk etymology believes the source of almost any short word lies in an acronym.

In reality, it's a most interesting word. There are three distinct senses of *tip* in English: the one for an extremity probably comes from Old Norse; the one with the sense of overturn possibly also comes from a Scandinavian language, though nobody is sure. Our sense may derive from the German *tippen*, or possibly may also be connected with the idea of an extremity, though authorities in language history are hedging their bets through lack of evidence.

It turns up first in the thirteenth century, meaning to touch lightly (as in the game *tip and run*). By the early 1600s it had become thieves' cant with the sense of handing something over, or passing something to another person surreptitiously. This may derive from the idea of lightly touching somebody's arm in order to communicate. (This is supported by other appearances of the word in phrases like *tip the wink* and *tip off* and the noun *tip* for a piece of inside information, say on a horse race.)

One specific thing that was passed was a small sum of money. By the beginning of the eighteenth century it had taken on its modern meaning, at first as a verb; the first recorded use is in George Farquhar's play *The Beaux' Stratagem* of 1706 ('Then I, Sir, tips me the Verger with half a Crown'). By the 1750s it could also mean the gratuity itself.

Toe the line

A common mistake is to write this as 'tow the line'. It's a homophonic error that's all too easy to make when in a hurry. In this case, the association of ideas between *tow* and *line* (in the sense of a rope) is often too powerful to overcome. The lack of any clear mental image of where it comes from is a contributing factor.

This has led to at least a couple of ingenious explanations:

- The phrase comes from the lines in front of the opposing rows of seats in the House of Commons (traditionally lines beyond which MPs were not permitted to step in order to keep the two sides at least a sword's thrust apart and so prevent emotion-laden fatal encounters).

- It was first used by a British executioner who drew a chalk line on the trap door of the gallows. Those about to die were instructed to put their toes against the line. Obedient prisoners would comply, but defiant ones would not, and they would be punished with a less comfortable death.

The one thing these stories have correct is that the true spelling of the first word is *toe*. *Toe the line* is the survivor of a set of phrases that were common in the nineteenth century; others were *toe the mark*, *toe the scratch*, *toe the crack* or *toe the trig*.

In every case, the image was that of men lining up in a row with the tips of their toes touching some line. They might be on parade, or preparing to undertake some task, or in readiness for a race or fight. Even the earliest recorded form, dating from 1813, already had the modern figurative sense of conforming to the usual standards or rules: 'He began to think it was high time to toe the mark.' Many early examples are from the British Navy, which is where it may have originated.

Toe the crack is an American form of the 1820s, in reference to a crack in the floorboards that delineates a straight line; *toe the scratch* is from prize fighting, where *scratch* was the line drawn across the ring (often in the earth of an informal outdoor ring) to which the fighters were brought ready for the contest – it's a close relative of *to come up to scratch*. In *toe the trig*, *trig* is an old term for a boundary or centre line in various sports.

Toerag

This expressive insult is basically British, though it is also well known in Australia. It means that the person addressed is contempt-ible or worthless, a scrounger. It doesn't turn up in print much, being considered slang that's too coarse for even semi-formal prose. When it does appear it is sometimes written as *tow-rag* or *towrag*, as in this sentence found online: 'Some little towrag stole the CD player while we were having a curry the other week.'

The original form – in the nineteenth century – was certainly *toe rag*. It referred to the strips of cloth that convicts or tramps wrapped around their feet as an inadequate substitute for socks. The first recorded use is by J. F. Mortlock in his *Experiences of a Convict* of 1864: 'Stockings being unknown, some luxurious men wrapped round their feet a piece of old shirting, called, in language more expressive than elegant, a "toe-rag".' It didn't take long to become a term of abuse – in 1875 a book on British circus life said that 'Toe rags is another expression of contempt . . . used . . . chiefly by the lower grades of circus men, and the acrobats who stroll about the country, performing at fairs.'

It seems to have come to wider British knowledge and use from the 1970s on, largely because it was aired in the ITV police series *The Sweeney* about the London mobile detective force called the Flying Squad (rhyming slang: *flying squad = Sweeney Todd*, the demon barber of Fleet Street), a programme that delighted in using London slang.

The *towrag* spelling appears because the link to the original sense has long since vanished. A series of letters in the *Independent* newspaper in 1997 indeed sought to justify that spelling by relating it to *tow*, a bundle of untwisted fibres often used to wipe up spills. Good try, but no.

Tote

In the book *Behind the Scenes: Thirty Years a Slave*, first published in 1868, Elizabeth Keckley records an eyewitness report of President Lincoln visiting Richmond, Virginia, just after it had been captured by Unionist forces in 1864. He met a little ragged black boy who used the word *tote*. The President discovered this meant 'to carry'. He asked Charles Sumner, the Senator from Massachusetts who was with him, what its origin was; he hazarded a guess that it came from Latin *totus*, everything. President Lincoln very reasonably pointed out that the boy's word had nothing to do with that meaning, and the Senator, somewhat abashed, agreed and remarked that 'Tote in this sense is defined in our standard dictionaries as a colloquial word of the Southern States, used especially by the negroes'. He was right on the second point but his *ad hoc* etymology from Latin was as wide of the mark as that of a modern writer I've encountered who derived it from the Hebrew word *thet* for a basket, and those in the nineteenth century who suggest it had an American Indian origin.

Even today *tote* is commonly considered to be characteristic of the southern states of the USA. Dr James Kibler summed it up in *The Southern Patriot* in 1997: 'We Southerners *tote* water and *tote* packages and *tote* the vegetables from the garden in summer. Southern students *tote* their books to school. Southern policemen *tote* guns. Southern workers *tote* their dinners to work.' However, compound terms like *tote bag*, known from the end of the nineteenth century, are more widely distributed.

The Senator was right in that the word is indeed associated in particular with Black American English speech. The archetypal use, one that introduced it to a lot of people outside America, was in the song *Old Man River* from *Showboat*:

Tote dat barge! Lif' dat bale!
Git a little drunk, An' you land in jail . . .

This Southern black association has led people to assume an African origin. Specifically, it is said to come from Kikongo *tota*, to pick up, or Kimbundu *tuta*, to carry or load, both related to Swahili *tuta*, to pile up or carry. It's also argued that it came into American English through *tot*, a Gullah word meaning to carry, which is traceable to a West African origin.

There's a problem here, because the word's antecedents aren't nearly as clear as proponents of the out-of-Africa theories would like. It appears first in 1676 in Virginia in reference to grievances among members of the Governor's out-guard, racial origin unknown. Later it's found in the New England states, to the extent that one writer in 1809 took it to be a 'native vulgarism of Massachusetts'. This has led some writers, including the editors of the first edition of the *Oxford English Dictionary*, to pooh-pooh an African origin and to suggest that it really came from some English dialect word that is now lost to us.

There were African slaves and indentured workers in Jamestown, Virginia, from 1619 onwards, half a century before the word is first recorded. It is by no means unlikely that a word from an African language might have permeated the local vocabulary in that time.

Lacking early evidence, though, we have to class this origin as unproven.

Trivial

It was only too appropriate that the question master of a pub trivia quiz recently ruled that this word came from the Latin *trivium*, the word for a crossroads or a public street (strictly, a place where three roads meet, from *tri-*, three, plus *via*, way or road). Such places, he said, were where ordinary people would congregate in their daily lives, so that the word also had the implication of affairs that were commonplace or of little importance.

There's support for it in that the related adjective *trivialis* in Latin did mean something that was common or popular. And our word does come from Latin *trivium*. But the path to the modern sense comes through a different route.

In the medieval educational system, learning was divided into seven liberal arts that were split into two groups. An introductory course was called the *trivium*. This comprised grammar, logic and rhetoric; a more advanced set called the *quadrivium* consisted of the mathematical sciences – arithmetic, geometry, astronomy and music. The Latin names for these came from *via*, way, and may be translated as 'the threefold way' and 'the fourfold way'. *Trivial* was the usual adjective applied to the trivium.

Because the four mathematical sciences of the quadrivium were considered to be much more difficult to learn than the others and dealt with matters that were less commonly met with in daily life, the subjects of the trivium came to be thought of as the ones that were ordinary, familiar or simple. Over time, this sense of *trivial* evolved into our modern one.

Those with a knowledge of Latin – that was everybody involved in education at the time, of course – also knew what Romans of the classical period had meant by *trivialis*. That sense may well have influenced the development of the modern sense of *trivial* but isn't the foundation of it.

Turn the tables

If you *turn the tables* on someone you reverse your relationship with them, to your advantage. But what tables, and how by turning them do you improve your situation?

Forward inventive amateur etymologists. One suggestion connects the phrase with wealthy Roman collectors of antique furniture; when such a man complained about his wife's extravagances, she had merely to turn to the tables he had collected and remind him of his own excessive expenditure. Another story connects it with the parsimonious behaviour of old-time British households. The tops of their tables only had one finished side, a less expensive alternative to having both completed to a high standard. When the family was alone, they ate on the rough side to keep the finished one in good condition. When company came, they turned the table-top to its good side to impress the visitors.

Don't believe either of these for a moment.

The phrase seems to have had its real origin in gaming. The details are not wholly certain, but it is sometimes suggested that it refers to some board game, such as chess or draughts, in which turning the tables means literally turning the board around to shift the advantage from one player to the other. (Doing so does certainly make a difference in draughts, in which the pattern of playing squares is different for the two players, but would hardly alter the situation in chess.)

A much more likely board game is backgammon, which was known as *tables* from medieval times up to about 1750. (The *Oxford English Dictionary* suggests that the Latin word *tabulae* from which it derives may have referred to the 'men' or counters.) *Tables* in the expression might also or instead be linked to the traditional division of the board into four distinct playing tables, an outer and an inner table for each of the two players. It seems that *to turn the tables* referred to one of the sudden reversals of fortune players can experience.

Twenty-three skiddoo

This American slang expression is now almost totally defunct as an item of daily speech, though it is still widely remembered and writers resurrect it on occasion to evoke the 1920s; *skiddoo* as a slang term by itself has a faint residual existence. That word, and the full phrase, is usually taken to mean 'go away', 'beat it' or 'scram'.

The usual story told about its origins takes us to the corner of Twenty-third Street and Broadway in New York City. This is the location of the famous Flatiron Building, constructed in 1902 and later nicknamed for its triangular shape that resembles an old-fashioned flat iron. This corner – it is said – became notorious as an especially windy spot, partly because of the shape of the building. It is also said that young men would gather there in the hope that a gust would blow a woman's skirt up to provide them with a momentary voyeuristic thrill. The local cops would chase them away with the phrase 'Twenty-three skiddoo!'

It doesn't sound a likely story. The problem in this case is that nobody has tracked down the true story, and indeed we may never know.

There's no difficulty over *skiddoo*, which is almost certainly a variation on *skedaddle*, with the sense of 'go away, leave, or depart hurriedly', as the *Oxford English Dictionary* puts it. This is recorded from 1906, though it is almost certainly older. The first recorded appearance of the full phrase *twenty-three skiddoo* is in 1926 (though a book in 1906 alludes to it), but there is considerable anecdotal evidence to show that it was around at the turn of the century. C. T. Ryan, writing in *American Speech* in 1926, claimed to have remembered it from about 1901. Harold Wentworth and Stuart Flexner, in their *Dictionary of American Slang* (1975), say of it that 'It was in male use c1900–1910, originally among students and sophisticated young adults. It was perhaps the first truly national fad expression and one of the most popular fad expressions to appear in the US.' They note that, despite its heyday being the first decade of the century, it usually evokes the 1920s, long after the fashion for it had declined.

The etymological problem lies with *twenty-three*. Some of the more plausible theories that have been put forward are these:

- It's a hangover from telegraphists' slang, which employed numerical codes as abbreviations of common expressions; 30 was 'end of message', for example, one which American journalists still on occasion put at the end of pieces. It is said that 23 meant something like 'away with you!'

- It is similarly restaurant and bar staff code for 'get out of my way, I'm busy', which would put it in the same group as EIGHTY-SIX.

- A writer in 1906 suggested a link between leaving hurriedly and Twenty-third Street, as the latter gave access to 'ferries and depots for 80 per cent of the railroads leaving New York'.

- *The Only Way*, a stage adaptation of Charles Dickens's *A Tale of Two Cities* by two Irish clergymen, Freeman Wills and Frederick Langbridge, was widely performed in America at the end of the nineteenth century. In the last act, a woman knitting at the guillotine counted off the victims as they were executed and the hero Sydney Carton was the twenty-third. A writer in 1929 claimed that the number became a fashionable slang term for 'let's get out of here', with *skiddoo* being added to help those who didn't get the original theatrical reference.

As matters stand, there's no evidence that allows us to choose between these possibilities.

The one explanation that nobody has essayed, so far as I know, is that it comes from a very early Thomas Edison film, of August

1901, *What Happened on 23rd Street, New York City*. A young couple deep in conversation walk towards the camera; the woman steps on a ventilation grille in the pavement, which blows her skirts to knee height. This was a titillating image for the period that aroused some controversy when it was shown around the country (it was still a little naughty when something similar happened to Marilyn Monroe in *The Seven Year Itch* half a century later). The Edison catalogue of the time described it like this: 'The young lady's skirts are suddenly raised to, you might say an almost unreasonable height, greatly to her horror and much to the amusement of the newsboys, bootblacks and passersby. This subject is a winner.' That salacious comment says it all. Even if it wasn't a direct influence on the development of the expression, I'll bet my bottom dollar it's the origin of the most common story about it, linking it with voyeurs on Twenty-third Street.

Upper crust

If I had to point to a single group that does most to propagate false beliefs about word origins, it would have to be tourist guides, a useful and on the whole excellent body of people, but prone to a lack of critical faculty where etymology is concerned and with a tendency to embroider a story in the interests of playing to the gallery. I've heard more daft ideas about word origins put about by this group than anybody else.

In this instance, my disgruntlement is directed especially towards those working in historic properties who claim that upper crust – a term for the upper social classes or aristocracy – derives from the poor performance of bread ovens in olden days. They heated so unevenly, it is said, that the bottom part of the loaf burned, while the top was properly baked. As a result, the burnt portion was given to the servants, while the upper crust was reserved for their superiors. The big problem with this idea is that it assumes old-time bread ovens were heated from below. In fact they were first filled with wood (gorse branches were the favourite), which were burned in the oven and the ashes raked out. Only then was the bread dough put in to bake. So the loaves would have been heated pretty evenly all round, which was the main reason why this indirect method was adopted in the first place.

There's another, slightly more subtle, version of this tale that refers to an historical document, John Russell's *The Boke of Nurture*, a work of etiquette written about 1460. This says (in modernized spelling), 'Cut the upper crust [of the loaf] for your sovereign', which has led to the idea that it was then regarded as good manners to cut the top crust off a loaf of bread and offer it to the ranking person at the table.

The phrase *upper crust* has indeed been around since the fifteenth century in its literal sense of the top part of a loaf of bread (John Russell's book contains its first recorded use). It turns up in British slang for a while from the 1820s on, but in the sense of the head or the hat; in the latter sense it appears in Pierce Egan's *Boxiana* of 1829: 'Ward . . . threw his upper-crust into the ring.'

The slangy sense of the upper classes seems, perhaps surprisingly, to be North American. In 1848, John Russell Bartlett included the term in his *Dictionary of Americanisms*, quoting a work by the Nova Scotian judge Thomas Chandler Haliburton, *Sam Slick in England*.

The idea might indeed be that the upper crust of a loaf was the finer part, though I suspect that the underlying image was that of cream floating to the top of fresh milk with no connection to bread at all. This is supported by its first recorded use in 1836, in an earlier work of Haliburton's, *The Clockmaker*: 'I actilly have nothin left to set afore you; for it was none o' your skim-milk parties, but superfine uppercrust real jam, and we made clean work of it.'

There's certainly no connection with royalty or medieval etiquette.

Wagon *See* ON THE WAGON

Welsh rabbit

This curious name for what is basically cheese on toast has created some folk etymological confusion. Almost as soon as it first appeared in the language, in the eighteenth century, it was misconstrued as *Welsh rarebit*, making the decoction sound much more exotic and refined than it actually is.

The *Welsh rarebit* version is so common today that some dictionaries give it as the main one, taking the reasonable view that the error is of such antiquity and so widespread that it has become standard. Other dictionaries firmly correct the reader, suggesting either that confusion is rife, or that pedagogy and pedantry remain the special preserve of only certain groups of lexicographers.

Though there's some doubt over the origin, it seems likely that it's a jocular and mildly racist English term pointing up the perceived poverty of the Welsh people. The wild rabbit was once a common source of meat for poor English farm labourers. So the idea may have been that for the Welsh to be forced to substitute humble toasted cheese they must have been even more deeply impoverished.

Wet one's whistle

An odd origin is sometimes put forward for this phrase, which may be summed up by quoting one of those anonymous e-mails doing the rounds: 'Many years ago in England, pub frequenters had a whistle baked into the rim or handle of their ceramic cups. When they needed a refill, they used the whistle to get some service. *Wet your whistle* is the phrase inspired by this practice.'

Foreign visitors to Britain may be saddened to hear that no pub cup or mug ever really had a whistle fitted for this purpose. If you wanted another drink, you went up to the bar and asked for it; if the place was posh enough to have table service, you most certainly wouldn't blow a whistle to get attention. You do sometimes see such mugs today, but they're the pottery equivalent of the e-mail, a joke on a long-established saying.

The word *whistle* here is just a joking reference to the mouth or throat and to the fact that you can't easily whistle when your mouth is dry. So *to wet one's whistle* is just to drink, especially after a hard day's work. It's a very old expression: its first recorded appearance is in Chaucer's *Canterbury Tales* at the end of the four-teenth century, and it must surely be even older.

You can sometimes see the phrase as *whet one's whistle*, as though it is in need of sharpening. This has led one writer to speculate that the final word was really *whittle*, an old English dialect word for a scythe. Farm workers at harvest time would stop to whet their whittle (and perhaps wet their whistle at the same time). The problem here is that a whittle was a large knife, not a scythe.

It would seem that those who first wrote it as *whet one's whistle* – more than 300 years ago – were as unsure of the real source of the expression as many of us are today. I shudder to think what the anonymous writer of the e-mail message might make of the *whet* version.

While

Do you while away the time in some leisurely pursuit, or do you wile it away? It's hardly an earth-shattering question, though many people would argue that the second spelling is wrong. But investigation of the matter does illuminate how words can change their alphabetical spots without any obvious cause.

Historically and formally, while is the correct spelling. But wile is not only found today but has been used in the past by some good writers. As a result, some British dictionaries allow wile as a variant, and several American ones offer it as valid without any comment. The only style guide I can find that mentions the matter is the second edition of Fowler's Modern English Usage (1965), which says that while the time away is now the standard form but that wile was formerly not uncommon.

A little delving into word history might be helpful to make this clearer. Writers in the early sixteenth century borrowed the conjunction while and turned it into a verb. The first known user of it in the modern sense of passing time leisurely or idly was Francis Quarles, in a poem of 1635 called Emblems:

> Nor do I beg this slender inch, to while
> The time away, or falsely to beguile
> My thoughts with joy.

So far, so good. The problem began at the end of the following century, when writers started to spell it wile instead. The OED's editors suggested this might have been because people were thinking of beguile the time, a related phrase that goes back to Shakespeare. Its users may have been thinking of the sense of wile that means deceit or deception, so that the idea in to wile away time was to steal time illicitly from one's proper duties. The French expression tromper le temps and the Latin decipere tempus both mean to 'deceive' time in the same way.

The first recorded user of the *wile* form was Fanny Burney, in her novel *Camilla* of 1796: 'He persuaded his sisters, therefore, to walk out with him, to wile away at once expectation and retrospection.' In the following century it was used by writers such as Sir Walter Scott, Charles Dickens and Rider Haggard. Rather later, Sir Arthur Conan Doyle had Sherlock Holmes say, in *The Adventure of the Second Stain*: 'Yes; I will wile away the morning at Godolphin Street with our friends of the regular establishment.'

With that phalanx of worthies in the background, it's hard for modern works on language to assert that *wile* is wrong. But my advice would be to stick with *while*, since you can't be faulted spelling it that way.

Whole ball of wax

The *whole ball of wax* is everything (and so means essentially the same as other American expressions like THE WHOLE NINE YARDS, *the whole shooting match*, *the whole megillah*, *the whole shebang* and *the whole enchilada*). Until recently, its first appearance was in the ninth edition of *Webster's New Collegiate Dictionary*, published in 1953.

It has been suggested, by a writer with too serious a demeanour to be accused of pulling our leg, that it comes from the workers at the famous waxworks of Madame Tussaud, though quite how is not made clear. We can dismiss this supposed connection out of hand: it's the product of an unoriginal mind which has linked *wax* with *waxworks* and done the verbal equivalent of making two and two equal five.

Another story appeared in William and Mary Morris's *The Morris Dictionary of Word and Phrase Origins*. They quote an English legal text from 1620 which describes the allocation of land among the heirs to an estate by a process very much like a lottery. Each parcel of land was listed on its own piece of paper, sealed inside a small ball of wax, and placed in a hat. Each heir then pulled out one of the balls to discover which part was his. The Morrises were strangely credulous about this story in view of the nearly 400-year and more than 3,000-mile gap between that description and the first appearance of the phrase. Whatever the origin, this certainly isn't it.

A graphic artist, a subscriber to my *World Wide Words* newsletter, reported that he heard in a seminar on typography that the phrase comes from typesetting. He was told that, in the days when type was made of metal, small pieces of gold would flake off the typesetting equipment. The typesetter would collect the gold flakes in a ball of wax to later melt down and reclaim the gold. Very often, someone would make off with the whole ball of wax. I don't believe that either. So far as I know, no gold is used in typesetting, though the story might be valid for goldsmithing or jewellery manufacture. However, I can't find a reference anywhere to that method having been used to gather up flakes of waste gold.

I did find what seemed to be a clue to its origins, in a disintegrating paperback in my library – a science-fiction novel of 1954 by Shepherd Mead, who two years before had written *How To Succeed in Business Without Really Trying*. Called *The Big Ball of Wax*, it's a futuristic satire on business and advertising in America and contains this line from the narrator, a market research man, about the story to come: 'Well, why don't we go back to the beginning and roll it all up, as the fellows say, into one big ball of wax?', that is, put everything together to make a coherent and complete whole. This sounds too much like a fuller and less elliptical early version of the saying to be a coincidence. However, many old newspapers have now been digitized, so that they can be readily searched electronically. This has thrown up a number of much older appearances of the phrase. The earliest found so far is from the *Atlanta*

Constitution of 25 April 1882: 'We notice that John Sherman & Co. have opened a real estate office in Washington. Believing in his heart of hearts that he owns this country, we will be greatly surprised if Mr. Sherman does not attempt to sell out the whole ball of wax under the hammer.'

The origin has been taken back so far that it is beginning to look as though another often-told story might be the right one. It is said that *whole ball of wax* is a humorous modification of *whole bailiwick*, perhaps because of a mental association between *bail* and *ball*, and between *wick* and candle wax.

Whole nine yards

If you're hoping for a definitive answer on the origin of this expression, you'd better buy a crystal ball. I have to say straight away this is one of the great unsolved mysteries of modern etymology, for which many seek the truth and almost as many find explanations, but for which nobody has a real clue based on evidence. What we do know is that the phrase is recorded from the 1960s, is an Americanism (it's nothing like so well known in Britain, for example), and has the meaning of 'everything; all of it; the whole lot; the works'. But there are no leads anyone can discover to a reasonable idea of where it came from.

What is most remarkable about the phrase is the number of attempts that have been made to explain it. This may be because it's an odd expression. But perhaps the need to make sense of this saying in particular is because it came into existence only during the lifetime of many people still with us, and so lacks the patina of age that turns phrases into naturalized idioms that we accept without question.

While looking into it, I've seen references to the size of a nun's habit, the amount of material needed to make a man's three-piece suit, the length of a maharajah's ceremonial sash, the capacity of a West Virginia ore wagon, the volume of rubbish that would fill a standard garbage truck, the length of a hangman's noose, how far you would have to sprint during a jail break to get from the cellblock to the outer wall, the length of a standard bolt of cloth, the volume of a rich man's grave, or just possibly the length of his shroud, the size of a soldier's pack, the length of cloth needed for a Scottish 'great kilt' or a traditional Indian sari, or some distance associated with sports or athletics, especially the game of American football.

None of these has anything going for it except the unsung inventiveness of compulsive explainers. For example, a man's suit requires about five square yards of material; anyone who thinks a soldier's pack could measure nine cubic yards needs to take a good look at a tape measure; and I'm told it takes ten yards to earn a first down in American football, not nine.

One particularly bizarre story that turns up more frequently than any other is that it represents the capacity of a ready-mixed cement truck, so that the whole nine yards might be a reference to a complete load. It does seem rather unlikely that a term from such a specialist field would become so well known throughout North America, but one or two writers are convinced this is the true origin. However, the capacity of today's trucks varies a great deal, and few of them can actually carry nine cubic yards of cement. Matthew Jetmore, a contributor to the urban folklore online newsgroup, unearthed evidence from the August 1964 issue of the *Ready Mixed Concrete Magazine* that this could not have been the origin: 'Whereas, just a few years ago, the 4.5 cubic yard mixer was definitely the standard of the industry, the average nationwide mixer size by 1962 had increased to 6.24 cubic yards, with still no end in sight to the demand for increased payload.' That makes it clear that at the time the expression was presumably coined the usual size was only about half the nine (cubic) yards of the saying.

Another relates to the idea of *yards* being the long spars on a ship rather than units of measurement. The argument is that a three-masted ship had three yards on each mast for the square sails, making nine in all, so that a ship with all sails set would be using *the whole nine yards*. The biggest problem here is dating – by the time the expression came into use, sailing ships were long gone; even if the phrase were fifty years older than its first certified appearance (unlikely, but not impossible), it would still be right at the end of the sailing-ship era, and long after its heyday. Other problems are that big square-rigged sailing ships commonly had more than nine yards and that the expression ought in any case to be *all nine yards* rather than *the whole nine yards* (the same objection could be made about any suggestion that involves numbers rather than areas or volumes). Another attempt at relating the expression to sailing ships has it that *nine yards* is somehow related to the area of canvas, but a full-rigged ship had vastly more than nine square yards of sail.

Yet another explanation is that it was invented by fighter pilots in the Pacific during the Second World War. It is said that the .50 calibre machine gun ammunition belts in the Spitfire fighter measured exactly 27 feet. If the pilots fired all their ammo at a target, they would say that it got 'the whole nine yards'. Others say it wasn't the Spitfire, an uncommon plane in that theatre, but the Boeing B-17, the Flying Fortress. A merit of this claim is that it would explain why the phrase only began to be recorded after the War. Variations on this story suggest that the origin was either the Korean War, or ground-based machine guns in the First World War. But some writers dispute the central fact and say that the belts were in practice variable in length so that no such saying could have been generated.

Some writers argue that the number isn't actually a dimension of any kind: in the *Cassell Dictionary of Slang*, Jonathon Green suggests that it's more likely to represent a use of *nine* as a mystic number, after the fashion of *nine tailors*, the *nine muses*, and several other expressions; Jesse Sheidlower, in his book *Jesse's Word of the Day*, thinks that it may be related in this way to the number in the equally odd expression DRESSED TO THE NINES.

What do I believe? I feel that, failing the discovery of the lexicographical equivalent of the crock of gold at the end of the rainbow, we are unlikely to find out the truth about this one.

Windy City

Most Americans know that this is an epithet for Chicago. The obvious assumption is that it refers to the notorious winds that gust through the city (though there are actually other cities in the USA that are more windy, Chicago's folk reputation as the worst seems secure).

Anyone who enquires more deeply about its origins is likely to be told that it dates to shortly before the great World's Columbian Exhibition of 1893. Chicago was putting forward its claim to host it with verve and bombast. This got up the noses of people in New York, which was competing with Chicago to do so. The animosity became so great that Charles A. Dana, editor of the *New York Sun*, wrote an editorial telling New Yorkers to pay no attention to the 'nonsensical claims of that windy city. Its people could not hold a world's fair even if they won it.' The history books tell us that Chicago did win it and did hold it (and even made a profit from it). Many authorities tell us that the nickname of *Windy City* dates from that editorial.

This story is wrong. There are numerous recorded instances of Chicago being called the *Windy City* before Mr Dana put his pen to paper. That we now have what looks like the real story is owed, as so often with American sayings, to researcher Barry Popik.

For example, he found this in the *Chicago Tribune* for 11 September 1886: 'The name of "Windy City," which is sometimes used by village papers in New York and Michigan to designate Chicago, is intended as a tribute to the refreshing lake breezes of the great summer resort of the West, but is an awkward and rather ill-chosen expression and is doubtless misunderstood.' He has since discovered that the term appears even earlier, in newspapers going back as far as 1877; an example is in the *Cincinnati Enquirer* of 7 October 1882: 'All talk that the triumph was secured through the generosity of the chaps from the Windy City is buncombe of the worst sort.'

It would seem that Charles Dana was slyly slipping in a reference to a nickname already well known, either as a figurative reference to the blustering of Chicago politicians or to its reputation as a notoriously windy place. He could not have known what misunderstandings would follow.

Wiseacre

The spelling here seems to connect the word to the countryside or farming, perhaps to some know-all farm labourer or to the oldest local inhabitant, who might be found dispensing spurious wisdom from the warmest settle in the village pub's inglenook.

In truth, the word has nothing to do with rolling acres. The English got it from the Dutch word *wijsseggher* in the late sixteenth century. In that language it meant a soothsayer.

The first part was no trouble for English speakers – it's the same word as our *wise*, from the same source and pronounced the same way. But the second part was a problem. English did once have a related word *segger*, though it's not well recorded, which literally meant a sayer, but seems to have been used to describe a braggart. The Dutch word could have been literally translated as *wise sayer*, which is close enough to the English *soothsayer* (*sooth* here being an Old English word meaning truth) to have merely created a synonym.

Instead, the English seem to have borrowed *wijsseggher* under the influence of linguistic or nationalistic chauvinism, not in the literal sense, but to identify somebody who pretended to wisdom. In the process they creatively mangled the final part into *aker* or *acre*, thereby creating a fertile field of misunderstanding for later generations.

In seeking a culprit, though, we might with some justice accuse the Dutch, who were guilty of a folk etymology of their own, since they derived it from Old High German *wizzago*, also meaning a soothsayer. This has no word history connection with *wise* or *segger*.

Wog

This offensive British slang term first appeared in the 1920s as a term for Indians, Asians, Arabs and other 'non-white' persons in the last days of the Empire. Later on, it was extended to any foreigner (as in the notoriously xenophobic phrase 'the wogs begin at Calais').

We're not entirely sure where it comes from, and the acronymizers have been at work, arguing that it's the initials of such phrases as 'Wily Oriental Gentleman', 'Westernized Oriental Gentleman', or even 'Working On Government Service', a phrase supposedly written on the backs of uniforms worn by workers digging the Suez Canal. All nonsense, of course.

The most plausible suggestion, which was put forward by Eric Partridge in his *Dictionary of Slang and Unconventional English*, is that it's an abbreviation of *golliwog*, the name of the black-faced doll that is itself now regarded as a symbol of an unacceptable racist past. The dates fit, since *golliwog* became widely known in Britain after Robertson's, the jam makers, adopted it in 1910 as a trademark (they finally abandoned it in 2001 after a sustained campaign of protest by race relations groups).

We're fairly sure where *golliwog* came from. Its primary source was the name of a doll in a series of children's books by the American writer Bertha Upton, starting in 1895, which became highly popular, inspiring many merchandising spin-offs. She is thought to have invented it by combining the interjection *golly!* (a disguised reference to God), plus *pollywog*, a name for a tadpole known from American English and British dialect, which comes from Old English *poll*, meaning head, plus *wiggle*.

Woman

You will sometimes see it argued that *woman* is a corruption of *womb-man*. It isn't.

In Old English, before the Norman Conquest, the word was *wifmon* or *wifman*, the two halves being *wif* and *man*. Though they strongly remind us of their modern equivalents *wife* and *man*, their senses were subtly different: *wif* could refer to any woman and *man* was the general term for any human being, male or female (as it still is in words like *mankind*). So *wifman* meant no more than a female human being. It may be that the shift of *wif* towards its modern sense of *wife* had helped the acceptance of *wifman* as a more general alternative.

By about 1200, the word had become *wimman* and further changes in the way people said it in various English dialects led to it taking on its modern form of *woman* by about 1400.

See also FEMALE.

Wonk

The boring facts first: wonk is a disparaging term for a studious or hard-working person. It is first recorded, according to the Oxford English Dictionary, in an article in Sports Illustrated in December 1962, though Fred Shapiro of Yale Law School has more recently turned up an example from Time in 1954. It gained wider exposure through being used in Erich Segal's Love Story of 1970: 'Who could Jenny be talking to that was worth appropriating moments set aside for a date with me? Some musical wonk?'

The clue to its origin may be in that article in Sports Illustrated, in which it is explained that in Harvard slang there was a tripartite classification of students into wonks, preppies and jocks. It seems that all three terms were around in the 1950s (jock possibly even earlier) and that they have moved into mainstream use in the decades since. The word was presumably taken to Washington by Harvard graduates and formed the basis for the modern term policy wonk, which is where most of us encounter it. There it acquired the meaning of 'a policy expert, especially one who takes an obsessive interest in minor details of policy', with a disparaging implication of someone immersed in detail and out of touch with the real world.

Now to the sixty-four thousand dollar question: where did the word come from? This is where we step on to shaky ground and where the amateur etymologists have had free run. Some have suggested that it may be know written backwards or an acronym for WithOut Normal Knowledge. More seriously, others find an origin in the British word wonky, meaning something or someone unsteady or unsound; even if a connection is found, which seems unlikely, it just takes the problem back a few decades, since we don't know where wonky comes from either. A source in wank, for masturbation, has also been suggested. A popular derivation links it with Willy Wonka and the Chocolate Factory, but though Roald Dahl's original story *Charlie and the Chocolate Factory* dates from 1964, the name *Wonka* was really only popularized by the film; and *wonk*, as we've seen, is anyway older than either.

Others suggest links with other known senses of *wonk*: as 1920s slang for a useless naval cadet or midshipman; a disparaging Australian aboriginal word for a white man (much like the Black American *honky*, with which it is not connected); 1940s Australian slang for an effeminate or homosexual man (also known in that period as a *gussie* or a *spurge*); or from a Chinese word for a dog, which may be from *huang gua*, yellow dog (this is a favourite suggestion among American politicos because of associations with *yellow dog* to mean opposition to trade unionism, and with the unconnected *Yellow Dog Democrat* for a Democratic Party loyalist).

None of these has solid evidence in its favour, and only the naval slang sounds even moderately plausible. We really don't know.

Wop

This derogatory but rather outdated American term for an Italian or other southern European immigrant is often claimed to be another example of an acronym.

The usual story goes like this: an illiterate Italian immigrant presents himself off the boat at Ellis Island without the right documents, as a result of which the immigration officer describes him by the initials WOP, meaning 'WithOut Papers' or 'WithOut Passport'. As an alternative story, a Canadian book, seriously meant, expanded the initials to 'Working On Pavement', describing Italian labourers who were relaying roads in Montreal during the Second World War. I've also seen it suggested that it stands for 'Western Oriental Person', or 'Worthy Oriental Person', which suggests the word is being confused with the equally derogatory British slang term WOG.

As so often, folk etymology is filling a gap in knowledge. It isn't entirely clear where *wop* comes from. An early example appears in New York in 1912, in a book by Arthur Train entitled *Courts, Criminals and Camorra*: 'There is a society of criminal young men in New York City . . . They are known by the euphonious name of "Waps" or "Jacks". These are young Italian-Americans who allow themselves to be supported by one or two women . . . They form one variety of the many gangs that infest the city.' But it also appears in a song by Irving Berlin, also of 1912, called *My Sweet Italian Man*:

> *My sweet Italian man,*
> *I'm-a sick, I'm-a sick, Love-a me much-a quick,*
> *Come here and squeeze-a my hand;*
> *Say you love me, wop-a,*
> *Like you love your barber shop-a*

which implies either that it wasn't thought to be insulting at that date, or that Irving Berlin had naively misunderstood its implications.

Our best guess is that the word comes from the Neapolitan dialect, in which *guappo* is a swaggering person, which sounds innocuous enough until you know that it's probably connected with the Spanish *guapo* for a pimp or ruffian and that both words may derive from Latin *vappa*, wine that has gone flat or, figuratively, a worthless person.

So it looks as though the term was at first applied by Italians as an insulting term to some of themselves and was only later taken over by Americans as a derogatory term for all Italians.

Woodchuck

Most people outside North America know this fellow through the old tongue-twister: 'How much wood would a woodchuck chuck if a woodchuck could chuck wood?' They are sometimes surprised to learn that he's the same animal as the *groundhog*, the one that's reputed to pop out of his burrow after winter hibernation on 2 February to check if he throws a shadow; if he does, he goes back to sleep because another six weeks of bad weather will follow. (Most groundhogs actually stay firmly asleep until March, but *Groundhog Day* – a variation on the old British *Candlemas Day* for the same date, about which weather legends are also known – is too fixed in the round of the American year to be bothered by little things like that.)

The groundhog – also known in areas such as the Appalachians as the *whistle pig* from the whistling alarm calls it makes – has nothing porcine about it, though it does indeed live on and in the ground. It's actually a marmot, a type of squirrel. Nor does it have anything to do with wood, though it is a vegetarian. The name *woodchuck* is a typical example of folk etymology, one of many by which early European settlers of North America converted a Native American name into something that seemed to make more sense. In this case the original was either the Ojibwa *otchig* or the Cree *otchock* or *wuchak*.

Yankee

The British use its abbreviation *Yank* for any American, southerners in the USA prefer to restrict it to a northerner from above the Mason–Dixon line, while those in the north apply it to New Englanders, who are generally happy to be so called, though some prefer to limit it to the inhabitants of Vermont. This progressive narrowing of naming illuminates the cultural complexities of the term, which are mirrored by arguments about where it comes from. These are as eclectic as the tales that surround OK, but less easy to refute.

These are a few of the stories I've come across:

- It is from Cherokee *eankke*, a slave or coward, applied to New Englanders by the Virginians for not assisting them in a war with the Cherokees. Or it comes from the Algonquinian *awauna-guss*, 'this stranger'.

- It was created by American Indians who had difficulty pronouncing the word *English*, a view put forward by the Reverend John Heckewelder in 1819 and supported by James Fenimore Cooper in his *Deerslayer* of 1841. Others have argued that it was the French word *Anglais* that was corrupted.

- It derives from the name of a tribe of Indians, the *Yankos*, the invincible ones, of which no records exist.

- It is from the Scots *yankie*, meaning a gigantic falsehood.

Just to complicate the story, a couple of humorists got in early on the game. In 1809 an anonymous hoaxer had a letter published in the *Monthly Review and Boston Anthology* that was supposedly from Noah Webster, suggesting an origin in a Persian word *jenghe* for a warlike man or swift horse. And twenty years later Washington Irving, in *A History of New York . . . by Dietrich Knickerbocker*, proposed an origin in *yanokies*, 'which in the Mais-Tschusaeg or Massachusetts language signifies silent men'. Unfortunately, some people took these tongue-in-cheek writers seriously.

The early written evidence is sparse. There are three references in the 1680s to a pirate captain named Williams, whose nickname was *Yankey* or *Yankey Duch*. A later inventory in Carolina in 1725 includes 'Item one negroe man named Yankee to be sold'. General James Wolfe used *Yankee* as a pejorative reference to his colonial troops in a letter in 1758. We know that British soldiers in the early years of the American Revolution borrowed it as a dismissive term for the colonists, in particular in the song 'Yankee Doodle Dandy', which the colonists appropriated after the battles of Lexington and Concord.

It seems most likely that it came from a nickname, *Janke*, a diminutive form of *Jan*, the Dutch equivalent to *John*. In turn this may be from *Jan Kees*, a term for a Dutch everyman (rather like *John Doe*), which came from *Jan Kaas*, literally John Cheese, roughly the Dutch equivalent of the eponymic *John Bull* for the English. The suggestion is that it was first applied as a nickname to the early Dutch colonists in New Amsterdam (later renamed New York) and was then transferred to English settlers in New England, and later extended more widely.

Yonks

You must be from Britain or Australia to know this word for a substantial but indefinite period of time. It puzzles everyone. We know very little about it for certain except that it first appeared in Britain in the 1960s. It usually turns up in the phrase *for yonks* ('I haven't seen him for yonks').

As an inevitable consequence of its being a strange word with no apparent link to any other word in the language, people have been inventively seeking possible origins. The most common misapprehension is that it's a complicated acronym from 'Years, mONths, and weeKS', so indicating a long period of time. As I've said elsewhere, we have to be suspicious of acronymic origins, since they almost invariably turn out to be specious. This one seems particularly stretched and improbable.

On the other hand, proponents of the idea may well argue that the tentative origin put forward in reference books is equally outlandish. The experts suggest you should start with *donkey's years*, a much older informal term for a long period of time, Spoonerize it into *yonkey's dears*, and then clip it to *yonks*.

I know, I know, but it's the best we have.

Zzxjoanw

This is rather different to most of the other entries in this book, because it isn't a folk etymology but a hoax, one that has fooled several generations of writers on word history. But it provides an intriguing final entry, as it did through several editions of Rupert Hughes' *The Music Lovers' Encyclopedia*, first published in 1903. He claimed that it was a Maori name for a drum and I can point to at least three recent popular works on etymology that cite the word with this meaning. Unfortunately, it was demolished as a real word by Philip Cohen in the November 1976 issue of *Word Ways*. Not the least part of the case against it is that there is no Z, X or J in the Maori language, which makes one wonder how it managed to survive unchallenged for so long. That it still appears is a testament to the tendency of writers to borrow from each other, not the least important way by which folk etymologies propagate.

Select Bibliography

This is a short list of books that may be of interest if you want to pursue the history and evolution of words. The choice is decidedly personal and eclectic, but it does include some of the more recent and easily accessible works I found useful while researching this book.

Ayto, John, *The Oxford Dictionary of Rhyming Slang*, Oxford University Press (2002).

Barnhart, David K., and Metcalf, Allan A., *America in So Many Words*, Houghton Mifflin (1997).

Barnhart, Robert K., *The Barnhart Dictionary of Etymology*, The H. W. Wilson Company (1988).

Cohen, Gerald Leonard, *Origin of the Term 'Shyster'*, Forum Anglicum 12, Verlag Peter Lang, Frankfurt am Main (1982).

Edelstein, Stewart, *Dubious Doublets*, John Wiley (2003).

Green, Jonathon, *The Cassell Dictionary of Slang*, Cassell (1998).

Klein, Ernest, *A Comprehensive Etymological Dictionary of the English Language*, Elsevier (1971).

Lighter, Jonathan, *The Random House Historical Dictionary of American Slang*, volumes I (A–G, 1994) and II (H–O, 1997), Random House.

Merriam-Webster's Dictionary of English Usage, Merriam-Webster (1994).

Morris, Evan, *The Word Detective*, Algonquin Books (2000).

Morris, William, and Morris, Mary, *Morris Dictionary of Word and Phrase Origins*, HarperCollins (1988).

Oxford English Dictionary, second edition, Oxford University Press (1989); CD-ROM edition 1992.

Partridge, Eric, A Dictionary of Slang and Unconventional English, eighth edition, edited by Paul Beale, Routledge (1984).

Rawson, Hugh, Devious Derivations, Random House (1994).

Sheidlower, Jesse, The F-Word, Random House (1995).

— Jesse's Word of the Day, Random House (1998).

Select Webliography

The following are just a few of those websites that deal with language:

Ask Oxford <http://www.askoxford.com/>   A British-based compendium of information about words, including Word of the Day, Quote of the Week, Ask the Experts and word games.

Mavens' Word of the Day <http://www.randomhouse.com/wotd/> From the Word Mavens of Random House. This closed at the end of 2001, but an archive of past pieces gives answers to queries about the meanings of words and expressions.

Urban Legends Archive <http://www.urbanlegends.com/language/ etymology/> This discusses, and debunks, some of the stranger stories about the origins of words that circulate online and off.

Verbatim <http://www.verbatimmag.com/>   The online archive for the quarterly magazine which investigates the (often odd) byways of language.

Vocabula Review <http://www.vocabula.com/>   A monthly online magazine that celebrates the 'opulence and elegance' of the English language.

Word Detective <http://www.word-detective.com/>   The online equivalent of Evan Morris's newspaper columns and book.

Word for Word <http://plateaupress.com.au/wfw/articles.htm> Articles on words and phrases by Australian writer Terry O'Connor.

World Wide Words <http://www.worldwidewords.org> My own site, currently with some 1,400 articles on aspects of language and word history.